Bayou Justice:
Southeast Louisiana Cold Case Files

Bayou Justice, Year 1

HL Arledge

Published by Bogart Books, 2019.

Table of Contents

Introduction 1

The Hi-Ho Murder 2

Kassie Federer 6

Tarred and Feathered 11

Murder Cleared by Exception 16

Rube Rogers 20

Oswald from New Orleans 26

Grinch Who Stole Guns 31

Maybe Bonnie & Clyde 34

Daytra and Robert 38

The Panama Bandit 41

The Mob Collector 45

Selonia Reed 48

Coffee with Victims 52

Willie Jones 55

Henry Forrest 59

Roy McCrory 62

Charles Ray Spears 66

The Goodyear Killer 69

The Axe-man of Tangipahoa 72

The Kentwood Shoot-out 76

Edward Toefield, Jr. 80

The Lynchings 83

Eric Walber 87

Michael Wearry 91

The Cazan Crime-fighters 95

Hermina Reed 99

Huey Long 101

Uncle Jerry 105

The Naked Hitch-hiker 109

Modern-day Bonnie and Clyde 113

The Poultry Pioneer 116

Reginald Reed 120

Jimmy Ray Barnes.. 122

Pleading the Reed murder 127

Clay Bertrand 2019.. 129

Clay Bertrand 1967.. 132

Donna Lynn Bahm.. 136

Al Daniels, Private Eye 140

Ed Bahm and the Extortionist.. 144

No Justice for Donna.. 148

Margaret Ann Coon 153

The Jogger... 157

Sandra Davis 162

Irma Jean and Margaret... 166

The LSU Murder 170

Dr. Mary Sherman.. 173

Dallas Calmes.. 178

The Bootleggers... 182

Courtroom Burlesque... 187

Tony Carollo 191

Lynn Nunez 196

Peter Revere 200

Judge Brady Fitzsimmons 204

Walter Reed 208

Frankie Richard... 213

Jennings 216

The Boudreaux Inn... 220

The Other Suspects 225

The Luling Ferry 229

Girl in the Yellow Raincoat 232

Skulls, Ghosts, and Devils... 236

Cattle Mutilation.. 240

The Cemetery Slayer 244

The Devil Cult 248

The Bad Cop... 253

The Mailbox Skull 257

Voodoo Man and Other Suspects 261

Louisiana's Robin Hood.. 266
Colonel Hobgood 271
Jimmy and Diddie 275
Goodbye, Diddie Cooper.. 280
The Carwash Witness.. 284

THIS BOOK IS DEDICATED to my wife, Janna.

Thank you for supporting me in everything I do.

Also, to my editor, Lil Mirando for her patience.

Both remind me regularly to keep my life insurance current.

Introduction

Louisiana is home to some of the most unusual true-crime events in history. From rogue voodoo priests to swamp cults, spurned lovers with knives, or renegade mobsters, even kidnapping, murder, rape, and burglary have hot and spicy flavors on the bayou.

I should know. As an investigative reporter in South Louisiana, I've been writing about these events since 1979, and I'm obsessed with finding the truth, and not just in current crimes. My passion is revisiting historic headlines in search of clues long forgotten. Our train robbers, con-men, and bank bandits are a special kind of colorful.

Within the pages of this book, you'll find year one of Bayou Justice, a twice-weekly true-crime newspaper column inspecting cold case files from Cajun Country, each report detailed from interviews with key players, among them: police investigators, lawyers, victims, and their families.

Bayou Justice: Southeast Louisiana Cold Case Files compiles year one of the award-wining newspaper columns with updates, recent developments, to each true-crime installment.

Some of these stories will make you smile, others will make you angry, and some will make you cry, but I'm confident you'll be thrilled by the ride. After you read this book, drop me a line. Let me know what you think, especially if you have clues or secrets from our next adventure.

The Hi-Ho Murder

With new information from readers and other sources, this chapter evolved from the *Bayou Justice* column entitled "*Even Hoodlums eat at Hi-Ho Barbeque*," initially published in south Louisiana newspapers on Tuesday, October 15, 2018.

THE FIRST CORPSE I ever saw belonged to a party barge captain named John George Trathen.

At nine years old, I watched nine Livingston Parish sheriff's deputies pull his body from a briar patch at the base of the Courtney Bridge in Holden. Bright sun. Chilly air. I'm squinting, standing next to my mom and a few other nosy neighbors.

According to the Associated Press:

"Trathen's body was found by a swimmer, Sunday, August 8, 1973, shortly before noon, behind a clump of bushes next to LA 1036 and a bridge over the Tickfaw River. Authorities identified the body as John George Trathen, 41, a party barge captain and professional sports angler from Miami Beach, Florida."

Trathen was also a veteran of the Korean War and the United States Coast Guard.

"He was shot four times — in the chest, side, leg, and chin. His rig amortized right hand still held a cigarette butt in between two fingers when deputies reached the body."

I did not see the cigarette, but I did see his wool cap. It fell from the stretcher as the deputies pushed through the brush and lost their balance on the sandbar.

Within days of the murder, the first of five men arrested were behind bars.

Two weeks later, the Livingston Parish Sheriff's Office dropped all charges and released them.

The following year, WAFB-TV invited my Cub Scout troop to Baton Rouge to appear on the Buckskin Bill television show. We arrived promptly that afternoon to bad news. Buckskin Bill Black had taken the day off, Den Mother Joyce Hoover told us. Weatherman Sid Crocker would host, or so she thought. Three hours later, the Watergate hearings pre-empted the show.

For three long hours, twenty-three third-graders raced around the Channel 9 studios, while I watched the live feed from CBS. My troop complained loudly, but not me. The escapades of Bob Woodward and Carl Bernstein mesmerized me, and that day I decided to become a news reporter.

Ten years after the Courtney Bridge Murder, I was a Journalism major at Hammond's Southeastern Louisiana University, lunching at the Hi-Ho Barbeque restaurant, and talking to Celeste Alexander about John George Trathen's last meal.

For decades until her death in 2002, "Miss Celeste" worked the counter at the Hi-Ho on West Thomas Street without a cash register of any kind. The trait patrons today remember most about her is her near-photographic memory.

"He sat right over there," she said. "With those two mafia types." She told me the story in 1982, but she described it as if it happened that morning. "He had pork with cheese. The other two had beef dressed, but the dead man had pork."

Going to SLU, I ate lunch daily at Hi-Ho. Their prices were a little lower than Mr. Cook's or anything else near the campus and much lower than Lee's Drive-in or the Tropic Café downtown. Besides, everyone ate at Hi-Ho, and everyone loved to talk with Miss Celeste.

"Narcs coming through here say he was undercover," Miss Celeste said. "Some crazy drug thing. Watch. They won't catch them. Not ever. Mark my word. Somebody big covered up the whole thing."

Shortly after Trathen's murder, meeting with police, Miss Celeste identified Leonard L. "Curly" Shipley, 48, of Kenner as one of the men eating barbeque beef. They booked him as a material witness, and after a few days of questioning, Sheriff Taft Faust charged Paul Wayne George, 27, of Shreveport with the murder.

Faust also charged three New Orleans residents, Louis Matranga, Leonard B. Johnson, and Jessie A. Martin, as accessories after the fact.

With the help of the Federal Bureau of Investigation, the LPSO discovered quickly what these men had in common. All had prior arrests for either armed robbery or transporting illegal drugs. Additionally, all worked at nightclubs controlled by Carlos Marcello; the man FBI Director J. Edgar Hoover called the New Orleans' "top hoodlum."

Louis Matranga — once arrested with $36,000 and a stolen safe in the back seat of his car — was having lunch at Marcello's Town and Country Motel when Jefferson Parish sheriff's deputies arrested him.

"Louie" Matranga was a descendant of Tony Matranga, the man credited with bringing the mafia to New Orleans in 1857. According to Wikipedia, Tony's son, Charles Matranga, led the family from 1881-1922. Underboss, Sylvestro "Silver Dollar Sam" Carolla took over. The government deported him in 1944, leaving his underboss, Carlos Marcello, in charge.

On August 22, 1974, *The Acadiana Advocate* reported that an unidentified assailant shot Paul Wayne George — the man charged with John George Trathen's murder — "gangland-style."

"He was shot six times outside a nightspot he owned on US 167 southwest of Lafayette at about 10:30 p.m. Lafayette Parish Sheriff Carlo Listi said everyone knew George was involved in organized crime."

But what of Shipley, the man Miss Celeste saw dining with Trathen?

In 1997, former Hattiesburg, Mississippi Sheriff Leroy Hobbs — serving time for attempting to bribe Governor Edwin Edwards into pardoning convicted hitman Kirksey Nix, Jr. — identified Leonard "Curly" Shipley as the "racketeering representative" that paid him to approach Edwards.

Nix, by the way, was the hitman who killed New Orleans Grocery Magnate Frank Corso and the wife of Sheriff Buford "Walking Tall" Pusser. Nix also started a sex-for-sale business from within Angola State Penitentiary in the 1990s, but those are stories for another week.

On October 10, 1973, the LPSO cleared Paul Wayne George, Leonard "Curly" Shipley, Louis Matranga, Leonard B. Johnson, and Jessie A. Martin of all charges related to the death of John George Trathen. Chief Deputy Odom Graves told reporters there was not enough evidence to hold the men any longer.

After all, there is no crime in eating a Hi-Ho sandwich — unless, of course, you down it with anything but a beer or a thick-bottled Barq's.

Kassie Federer

With new information from readers and other sources, this chapter evolved from the Bayou Justice column entitled "Kassie Federer mystery still unresolved," initially published in south Louisiana newspapers on Tuesday, October 23, 2018.

DEFENSE ATTORNEY JOHNNY Cochran had a simple definition for reasonable doubt: "If the story doesn't make sense, you must find for the defense."

Last week, the Baton Rouge Police Department charged a suspect in the 1999 shooting death of Ponchatoula native Kassie Lynn Federer. DNA found inside a glove at the crime scene, detectives said, matched that of Travis Dwight Green, a 49-year-old death row inmate in Livingston, Texas.

BRPD issued a routine warrant, but Texas has Green confined to the Polunsky Unit — Polk County's infamous "concrete tomb" — locked-down 22-hours-a-day with no phones, no media, and no contact between inmates or with the outside world. Green may not even know police have charged him with another murder.

On death row, the District Attorney's office cannot extradite him to Louisiana. Unless the courts overturn his death sentence, he will never stand trial for Kassie Federer's murder.

He is presumed guilty. End of the story. Case Closed.

But an important question remains: did Green kill Kassie Federer?

In the real world, police investigations have more in common with the O. J. Simpson trial than with CSI. Real-life forensic testing is far from infallible, and DNA found on gloves at crime scenes often proves nothing.

The Louisiana State Police Crime Lab has an impeccable reputation.

However, the Houston Crime Lab collected and tested Green's original DNA sample. Their technicians entered Green's markers into CODIS — the FBI's Combined DNA Indexing System — where the Louisiana State Police Crime Lab eventually found a match to the DNA in the glove found at Kassie's apartment.

Unlike the LSP Crime Lab, the Houston lab's record is less than pristine:

- In 2002, the Houston Police Department closed the Houston Crime Lab after an independent audit revealed hundreds of convictions obtained based on incomplete or flawed testing.
- In 2003, an independent DNA retest released Josiah Sutton after he served four years of a twelve-year sentence for a sexual assault.
- In 2004, internal police investigators uncovered 280 boxes of lost evidence that included a fetus and body parts involved in some 8,000 cases, including rapes and murders going back to 1979.
- In 2005, the Houston City Council authorized an independent investigation of the lab, revealing that analysts faked tests and hid evidence.
- In 2006, the Houston Police Cold Case Squad used DNA provided by the Houston lab to charge Travis Dwight Green with the 1988 rape of 82-year-old Margaret McGinnis, only to discover later that Green was incarcerated during the attack.
- In 2007, a judge released Ronnie Taylor after new DNA tests proved him innocent of rape. He had served 12 years in prison.
- In 2008, Houston's Lab Chief resigned in an accreditation scandal.
- In 2009, a judge released Gary Alvin Richard, 53, after he served 22 years in prison for a rape and robbery he did not commit.
- In 2012, the lab reopened as the Houston Forensic Science Center, where a backlog of 6,600 untested rape kits persisted into 2013.
- In 2014, Crime Lab Technician Peter Lentz resigned after an internal investigation cited him for lying, improper procedure, and tampering with official records. Lentz worked 185 cases between January 2012 and March 2014.
- In 2016, a new audit found 298 wrongful convictions and errors in 65 cases, including 26 homicides and eight officer-involved

shootings.

Reviewing this lab's history, we can deduce two things: (1) DNA testing by humans is far from infallible, and (2) we do not want the Houston lab testing anything important.

Fortunately, detectives at the Baton Rouge Police Department reached the same conclusions. According to BRPD, Sergeant Don Copolla, Jr., after the LSP Crime Lab alerted them to the match, BRPD detectives traveled to Livingston, Texas, and personally obtained a fresh DNA swab from Green.

BRPD's Affidavit for Warrant says, "This [new] DNA swab was provided to the Louisiana State Police Crime Lab where it was determined that the defendant's DNA was the DNA located in the glove found at the scene."

Lieutenant Nick Manale, with LSP Public Affairs, explained. "The evidence in the 1999 case was analyzed by the LSP Crime Lab DNA Unit in 2002 and then again in 2014 to obtain additional DNA information. We entered the profile into CODIS with no resulting CODIS hit. With the growing size of the National CODIS Database, which has reached an estimated 17 million DNA profiles, the FBI recently modified its searching parameters on August 20, 2018, to more effectively search within DNA profiles. This change in search parameters resulted in the CODIS hit in the 1999 case. This investigative lead was then released to BRPD."

I asked him precisely what tests their lab performed and how many of the 20 CODIS-required loci (genetic markers) matched between the two samples. He said he could not release that information at this time as the case is still being prepared for the District Attorney's Office.

In the rare case that all 20 genetic markers match, there is also the problem of Green's irregular timeline. Any case the DA will want to build hinges on Green's abrupt detour to Baton Rouge and a glaring lack of motive.

Travis Green's alleged 1999 timeline:

- **September 2** — At 7:30 AM, Green rapes, strangles, and beats 19-year-old college student Kristin Loesch, while her boyfriend sleeps on her couch.
- **September 10** — Houston detectives interview Green regarding the murder of Kristin Loesch.

- **September 13** — Green kicks in an apartment door in Baton Rouge and shoots 19-year-old Kassie Federer. He drops a single glove on the floor and leaves, taking the victim's book-sack with him.
- **September 16** — Houston detectives arrest Green at his Houston residence and obtain a DNA swab.
- **September 20** — Representing himself before Judge Johnson, Green pleads guilty to the murder of Kristin Loesch, testifying that he met the couple the night before the killing and bought them marijuana.

If Green fled from Houston for Baton Rouge, why the immediate return?

The question warrants a closer look at September 13.

Early that afternoon, Kassie, a Louisiana State University psychology major, returned to her Park Boulevard apartment from classes at LSU. Shortly before 3: PM, someone kicked-in her deadbolt-locked door.

Investigators believe Kassie ran towards the kitchen to escape. Her assailant fired behind her repeatedly until a bullet punctured both lungs and her heart, killing her instantly.

Multiple shots pierced the living room wall, damaging the property next door. Hours later, Kassie's neighbor arrived and called the apartment manager, who found Kassie's door partially open, her body inside, and a phone in her hand. Her body was fully clothed, and her apartment appeared orderly.

Only the blue book sack she carried daily was missing.

If Travis Green was the assailant, why did the admitted rapist flee with only a book-sack? Why did he use a gun? What was his motive?

Travis Green's rap sheet is long. Incarcerated from 1984 to 1989 for receiving stolen movables, and 1991 to 1998 for aggravated assault, the state discharged him from parole four months before he admitted to killing Kristin Loesch.

I am not suggesting that Travis Green is an innocent man, but I am questioning whether he killed Kassie Federer. Yes, Kassie's family needs closure, but they also need certainty.

As I wrap this up, I wonder if the glove found in Kassie's apartment would fit the accused 230 pounds, 6' 2" black man, and I imagine what Johnny Cochran might say.

Tarred and Feathered

With new information from readers and other sources, this chapter evolved from the Bayou Justice column entitled "Hammond dentist tarred and feathered downtown," initially published in south Louisiana newspapers on Tuesday, October 30, 2018.

"YOU CAN'T RIGHTLY CALL it tarring, Your Honor. We used a cold creosote and tar mixture, stuff we use on corn to keep the crows off. It ain't hot, so it doesn't burn the skin. Well, not if it's cleaned off before the sun comes up."

"Mr. Starns, call it what you will," said Judge Nat Tycer. "The fact remains. It is illegal to strip a man naked, stick feathers to his body, and drop him on a crowded street."

"But Nat, I brought him home. It's not my fault he lives above the dentist's office, and I didn't put his office across the street from the Tropic Café."

"And I suppose you were not aware that the restaurant was open all night?"

"I wanted to drop him at the hotel and make him walk to his place, but my brother Newton said that would be cruel because he might not make it home before sun up."

"Where were your brothers in all this?"

"Oh, they didn't do any feathers. No, sir, they just watched. My brother, Henry, came up with the idea, though. Me, I just wanted to shoot the bastard."

When someone says "Bayou Justice," I usually think of this story. My great-grandfather, W. O. "Paw Bill," Courtney retold it weekly when I was a kid. My grandmother, "Maw Telliua," insisted he had embellished some of it. I never cared. I loved the story, regardless.

Imagine my surprise, decades later, finding these headlines from 1930: "Hammond dentist tarred and feathered," "Starns admits tarring, labels dentist homewrecker," "Tar and feather witnesses under guard," "Crowds fill tar and feather courtroom," "Tar and feather mistrial!", and "U. S. court refuses to hear tar and feather appeal."

These headlines screamed across the front pages of New Orleans and Baton Rouge papers and made their way into newspapers across the country. The story was big news for quieter times, but like most true crime stories, this one ends in sadness and gunfire.

The trouble started Sunday, May 25, 1930.

Isaac G. "Ike" Starns returned home from a Mississippi Shriner's convention to neighbors, whispering that his wife had spent a few nights with Dr. Sedgie L. Newsom, the family dentist. The following Monday evening, Dr. Newsom answered a house call at the Tangipahoa-Livingston parish line, only to be forced off the road by Starns' canary-yellow, wire-rimmed Ford Chrysler.

A .38 revolver in his hand, Starns ordered Newsom into the car and drove him into the woods near Albany. There, Newsom stood facing a roaring fire, surrounded by five men. Ike Starns held a pillow in his hand.

Starns would later tell a packed courtroom, "I told him the pillow came from my wife's bed and ordered him to smell it before we stripped off his clothes. I said, 'you want to be naked against my wife's pillow; I'm going to grant your wish.' I painted him up with the creosote. Then I ripped the pillow apart and stuck the feathers to him. Duck feathers, too. Really expensive."

On May 27, 1930, Hammond Police Chief W. H. Rimmer said the case was under investigation and that Dr. Newsom, then staying with relatives in Mississippi, had not suffered any physical injury after a physician-assisted him removing the feathers.

Tangipahoa Parish Sheriff Frank M. Edwards told *The States-Item* that he was "working with the sheriff in Livingston Parish and expressed his determination in arresting members of the Tar and Feather Mob within 24 hours."

The next day, deputies in two parishes arrested the five Starns brothers, all prominent and wealthy citizens, well known in Hammond. Berlin Starns owned the largest furniture store in South Louisiana. Ike Starns, 42, had a lumberyard and general store in Livingston. His brother, Newton, 39, owned two general stores, one in Frost and another in Springville. Charles, 36, owned a flour distribution business in Baton Rouge. Henry, 25, owned a store in Holden, and Gordon, 22, worked at his father's store in Hammond.

Following the arrest and news coverage that followed, Representative Marcus Rownd of Livingston spoke from the floor of the house, chastising a New Orleans newspaper who described the Starns brothers as "outlaws from the free state of Livingston."

"This article went on to say that nightrider activities are still carried on with the frequency of earlier days. That is untrue. Livingston Parish is one of the most peaceful in the state. We have schools. We have churches and lodges of various kinds, and any man, woman, or child would be safe in this parish — at least as far as the citizens of the parish are concerned."

"I want it on the record. My people are not outlaws," he said. "The people of Livingston Parish are honest and law-abiding. The staff of these newspapers should visit and get acquainted with people before they slander them. I take this as a personal insult to my people and demand that this newspaper apologizes."

When the trials began, the case made national news.

The 21st Judicial Court tried the Starns brothers living in Livingston Parish in Springville, and those in Tangipahoa stood trial in Amite. Amite Defense Attorney Amos L. Ponder represented all five, arguing each time that Louisiana's "unwritten law" was their best defense.

"I found it difficult to advise my clients against doing what I — or any judge or juror here today — would have done if their family were under attack. When the day comes that morality and marriage do not come first, this country will go to hell flying."

Ponder said that the breaking up of the Starns home by the misconduct of Dr. Newsom and Gladys Starns was a mental punishment to Ike and that the brothers chose the retaliation to inflict a similar psychological punishment.

"My clients wanted the punishment to fit the crime, Your Honor."

The lawyer said he had no objection to a man womanizing provided he "confined himself to targets that did not attack girlhood or the sanctity of the home."

Ike Starns also testified. "Yes, I did tar and feather Dr. S. L. Newsom. I put the tar and feathers on him with my own hand. Doing this, I decided, was better than what most men would have done to someone who breaks up happy homes. He should be thankful I spared his life."

After three criminal trials, a jury acquitted Ike and his brothers.

Dr. Newsom filed suit in civil court afterward, and the state awarded him $6,000.

As this story ends, I have vindicated my grandfather. Paw Bill's tale of the tarred and feathered dentist proved more fact than fabrication. Compared to the newspapers of the day, Paw undersold his story. He left out the saddest parts.

Ike Starns was a war hero, serving the 348th Infantry in France during the First World War, and after the war, he joined law enforcement in tracking down two of the six bank robbers hanged for the Independence murder of Dallas Calmes in 1924.

Starns never reconciled with Gladys, and he never forgave Newsom.

In 1934, an intoxicated Starns climbed out of his canary-yellow Chrysler in front of the Central Drugstore downtown and fired two .38 caliber rounds into Newsom's office window. The dentist stood in the stairwell of his building, frozen, holding his unfired pistol.

Hearing the shots, police officers crossed the street from the Columbia Theater, and Starns turned his gun on them. They returned fire, and Starns fell dead on Thomas Street, where the feathered Dr. Newsom had stood four years earlier in front of his locked office without keys or pockets to carry them in.

Today, we would call Starns' death suicide-by-police, but in 1934, most just said Ike Starns died from a broken heart.

Murder Cleared by Exception

With new information from readers and other sources, this chapter evolved from the Bayou Justice column entitled "Cold case murder prompts 4-parish data requests," initially published in south Louisiana newspapers on Tuesday, November 6, 2018.

HAMMOND POLICE FOUND Selonia Smith Reed murdered in August of 1987. Over three decades have passed without an arrest, but this week, Police Chief James Stewart said investigators closed the case years ago.

Last Thursday, I filed public records requests with 16 law enforcement agencies in four parishes, requesting definitive lists of all homicide victims in each jurisdiction along with the status of each investigation going back 30 years.

According to the Federal Bureau of Investigation's Uniform Crime Reports, from the period between 1987 and 2017, over 300,000 homicides remain unresolved in the United States — and 9,630 of those are in Louisiana. With the cooperation of these 16 agencies, in the months ahead, I plan to review each of the unsolved murders from Tangipahoa, Livingston, St. Helena, and St. Tammany Parishes and seek your assistance in resolving them.

In addition to reporting which cases are closed and which are open, these agencies will also note those cases somewhere in-between — cases where detectives believe they have completed an investigation to the best of their ability. Still, the prosecutor refuses to bring the alleged perpetrator to trial.

At a press conference last Wednesday, I watched Denham Springs Police Chief Shannon Womack describe the murders of Eugene and Patricia Gurley as "the most heinous and senseless crime" in the history of Denham Springs. His remark took me back to a Hammond City Council meeting in 1987, where Councilman Wilbert Dangerfield said the murder of a 26-year-old bank teller was "the most brutal in the history of the city." Dangerfield proposed that the city ask for assistance from the Louisiana State Police and hire an additional officer to allow someone to focus on the case fulltime. Councilman George Perkins supported the motion, also suggesting that the city sponsor free self-defense and anti-rape seminars for women.

In 1996, I asked Hammond Police Chief Roddy Devall what happened. He told me, "It's still an open case. As long as we get tips, we will continue to follow-up. That's all we can do."

Two weeks ago, I asked Hammond's current chief the same question. Chief James Stewart looked into it and ultimately told me the case had been "solved" years ago. However, he said his department could not provide details because the case had been "Cleared by Exceptional Means."

Unfortunately, I knew what that meant.

In Uniform Crime Reporting, the FBI defines an offense closed or "cleared" when the investigation results in the police arresting an alleged perpetrator or the case being "Cleared by Exceptional Means." This status or "disposition code" means that an agency has (1) identified the offender, (2) gathered enough evidence to support charges, (3) determined the offender's location, and (4) encountered an obstacle that prevents arrest.

For homicide cases, the fourth criterion originally meant the alleged offender had died, or another jurisdiction had incarcerated the alleged offender for a separate homicide. Still, according to a Southeastern Louisiana University Criminal Justice professor, that fourth criterion has ballooned into something else.

In 2007, Dr. John Boulahanis — along with now-retired SLU professor, Dr. Marc Riedel — conducted a comprehensive breakdown of homicides in Chicago over seven years and found approximately 20 percent of the agency's caseload exceptionally cleared. Developing *Homicides Exceptionally Cleared and Cleared by Arrest*, Boulahanis discovered a majority of cases had been "barred to prosecution," — meaning the prosecutor "decided against" filing charges.

"Homicide clearance rates appear to be going down nationwide, but those numbers are deceptive," Boulahanis said. "The decline is due largely to the allowance of barred to prosecution. That began in 1982, the year this steady decline started."

"Here's how it works," Boulahanis explained. "Most large police departments have something called Felony Review. Before investigators make an arrest, they call the prosecutor's office and provide a summary of the evidence they have. The prosecutor decides whether there's enough evidence to arrest. And sometimes the prosecutor says no. We need more."

"If law enforcement disagrees. They think they have enough evidence and have exhausted all of their means; they can then file paperwork under this barred-to-prosecution option that allows them to clear the case by exception. Once they clear a case, they don't go back to it."

Dr. Kimberly Lonsway, at the University of Illinois, who authored a follow-up study, found this alarming. In her paper, *Clearance Methods in Sexual Assault Cases*, she said that police who have conducted a thorough investigation should not be punished based on a prosecutor's decision not to file charges. Likewise, she said, "[clearances by exception] can mask a shoddy investigation where law enforcement has not completed their job and handed over a file that no prosecutor in the country could move forward on."

Boulahanis said there are three apparent problems caused by exceptional clearances: (1) a murderer is still at large and may kill again, (2) a murderer unpunished diminishes the deterrent effect of the criminal justice system, and (3) failing to prosecute the guilty deprives the deceased's family of closure.

At his office in Meade Hall, I told Dr. Boulahanis of the requests filed with local law enforcement. I asked what else the press or public could do to help alleviate this standoff between investigators and prosecutors.

"You've got the right idea," he said. "When clearance rates go down, exceptional clearances go up, especially when barred to prosecution comes into play. If you can divorce the two, Cleared by Arrest and Cleared by Exceptional Means, that's a step in the right direction."

He said only law enforcement and prosecutors working together could solve the problem, and to solve the problem, they have to accept ownership of the problem.

"Prosecutors have told me: wait a second. This is not our issue. We only look at what we're given from a legal perspective. If there isn't enough evidence, it's law enforcement's job to find more. When I asked police detectives, they're quick to say: it's not up to us. The prosecutor made that decision."

He said the real problem is their lack of incentive to fix the problem.

"Think about it. The situation is a win-win. Cases barred to prosecution still count as cleared, while prosecutors avoid potentially damaging their conviction rates. They both benefit from it," he said. "The police department gets credit for the case, and the prosecutor doesn't have to try a case that might lead to no conviction."

If Dr. Boulahanis is correct, compiling my homicide list may prove more difficult than I thought.

Rube Rogers

With new information from readers and other sources, this chapter evolved from the Bayou Justice column entitled "Legend Rube Rogers suffered heinous death," initially published in south Louisiana newspapers on Tuesday, November 27, 2019.

ON AUGUST 14, 2010, Rube Roger's white pickup truck pulled into a Days Inn in Hurricane Mills, Tennessee, 75 miles west of Nashville. The driver signed "Rube Rogers" on the registry and paid with a credit card belonging to Rube Rogers. In his hotel room, he rolled a marijuana cigarette and phoned the ranch of Country Music Legend Loretta Lynn.

Rube Rogers and Loretta Lynn had been friends since 1960.

On the phone, Eric Maurer asked Loretta's son, Ernest Ray Lynn, if they were hiring at the ranch.

Eric Maurer, 31, and his twin brother, Derrick, had lived with Rube Rogers since age 10. Ernest Lynn had known them all his life. He and his brother had spent Summers at Paradise, the Rogers farm near Springfield.

Ernest Lynn never imagined that — less than 12 hours earlier — Eric Maurer had shoved Rogers down a stairwell before slitting his throat with a kitchen knife.

If you've not heard anyone say "Rube Rogers was a legend," you haven't spent much time is southeast Louisiana.

From *Cash Box Magazine*, September 24, 1960:

"We just got wind of an interesting incident that happened out Louisiana way. It seems there's this kid announcer at WFPR in Hammond, Louisiana, by the name of Rube Rogers — affectionately tagged as the original Country Boy — who heard about the closing of the Louisiana Hayride and got busy on the phone contacting country artists all over these United States. He got up a package show featuring Red Sovigne and put it on in the Albany High School auditorium, just a few miles from Hammond. After sinking two paychecks into advertising and promotion, old Rube drew a crowd of 1,400 people. Next, he stays up day and night, working up another show, calling that one the Grand Ole Louisiana Hayride. And sure 'nuff, he puts it over big, drawing some 2,500 people — too many to fit in that auditorium. He's got to find a bigger place or book multiple sites to thin out the crowd."

From James H. "Jimmy" Morrison, in the United States Congressional Record, July 12, 1966:

"Mr. Speaker, it used to be that you would have to go to Nashville on a Saturday night to see and hear good old country western music played by famous artists at the Grand Ole Opry. But this Tennessee monopoly is being challenged as people come from miles around, from anywhere and almost everywhere to see Ponchatoula's pride and joy, the South Louisiana Hayride.

"Working with Rube Rogers and Stanley Cowen — who's father, Dunk, owns the building — is Lloyd 'Hank' Jones, a great MC with musical talent.

"On any Saturday night, it is not uncommon to see people from as far away as Florida or California. You might see Louisiana's governor, John J. McKeithen, with his family sitting right there in the front row, or a U.S. Congressman or a visiting U.S. Senator. They all come — sometimes as many as 2,000 or 3,000 at a time with folks of all ages from 2 to 92.

"At about 8 o'clock as the crowds pull in, those who cannot get a prize seat stay home and turn on the popular radio station, WFPR. That station has a listening audience of well over 100,000 folks, enjoying the talents of Rube Rogers, Terrel 'Foots' McCrory, and George Holly, all of the neighboring city of Hammond. The show is brought by this radio station, to all the armchair fans who sit at home listening to Rube opening each show with: 'Get comfortable, just take off your shoes, you'll feel better, get the coffee poured around 'cause here comes the show you have been waiting for.' "

By 1968, Rube Rogers served as a booking agent, promoter, and occasional host at the South Louisiana Hayride, the Loranger Opry, and the Old South Jamboree in Walker. Additionally, his self-syndicated weekly newspaper column, the Opry Spotlight, went out to newspapers in six states, promoting shows at each of these locations.

In 1968 alone, Rube's column described appearances by over 200 Opry stars, including Loretta Lynn, Porter Waggoner, Grandpa Jones, Ernest Tubb, Charlie Louvin, Willie Nelson, Merle Haggard, Dolly Parton, Bill Monroe, Conway Twitty, Jack Greene, Hank Williams Jr., George Jones, and Roy Acuff.

During this period, Rube Rogers recorded and sold records of his own, including duets with well-known local artists. On the radio, advertisers paid top dollar to hear his unique voice on their radio commercials. Because of those commercials, many locals today still smile when someone mentions the name "Tangi Meats" or the phrases "Going to Sunflower" or "It's Swap Shop time!"

I interviewed Rube Rogers for the first time in 1979. He told me that his first business was a non-profit that promoted gospel concerts in Springfield, long before the country music shows. He also talked of his extended friendships with Willie Nelson and Loretta Lynn, and he said that politics had ruined his life.

"All I ever wanted to do was help people," he said. "I thought public service would be the best way to do that. I was wrong. Everybody loves you on the music stage. On the political stage, there's always someone with a different agenda from yours — and that person will do whatever it takes to bring you down."

When Jimmy Morrison retired, Rube took leave from the radio station and ran for that seat. His campaign speeches insisted that Louisiana oil refineries pay their equal share of taxes, and he publicly identified politicians supported by reputed members of the mob. He lost the race to John Rarick, who accepted donations from both Carlos Marcello and Standard Oil.

In 1972, Rube campaigned for the Tangipahoa Parish Police Jury and won.

During his tenure in office, he chaired the Tangipahoa Bicentennial Committee and petitioned to get the town of Pumpkin Center added to maps and state road-signs. He fought the dredging of Lake Pontchartrain and the destruction of the Tangipahoa River through gravel mining. He led successful movements to widen Highway 22 from Ponchatoula to Springfield and to elevate portions of I-55 from a ground-level, shell-based road.

After leaving office in 1976, he led the campaign mostly responsible for replacing the police jury system with the current home rule charter.

In every instance, Rube leveraged his platform as a popular radio personality to educate the public and encourage all to make their voices heard.

In 1979, he ran for State Senate and again took on the oil companies.

"Recent oil and gas finds make the energy fields between Clinton and Covington the largest in America, yet our existing severance taxes are the lowest on earth. If our oil prices are not brought in line with the world market, the major oil companies will swallow our service station operators, and there will be no more privately owned stations," he said.

And again, he challenged voters to take a serious look at the mafia.

"It's time our state waged an all-out war on the cause of our social and economic ills: organized crime," he said.

And again, he lost the race.

That sums up the legend that was Rube Rogers. Unfortunately, with the successes of every legendary figure, there is an equal amount of tragedy.

In August of 1967, Rube's younger brother, Billy, died in a deep-sea diving accident in the Gulf of Mexico. That same month, the radio station that made him famous burned to the ground. And in 1980, his 18-year-old son, Carl Edward Rogers, committed suicide. Neighbors found him near his home in Pumpkin Center with a .22 caliber bullet in his chest.

The following year, John Rogers, Rube's second-born, was robbed at gunpoint, along with his two cousins, Larry and Terri Rogers. The three were working at Rube's Interstate Battery store when they were surprised by Donald Leach of Ponchatoula and Leonard Johnson of Albany.

One week after the robbery, the Tangipahoa Parish Sheriff's Office returned to the Rogers property and collected ten marijuana plants, charging Rube Rogers for possession and cultivation with intent to distribute. Rube ultimately pled guilty and received a suspended sentence of five years and paid a $4,000 fine.

Jurors deliberated for less than an hour before unanimously finding Eric Lane Maurer guilty of the second-degree murder of Rube Rogers, and on Tuesday, May 28, 2013. Twenty-first Judicial District Court Judge Doug Hughes gave him a life sentence at hard labor without benefit of probation or parole.

Prosecutor Brad Berner, representing the 21st Judicial District Attorney's Office, characterized the case as a calculated robbery that ended in murder. He used testimony from Tangipahoa Parish Sheriff's deputies and Humphrey Count, Tennessee Sheriff Chris Davis to show Maurer entered Rogers' home on Paradise Road south of Hwy 22 near the Tangipahoa/ Livingston Parish line to commit a robbery.

A garbled 911 tape played after lunch for the 12 jurors, with the beyond-the-grave testimony of Rogers, who identified "Eric" Maurer as his assailant on the night of Aug. 13, 2010.

Berner described the events leading up to Rube Rogers' murder:

- Maurer caught a ride to Rogers' house around 10 p.m. on the night of Aug. 13, 2010, and entered the home through an unlocked window.
- Maurer then climbed the stairs to the second story of the home, where he confronted Rube Rogers and ultimately kicked him down the flight of stairs.
- Maurer then takes all the cash and two credit cards from the victim's wallet, along with the keys to his white pick-up truck.
- Maurer observes Rogers on the phone calling 911, and sliced his throat with a butcher knife, before stabbing him around the neck "two or three times" more.
- Maurer leaves in Rogers's white pick up truck and picks up his father, Ricky Maurer. The two then ride north on I-55 to Tennessee.
- The suspect and his father are apprehended at a Days Inn motel in Humphrey County one day later.

As with all heinous crimes, there are outstanding questions.

In court — on the record — but away from the jury were allegations that the defendant's twin brother, Derrick Maurer offered to confess to the murder, and Eric Maurer alleged in taped statements to police that Ricky Maurer was the mastermind behind the plot.

Oswald from New Orleans

W*ith new information from readers and other sources, this chapter evolved from the Bayou Justice column entitled "Lee Harvey Oswald's escape pilot hid at SLU," initially published in south Louisiana newspapers on Tuesday, November 21, 2018.*

THIS WEEK MARKS THE 55th anniversary of the Kennedy Assassination. Whether a singular assassin, innocent patsy, or co-conspirator, Lee Harvey Oswald and his connections to southeast Louisiana in the summer of 1963 are fascinating.

Earlier this month, Covington's English Tea Room invited me to speak to a small group concerning Carnal Knowledge, my upcoming book detailing those connections and others throughout the state. That group discussion got me thinking I should share some of that information in this column.

On March 1, 1967, New Orleans District Attorney Jim Garrison arrested and charged Kentwood-born, Hammond-native Clay Shaw with conspiring to assassinate President John F. Kennedy. According to Garrison, Shaw worked closely with accused assassin Lee Harvey Oswald and David Ferrie, a former Eastern Airlines pilot, and self-proclaimed private investigator.

As the first shots struck President Kennedy on November 22, 1963, David Ferrie sat in a New Orleans courtroom next to the defendant — his employer, a Jefferson Parish business owner named Carlos Marcello.

After Marcello's acquittal, Ferrie picked up two teenagers and drove to Texas. While his friends ice-skated, Ferrie stood at the rink payphone, making and answering calls avoiding the long-distance tolls he would have paid in New Orleans. Ferrie told the FBI the calls were to potential investors in a business venture. He planned to open his ice-skating rink in New Orleans.

Ferrie told investigators from the New Orleans District Attorney's Office the trip was a hunting expedition. He said the trio was "hunting wild geese."

In 2007, Alvin Beauboeuf, one of Ferrie's traveling companions that day, told a New Orleans magazine reporter that Ferrie made the trip and the phone calls as part of his work for Carlos Marcello. Beauboeuf said he did not know whom Ferrie called or why, but he believed the calls had nothing to do with the assassination of the president.

In 1963, Ferrie explained to the FBI what happened after he left the skating rink. He said that following the trip to Texas, he, Alvin Beauboeuf and Melvin Coffey stopped in Alexandria to visit Coffey's parents. There, he called Marcello Attorney G. Wray Gill, who told him the police were looking for him with questions about the assassination. Gill instructed him to drop the teenagers back in New Orleans and lie low while Gill gathered more information.

On the morning of November 24, 1963, Southeastern Louisiana University Student Frank Chalona, Jr. awoke to a stranger sleeping in the bed next to his in the Holloway-Smith Hall men's dormitory.

Chalona described the event to Jim Garrison in 1967:

"His back was to me so I couldn't see his face. He was sleeping fully clothed with his hat on, and his hair looked odd. My roommate, Thomas Compton, said the man had gone bald and pasted theatrical hair below the point where his hat met his head. After he'd left, my roommate told me the guy's name was Dave and that he had been Lee Harvey Oswald's instructor in the Civil Air Patrol."

During his 1969 trial, Clay Shaw denied knowing both Lee Harvey Oswald and David Ferrie, but according to recently released government files, the United States Federal Bureau of Investigation knew otherwise.

Director J. Edgar Hoover never shared that information with Garrison.

On March 16, 1967, Hammond resident, Carroll S. Thomas, called the FBI and described himself as a friend of Clay Shaw. The FBI report reads:

"Carroll S. Thomas, owner, Thomas Funeral Homes, Inc., 300 South Cherry Street, Hammond, Louisiana, advised that he was a close personal friend of Clay Shaw. Thomas also stated that he knew David Ferrie through Shaw. Thomas advised that he did not feel that Clay Shaw had been involved in a plot to kill President Kennedy."

The FBI kept that information to themselves until October 2017 when the Assassination Records Review Board forced the release of files containing Thomas' statement.

"Clay Shaw ate at Hi-Ho all the time." Terrel "Foots" McCrory told me in 1982. "He bought his mother's groceries next door, at the Sunflower, and then he'd get food to go. A nice guy, I enjoyed talking to him."

"That Ferrie's been here, too." Hi-Ho Barbecue's Celeste Alexander added. "But I never saw them together. That Ferrie always came with a kid from the college. He never bought a sandwich. He'd get a sauce-bun and put chips and mustard between the bread. Nasty."

Before his murder, Kentwood gubernatorial candidate Clyde Johnson insisted that he had attended a meeting in Baton Rouge, where Clay Shaw introduced him to both Lee Harvey Oswald and Dallas Strip-club Owner Jack Ruby.

Jack Ruby killed Oswald shot and killed Oswald in a crowded Dallas police station on November 24, 1963. Ruby died of cancer in January of 1967.

David Ferrie died with a brain aneurysm one month later.

During Shaw's trial, the prosecution brought forth eight witnesses from Jackson and Clinton, Louisiana, two adjacent rural towns in East Feliciana Parish. The four witnesses from Jackson placed Lee Harvey Oswald in that town during the summer of 1963. The four Clinton witnesses testified that defendant Clay Shaw had driven a black Cadillac to Clinton, and three of the witnesses testified that Lee Harvey Oswald was with him. One witness identified David Ferrie as being with Shaw and Oswald. A second witness more tentatively identified Ferrie.

Last month, I reconnected with the last surviving Feliciana witness. I first met Edwin McGehee in 1981. In nearly four decades, the story he tells has not changed. The Jackson barber insists he cut Lee Harvey Oswald's hair in late August or early September 1963.

"But I'm through talking to researchers," he said. "The last three who've interviewed me changed my words to lies. I'm done."

He said that authors Patricia Lambert and Judyth Baker angered him most. "They try to write their history, but we were there. We saw what happened. No one's going to change that."

Clay Shaw's trial began on January 29, 1969, in Orleans Parish Criminal Court, and ended on March 1, 1969. The Orleans Parish jury took less than an hour to find the retired trade executive "not guilty."

Ten years later, the House Select Committee on Assassinations released the results of their investigation. They stated that the Committee had interviewed the East Feliciana witnesses and were "inclined to believe" that Oswald had been in Clinton "in the company of David Ferrie, if not Clay Shaw."

Today, 50 years after his trial, most have forgotten Shaw, but researchers everywhere are still asking questions about David Ferrie.

In 1993, Attorney Gerald Posner insisted Oswald was not in the New Orleans Civil Air Patrol during the time Ferrie led the group. The following year, the PBS television show, Front Line, aired photographs of the two serving together.

In his book on the subject, retired SLU Professor Michael Kurtz reported seeing Oswald and Ferrie together in Mancuso's Restaurant on Camp Street in New Orleans, along with Carlos Quiroga, a Cuban exile leader.

Various witnesses, including Lizzie Hines of Tickfaw, remembered seeing Oswald and Ferrie together at two Cuban Exile training camps in southeast Louisiana — one near Bayou Lacombe and another near Bedico Creek, east of Ponchatoula. However, the most intriguing evidence of their relationship is related to a flight plan filed by David Ferrie in 1963. It rightly lists Ferrie's red and white 1948 Stinson Voyager. The stated destination is Garland, Texas, with the Dallas airport as an alternative. One of the passengers listed is a known alias of Lee Harvey Oswald, and another bears the last name of a Cuban exile leader.

The four-person crew departed from the Hammond airport on April 8, 1963 — one day before Oswald allegedly shot at Texas gubernatorial candidate Edwin Walker at his home in Dallas.

Highland Park Airport — the airport in Garland, Texas — was seven miles from Dealey Plaza, where John F. Kennedy died. According to Dallas Researcher Jim Gatewood, the airport's owner claimed he once had another Ferrie flight plan.

Gatewood reiterated the story this way:

According to John Randy Brodenhead, two FBI agents learned he had a flight plan filed by David Ferrie, showing his departure from Garland in a rented twin-engine Apache Piper, ultimately landing in Havana, Cuba. Before the agents could return with a warrant to secure the plan, the airport office went up in flames, destroying the document.

The expected flight date on that plan was November 22, 1963, and the sole passenger was Lee Harvey Oswald.

Grinch Who Stole Guns

With new information from readers and other sources, this chapter evolved from the Bayou Justice column entitled "Local Grinch's death still troubles relatives," initially published in south Louisiana newspapers on Tuesday, December 18, 2018.

BACK IN OCTOBER, WE investigated a potentially tall-tale retold regularly by my great-grandfather, William Oliver "Paw Bill" Courtney, and — amazingly — we found the story of the tarred-and-feathered Hammond dentist to be 100% accurate. This month, I wanted to look into Paw Bill's account about a Livingston Parish "Grinch" who stole Christmas presents, had a change of heart, and then returned them all before morning.

Checking the archives of the Associated Press and United Press International, unfortunately, I did not find the story confirmation I had hoped more, but I did uncover evidence that this would-be Grinch's death remains a mystery after 30 years.

Before we revisit his death, let's first recount the story of "the Grinch Who Stole Shotguns."

In the late sixties and early seventies, most South Louisiana residents still felt safe in their homes. They seldom locked their doors — rarely the doors on their homes and never the doors of vehicles parked in their front yards.

Yes, I know this part is already difficult for some to believe, but standby. I've haven't gotten to the unverifiable part yet.

Parents in this period taught their children gun safety. Back then, this meant that kids learned to shoot — or they learned not to touch. Either way, guns caused little concern among parents.

Instead of gun vaults or safes, most homes had open gun "racks" in the dens or living rooms, and during hunting seasons, all pickup trucks featured in-cab gun racks mounted behind passenger's heads above the front seat.

Christmas always coincided with Deer Hunting Season, and quite often, folks would buy their spouse's rifles and shotguns as presents. Since this hunting season arrived before Santa, hunters usually got these presents early, long before Christmas Day.

The dedicated hunters of South Louisiana would take weeks off from work to hunt, spending every day at the hunting camp or in a tree stand, often enduring below-freezing temperatures. But this all stopped on Christmas Eve — at least for the married hunters who wanted to stay that way.

Now, we have set the stage for our story.

It was Christmas Eve, December 24, 1970, in the town of Holden, Louisiana.

The residents were all home, snug in their beds, with vehicles unlocked in their front yards — and new, shiny shotguns and rifles hanging like stockings in every cab.

Not a creature was stirring, except Huey Courtney, a man who loved mischief. His first arrest came at age 19. On April 20, 1950, the Louisiana Forestry Commission charged him with arson after he admitted to setting a series of forest fires in the Holden area.

On this Christmas Eve in 1970, Huey was driving a beat-up green Chevrolet truck with a bull's horns mounted to the hood. No one would mistake this pickup for a sleigh, but he was not worried. Holden had few streetlights in those days.

Huey found it a comfortable night's work, driving from house to house, collecting the guns from each truck, and by 2: AM, he had appropriated more than 40 firearms.

Back home, he built a fire in the fireplace and sat down next to the Christmas tree, listening to Christmas carols on the radio. He sipped on some eggnog with rum, but for some reason, he could not fall asleep.

No one knows what happened between that moment and dawn.

The town might have never known anything had ever happened if not for the mix-up.

According to Paw Bill, when everyone got ready to return to the woods on Christmas Day, they each found a neighbor's gun in their truck and their weapon in someone else's vehicle.

Paw Bill told Congressman John Rarick this story with Huey and I sitting next to him. Cousin Huey did not deny the story. Instead, he just laughed, winked, and said, "How do you know the switch wasn't planned all along?"

As I mentioned, this was not a story I could confirm from the newspapers of the day, but Huey's death was a different matter. The Associated Press circulated the following report on June 10, 1986:

"Two men shot and killed each other at a residence north of Holden Saturday night, according to Livingston Parish Sheriff Odom Graves. Killed were Larry F. Van Hoose, 47, of Albany and Huey P. Courtney, 55, of Holden.

"The sheriff said Van Hoose went to Courtney's home around 10:30 Sunday night, June 9, and the two men, both armed with pistols, shot each other in Courtney's living room.

"Detectives have been unable to establish a motive for the shooting, but are continuing their investigation."

Larry Van Hoose opened a seafood distributorship in Albany after moving to Louisiana from Florida, where his family buried him. His obituary there described him as a commercial angler and a military veteran, who had served as a Florida sheriff's deputy in the 1960s.

His Albany barber said Van Hoose told him that he worked for the Central Intelligence Agency.

Huey Pierce Courtney lived at the end of a long gravel road, approximately one mile from the intersection of Highways 441 and 1036. In the weeks that followed his death, I interviewed three neighbors who lived near the beginning of that gravel road.

All three heard the shots that night, and all three said they came two minutes apart. They also described the dark blue or back car speeding from the residence following the shooting. Today, more than three decades later, police have yet to discover who drove that car.

Maybe Bonnie & Clyde

With new information from readers and other sources, this chapter evolved from the Bayou Justice column entitled "Bonnie & Clyde kidnap Ponchatoula banker," initially published in south Louisiana newspapers on Tuesday, December 25, 2018.

ON SEPTEMBER 1, 1932, two shotgun-wielding bandits car-jacked a Ponchatoula bank president and his two daughters. Confronted by an angry mob in a roadblock near Springfield, the pair abandoned the car and their captives, fleeing on foot into a nearby swamp, where a posse of 300 volunteers searched fruitlessly for them over four days.

The banker, W. E. Mount, told sheriff's deputies his kidnappers were "two young men." However, several near the roadblock insisted that the driver fleeing the green sedan was a woman. One witness, Springfield Druggist Estelle Coates, positively identified the fleeing driver as Bonnie Parker, infamous bank robber, and leader of the Bonnie and Clyde Gang.

I first heard this story in 1979, when I was writing for *The Hammond Vindicator*, alongside Mildred Furbos, who's father owned Louisiana's longest-running weekly for over four decades.

George B. Campbell died in 1967. He had run the paper since 1919. Still, he was best known for "The Stroller," a simple folklore column chronicling Hammond's life in simpler times, keeping readers abreast of topics like who had purchased a new automobile or had a child or did not cut the grass regularly. He even wrote about potholes, locomotive noise, and the latest offerings at the downtown café or the feed-and-seed stores.

C. Howard Nichols, a retired professor of Louisiana history at Southeastern Louisiana University in Hammond, said of the column: "In its heyday, it was a wonderful window on life in Hammond."

Campbell sold *The Vindicator* in 1966, and *The Daily Star* obtained it in 2003. However, back in the late 70s and early 80s, Bryan T. McMahon owned the weekly and had given me the use of a back-office — provided I sorted through decades of accumulated storage to clean it out. Mildred Furbos was helping me do so when we found a large flat, green linen box.

"Oh my goodness," Miss Milly said. "This was Poppa's; We thought it long gone."

Inside the box, we found newspaper clippings taped to sheets of blank newsprint — essentially scrapbook pages without the binding. The second sheet in the stack included a wanted poster for Bonnie Parker and Clyde Barrow.

Miss Milly said the poster once hung in the Springfield Drug Store and that Estelle Coates had given it to her father in 1932. Coates had asked him to help her prove that the infamous duo had kidnapped W. E. Mount and his children.

Afraid of reprisal, Mount had long refused to identify his captors.

From the clippings:

"Two bandits, foiled in attempts to kidnap W. E. Mount, president of the Merchants & Farmers Bank of Ponchatoula, along with Mr. Mount's two small daughters, were believed to be hiding in the woods west of Springfield in Livingston Parish, after shooting their way through a roadblock with both citizens and deputies returning fire.

"The bandits are known to have shotguns and may have at least one machine gun. Posse-men were told to take no chances and shoot on sight, but deputies report the pair disappeared and theorized they might have blended secretly with their posse of over 300 men and women.

"The middle-aged banker said his would-be captors wanted access to the vault and that he fought them both, considerably younger men, in a long, strenuous tussle. He said he escaped with his two small daughters, Ruby and Clarabelle, ages 11 and 12, on a roadside just a mile outside of Ponchatoula."

"Mr. Mount, suffering from the shock of this experience, is still unable to give a precise account of just what happened. However, an observant neighbor witnessed the escape and fired a shotgun over the heads of the assailants, causing them to speed away.

"Afterwards, the neighbor telephoned ahead to Springfield, alerting the town that the bandits were headed in their direction. After the call, Deputy Sheriff R. S. Theard sounded the alarm, collecting citizens with guns to form the roadblock.

"Deputy Sheriff Bud Sullivan parked a large flatbed truck across the roadway between Ponchatoula and Springfield. However, when the bandit's green sedan came screeching along, it circled the truck with both bandit's shooting at the crowd. The crowd returned fire, but the car went through a ditch and continued down the road into Springfield. The car was later found abandoned a quarter-mile west of Springfield. A trace of the Texas plates found the car had been stolen three months earlier."

Two months after the attempted kidnapping, New Orleans police apprehended a gang of six would-be bank robbers. Sheriff's deputies escorted W. E. Mount to the city in an attempt to identify the men who had attacked him, but he failed to do so.

According to Campbell's scrapbook notes, Estelle Coates insisted until her death that Bonnie Parker was the driver of the sedan. The newspaper clippings said all witnesses interviewed described the gunman in the passenger seat as tall and slender, clean-shaven with brown hair — an approximate description of Clyde Barrow in 1932.

In the 1990s, Nicholas R. Murray leased *The Vindicator* from Owner Harrel Griffith and asked me to work for him. By then, the newspaper had moved to a different building, and Miss Milly had long retired. I asked Mr. Murray if he had heard about the green, linen box.

Mr. Murray, an amateur genealogist, grinned broadly. He said Miss Milly had it, but she had allowed him to scan its contents. He had spent months researching the names in the articles, tracking down descendants of those named, but like Campbell before him, he was also unable to solve the puzzle.

The incident at the Springfield roadblock occurred on September 1, 1932.

Ironically, Bonnie and Clyde died in a similar Louisiana roadblock, just two years later. Just before dawn on May 23, 1934, another posse — this one composed of law enforcement officers from Louisiana and Texas — concealed themselves in bushes along the highway near Sailes, Louisiana, and waited.

As before, Bonnie and Clyde appeared in another stolen automobile. Again, they attempted to drive around the roadblock, and again, the posse opened fire.

But this time, Bonnie and Clyde died instantly.

Daytra and Robert

W*ith new information from readers and other sources, this chapter evolved from the Bayou Justice column entitled "No suspects in Christmas Mother, Child homicide," initially published in south Louisiana newspapers on Tuesday, January 8, 2019.*

AT 6:30 PM, SUNDAY, December 23, 2018, residents of a neighborhood two miles west of Independence heard gunshots and began phoning 911.

Tangipahoa Parish Sheriff's deputies responded, discovering the lifeless bodies of 42-year-old Daytra Miller and her 13-year-old son, Robert West, II, inside their home at the corner of Labruzza Lane and Fontana Road.

This week, family members boarded the wood-frame house's windows and doors with plywood, too heartbroken to return to the home.

Miller's aunt, Gloria McGee, said her niece had lived in the area at least 15 years, many of them with her children in the home on Labruzza. She described Miller as "Hard-working, very respectful, full of life, and very loving."

She said Robert was an honors student. "Just an angel, a joy to be around. So loving, respectful," McGee said. "A life cut short."

Robert West told reporters last week that on the morning of Christmas Eve, he watched workers from the coroner's office carry his son from his home in a body bag.

He said his son's mother was his best friend and that she had been packing to bring his son to stay with him a few days.

"My son was being raised by all of us. He's the youngest of six, including four girls." He said his son's siblings were looking forward to spending Christmas with their brother.

"We were just trying to preach to them how important it is for them to stay together," he said sobbing. "Even if Daytra and I weren't getting along, or something happened to one of us. As long as they stayed together, they'd be okay."

Tangi Academy Principal Jackie Wilson released this statement regarding the younger Robert West:

"He was a kind, gentle, helpful, and caring young man who always put others before himself. In one of his latest assignments in Mrs. Garner's ELA class, he wrote about wanting to be a professional fisherman. He loved fishing because his grandfather taught him how to fish. Robert would always stop in my office to 'check out' my fish tank. He even gave me a few tips on the proper ways to care for fish since mine kept dying at the beginning of the school year. I finally got it right, and the two that remain have been going strong since early September, thanks to some of his advice."

Kristian Polk-Usey, one of Robert West's teachers, said he was a mentor for younger children, a football and basketball player, and that he gave the best hugs.

"He was everything you'd want your son to be," Polk-Usey said.

"People loved my son," the elder West said. "I love him. He was a good kid."

The grieving father said he is praying that someone who knows what happened will speak up soon.

"If anyone has any information about my son or about anything that has happened to him. Even if you even remotely know someone involved or know something about this situation, please contact any authorities."

Last week, TPSO's Chief Information Officer, Dawn Panepinto, said investigators believe the victims may have known the person who committed the "heinous crime" since there had been no sign of forced entry.

"At this point for investigative purposes, we're accepting any information anyone has about shots being fired in the area," she said, adding that investigators have been working on the case around-the-clock since the murders. She said the agency had received multiple tips from the public, but it will take time to verify the information provided.

West said investigators told him that they are still waiting on the Louisiana State Police Crime Lab to analyze the final pieces of evidence before they release information on a possible person of interest in the shooting.

McGee insisted last week that these crimes were not a product of domestic violence. "We don't know who did this, but on behalf of the Miller and West family, we need your prayers and support, and we need the community's help to solve this crime. Any tips, any information you have, please call the Tangipahoa Parish Sheriff's Office, the local office, the Independence police department."

To assist with funeral expenses, the family has set up a Go Fund Me account in the name of her deceased nephew. Still, McGee said the family's primary focus this week is on helping police locate those responsible.

Sheriff Daniel Edwards said, "We are hopeful that someone with relevant information will step up and help put those responsible for this horrific crime behind bars. One thing we do know is that there are people out there who have information about these murders. We want that information or anything that will lead us in the direction of the shooters."

His office is offering a $5,000 reward for information in the case. Anyone able to help collect the prize anonymously through Crime Stoppers of Tangipahoa by calling 800-554-5245.

"Crime Stoppers has proven to be a useful tool in these types of investigations," the sheriff said, "and we are hopeful that someone with relevant information will step up and help put those responsible for this horrific crime behind bars."

The Panama Bandit

With new information from readers and other sources, this chapter evolved from the Bayou Justice column entitled "Panama Bandit, murderer At large since 1958," initially published in south Louisiana newspapers on Tuesday, January 15, 2019.

AT NOON, JUNE 24, 1958, Detective Walter Holmes, a sergeant with the New Orleans Police Department, walked into the Amite jail, anxious to interview the suspect Tangipahoa Parish Sheriff's Deputies had called him about that morning. He had spent the last month exhausting leads in a multi-state search for a murderer — the killer newspapers had begun to call the Panama Bandit.

The search began six weeks earlier when a man in a Panama hat shot a 36-year-old bartender named Thomas Gagliano.

An article in *The New Orleans Times-Picayune* on May 14, 1958, reported that someone shot and killed Gagliano around 3: AM at his bar, the T&M, at 210 North Dorgenois Street in Mid-City. The article described the murder as a botched holdup attempt and detailed an anonymous telephone tip that said the assailant was "a transfer truck driver."

The prisoner in the Tangipahoa Parish Jail was a truck driver from Pennsylvania named Delbert William Eyer. However, witnesses at the bar described the assailant as approximately 30-years-old. According to the Tangipahoa Parish Sheriff's Office, Eyer was only 24-years old.

Holmes had fingerprints from the bar and three slugs from the assailant's gun. The coroner had removed one of the slugs from Gagliano's body, and the police extracted two others from the bar.

The Tangipahoa Parish Sheriff's Office had slugs from Eyer's gun, and Holmes had driven to Amite, hoping the evidence matched.

In the weeks prior, he had traveled to Kentucky and North Carolina, where he ruled out truck-driving suspects in both states — and since Gagliano's death, two other New Orleans bar owners had been robbed by the man in the Panama hat.

The month before Holmes' trip to Amite, witnesses said Gagliano's slayer entered his bar shortly after midnight, had a drink, and then left. At closing time, he came back, ordered another glass, and pointed a .25 caliber revolver at Gagliano.

Announcing the holdup, he backed away from the bar-raising a gun in the air.

When Gagliano laughed, the holdup man fired a slug into the ceiling.

"Okay, okay," the bartender said, "Don't get excited."

Gagliano then walked behind the register, opened a money drawer, and grabbed his pistol. Outside the view of the holdup man, he tried to cock it, but a penny from the drawer caused his gun to jam.

At that moment, 28-year-old Margie Simmons — Gagliano's barmaid and common-law wife   screamed. "Please don't use that gun, Tom."

And, of course, that's when the holdup man shot Gagliano.

Gagliano fell forward, knocking the locked cash register to the floor, and the holdup man fled the building.

In addition to Simmons, Barmaid Linda Pertuit, 38, and a customer, Louis Gallo, 41, also witnessed the shooting.

Gagliano was a former cab driver and had operated the bar for only seven months.

Police raided his home at 827 St. Charles Street on Valentine's Day in 1955, arresting Gagliano and charging him with pandering — commonly referred to today as "pimping" — along with six women who also gave their home addresses as 827 St. Charles Street.

Two days after Gagliano's murder, a police sketch artist interviewed the witnesses and developed a composite drawing later circulated by police, along with the following description:

"He is a white man 25 to 30 years old, 5 feet, 10 inches tall, weighing 160-175 pounds. He has straight dark hair, an olive complexion, and he was wearing a light plaid sports shirt and blue jeans with spots. He was wearing a Panama hat, was possibly a truck driver, could speak Italian, and he had good teeth."

Two additional bar holdups occurred in the area in the month that followed. A witness to one of those holdups also described a Panama hat, but at the third holdup, the surviving bartender described the bandit as wearing a wool cap and a stocking mask.

Saloon patrons all over the city began to panic, imagining Panama Hat Bandits in every alley and dark bar corner. That's when the Slidell robbery made the papers.

Shortly after lunch on June 23, 1958, Stenographer Paula Rivet, 44, attempted to enter a Five and Dime store in Mid-City when a man exiting with a handkerchief over his face and a gun in his hand met her. She said the man told her the store was closed and hurried away.

Rivet screamed for help, and C. A. Strickland, who operated an electrical repair shop, jumped into his truck and began chasing the running gunman. After three blocks, the man ran between two houses.

"I shouted for him to stop," Strickland said, "and he came back. That's when I saw the blood on the gun. He pointed it at me and said: 'Please don't shoot' and tossed the gun under one of the houses. At that point, he ran off again."

In the yard next door, the gunman confronted Mrs. Freda Magee, who was hanging clothes on a line in her yard. He ran past her to a heavy tank truck loaded with rice. Climbing into the cab, he drove away.

Back at the Five and Dime, Paula Rivet found the store's cash register on the floor with a broken pair of scissors jammed in the locked register drawer. In a corner, she found the body of the part-time cashier, 47-year-old Myrtle Jones Pichon.

Her body had been drug across the store in a trail of blood that measured 45 feet.

Slidell Police Chief Clarence Howze found the rice truck speeding west on Highway 190 and gave chase. The trucker tossed the bloody handkerchief from the cab, while leading Howze and four St. Tammany Parish sheriff's deputies on a ten-mile chase that lasted over an hour as the trucker weaved in and out of traffic, backtracking several times.

"It was the darndest thing," Howze said. "He was trying to change clothes as he drove. The way the truck was weaving, it made it dangerous for us to try and head him off."

Tangipahoa Parish Sheriff's deputies stopped the truck at the parish line.

Delbert William Eyer climbed from the cab, saying, "I don't know what you want me for. I don't know anything about what happened."

At that point, according to Howze, the man attempted to run again. Howze "bear-hugged" him until the sheriff's deputies could handcuff him.

Police recovered Eyer's pistol beneath a house near the crime scene and locked Eyer in the St. Tammany Parish jail. That night, a mob of angry citizens entered the lockup with pistols, shotguns, and a hangman's noose.

Before sunrise the following day, a judge transferred Delbert William Eyer to the Tangipahoa Parish prison, where sheriff's deputies called Detective Walter Holmes.

In Amite, Holmes discovered that Eyer had no olive complexion, he did not speak Italian, and he had rotten teeth. Holmes compared the slugs — .22 versus .25 caliber — and he compared Eyer's fingerprints to those found on an ashtray at Gagliano's bar.

No match.

Holmes ordered a polygraph test. Questioned about the Slidell robbery and homicide, Eyer failed the test, but regarding the New Orleans slaying, he passed.

Disappointed, convinced that Delbert William Eyer was not the Panama Bandit, Holmes packed his things and walked out of the Amite jail frustrated. Still, in the parking lot, halfway to his car, a man in a Tickfaw Police uniform stopped him.

"Are you Detective Holmes?" The officer asked, unfolding a crumpled newspaper clipping. "You might want to stop in Tickfaw." The excerpt showed the original drawing police had circulated of the Panama Bandit. "I play cards with this man every week. He's got family in Independence."

The Mob Collector

With *new information from readers and other sources, this chapter evolved from the Bayou Justice column entitled "Panama Bandit Killer Carlos Marcello collector," initially published in south Louisiana newspapers on Tuesday, January 22, 2019.*

LAST WEEK, WE RETRACED the footsteps of Sergeant Walter Holmes, a New Orleans Police Detective on the trail of a hold-up man wanted for the murder of Bar-owner Thomas Gagliano in 1958.

His search took him into Kentucky, then North Carolina, and finally, the Tangipahoa Parish Jail in Amite. In each location, he compared traits of truck-driving hold-up men. None of the three proved to be the killer.

Disappointed, Holmes loaded his car in Amite, preparing to leave, when Tickfaw Police Officer Louis Pigno approached him. Pigno recognized a police sketch of the bandit as a man called "Nofi," and according to Pigno, the so-called Panama Hat Bandit played poker in the rear of Angelo Nicotre's bar every Wednesday night.

The following week, Holmes and Pigno sat in an unmarked car outside of an Independence bar called The Greek, waiting for the suspect to show.

When "Nofi" stepped into the light, Pigno said, "Angelo says this guy's got relatives all over Independence. Do you want to question some of them?"

Holmes shook his head. "That won't be necessary. I recognize him. His name was Onofio Pecoraro. He changed it when we busted him for robbing a warehouse. Today, he's called Nofio Pecora and works as a collector for the mob."

The original police report on the Gagliano homicide described the killer as "a white man with an olive complexion, 5 feet, 10 inches tall, 160-175 pounds, straight dark hair, could speak Italian, and had good teeth."

Pecora matched the description, and he liked to wear Panama hats in the summer, but he was no "truck driver." The anonymous telephone tip had sent the New Orleans police in the wrong direction. Pecora could have made that call himself.

However, Nofio Pecora was 48-years-old in 1958. If Pecora did shoot Thomas Gagliano, three witnesses lied to the police.

According to the Federal Bureau of Investigation's 200-document file on Onofio Pecoraro, he began smuggling narcotics from Honduras and up the Mississippi River in 1935. Still, his first arrest did not come until December 21, 1937.

Federal narcotics agents indicted 88 people related to a "gigantic interstate narcotics ring." Of the 88 arrested, most were from New York, but five had New Orleans homes: James Campo, Thomas Siracusa, Philip, and Nicholas Bonura, and Onofio Pecoraro. Federal narcotics agents charged all five with "conspiracy to violate narcotics laws."

In 1942, Louisiana State Police arrested Pecoraro — along with Philip Bonura and "Dutch August" Terilleaux — for possessing $20,000 in furs stolen from a Louisiana Department of Conservation warehouse, after a night watchman found two co-workers bound and gagged with adhesive tape.

The three arrested claimed to be traveling poultry dealers and said they had assisted a stranded truck driver on the highway and was given them the stolen furs as a reward.

When the fur incident made national news, Onofio Pecoraro changed his name to Nofio Pecora and opened a used car lot. Eventually, he would manage some bars on Bourbon Street, open a restaurant and buy a mobile home park, all through loans from his wife's employer, New Orleans' most infamous tomato salesman, Carlos Marcello.

As bail bondsmen, Nofio Pecora's most famous client may have been a guy named Lee Harvey Oswald. According to the FBI, one of the last telephone calls Jack Ruby made before killing Oswald was to Pecora's office at the mobile home court.

Pecora's wife, Frances, eventually worked in Louisiana state government before going to jail for attempting to bribe Tangipahoa Parish Sheriff Eddie Layrisson — that was after sheriff's deputies busted her son with a warehouse full of narcotics in Loranger.

But those are all stories for another week.

Back in New Orleans, Detective Holmes tried to track down 28-year-old Margie Simmons, Thomas Gagliano's common-law wife, to show her a photo of Pecora and maybe ask why she lied about the age of the man who shot her lover. Unfortunately, though, Simmons had left town with no forwarding address.

Witnesses Louis Gallo, 41, was located but refused to answer Holmes' questions without a lawyer present.

Barmaid Linda Pertuit, 38, said she had not seen the shooter, but she recognized Pecora's photo. She said that he "collected dividends" weekly from Gagliano and other bar owners who hosted gambling activities in back rooms.

She said that she thought most bars in New Orleans opened their businesses with loans from the mob, but she never asked questions.

Holmes must have wondered about the Greek Bar back in Independence.

Nofio Pecora died in 1986.

Today, the Thomas Gagliano murder officially remains unsolved.

Selonia Reed

With new information from readers and other sources, this chapter evolved from the Bayou Justice column entitled "Selonia Reed case active, Reginald Reed indicted," initially published in south Louisiana newspapers on Tuesday, January 29, 2019.

LAST OCTOBER, HAMMOND Police Chief James Stewart said HPD had closed the investigation into the 1987 brutal murder of Selonia Smith Reed without making an arrest. So, I filed a Public Records Request with the department (as well as 15 other law enforcement agencies) requesting 30 years of data on all homicide cases closed without anyone paying for the crime.

Hammond Mayor Pete Panepinto dismissed Chief Stewart, and Assistant Chief Thomas Corkern informed me that the Selonia Reed case was now active with both the Tangipahoa Parish Sheriff's Office and the Louisiana State Police involved in the investigation.

In an unrelated case, 21st Judicial District Attorney Scott Perrilloux indicted Selonia Reed's husband, 58-year-old Reginald Reed of Hammond, with one count of aggravated rape on January 14 of this year. The office scheduled his arraignment one month later, on Valentine's Day.

Perrilloux's Public Information Officer Autumn Payton said the DA's office could not release any additional information due to the nature of the crime. She said it would be impossible to do so without publicly identifying the victim of the rape.

Reginald Reed became a public figure in 1998 when he ran for Mayor of Hammond, but he made headlines 11 years earlier when someone murdered his wife.

At 6:30 that Sunday morning, August 23, 1987, Reed phoned Gwen Smith at North Oaks Hospital to tell her that his wife, Selonia, had gone out with friends the night before and had not returned home.

Gwen Smith told him, "That's not like my sister. She wouldn't go out and leave Little Reggie at home."

Gwen Smith told me last week, "Even if Loni had done such a thing, she would have been home before Little Reggie got up. He was a momma's boy. She didn't go anywhere without him."

An hour after speaking to Gwen Smith, Reginald Reed phoned the Hammond Police Department and reported his wife missing. Another hour went by before a patrol unit found Selonia Smith Reed's car in the parking lot of a convenience store less than a mile from the police station; her mutilated body slumped in the passenger's seat.

Jackie Smith, Selonia Reed's younger sister, lived in the Reed home the week before Selonia Reed's death. "Reginald had gone to New York on business. Loni was off work from the bank — home on vacation — and she was afraid to be alone. When she picked me up, we stopped at our father's place, and she asked Dad if he would buy her a gun."

"I thought she was afraid of the neighbor, a maintenance man that did work for them sometimes. One night, I stepped out on the porch to smoke. Loni said 'No. Go into the bathroom.' She hated the smoke in her house. I knew something wasn't right. This was about 10:30 at night. Loni heard Little Reggie moving around in his room and went to check on him, and I went outside anyway. Just as I stepped off the porch, a man was standing in the shadows. He almost scared me to death. Loni came to the door, saw us talking, and told me to get inside. We were both shook up."

After Reginald Reed returned from New York, the family of three drove Jackie Smith back home to New Orleans. "That Friday night, we had dinner. Everything seemed fine. I had no idea that was the last time I'd see my sister."

Gwen Smith said she saw their sister the night before her murder.

"My car was in the shop, and Loni gave me a ride home from work. She didn't say anything about going out with any girlfriends. She said she was going to the mall to pick up some things and asked if I wanted to go. I told her I was tired and had to work early the next morning."

The next morning was the Sunday when Reginald Reed called her.

"I went straight to Loni's house from work. The police were there, but there was something else strange. Don't get me wrong, Loni was a good housekeeper, but this place looked and smelled unusually clean, immaculate. There was no trash in the cans. Even the dirty clothes hamper was empty."

"She was going back to work that Monday, so it made sense that she would clean-up. I just never saw her house like that before. I still think about that sometimes."

Tangipahoa Parish Coroner Dr. Vincent Cefalu said the autopsy showed Selonia Reed died of four puncture wounds to her heart. The killer inflicted her wounds with "an instrument larger than an ice pick, but smaller than a knife, about the caliber of a screwdriver," Cefalu said.

Cefalu visibly choked up in a press conference, describing how police found the 26-year-old with an umbrella forced into her vagina and her face badly beaten. "It was just a bad sight," he said.

The autopsy report showed the murderer spread a substance similar to white toothpaste or lotion on parts of her body that mixed with the blood.

At the same press conference, Captain Jim Richardson of the Hammond Police Department said Selonia Reed had been dead less than three hours when they found her body at 9:30 a.m. He told reporters that detectives had looked for some container that might have held the lotion, but they could not find one.

In 1987, I worked as a newscaster for WFPR and WHMD in Hammond. I also worked as a stringer for the Associated Press and as Investigative Reporter for *The Hammond Vindicator*. In those roles, I worked the murder of Selonia Smith Reed, a young girl I had met only once. She was a teller at Citizen's National Bank.

The week following her death, I took a walk. From the location of her abandoned car on Thomas Street, behind the Timesaver convenience store, I walked through the woods and came out in the neighborhood where Selonia Reed lived.

Today, I shudder to think how difficult the hike might prove with my arthritic knee, but 30 years ago, I made the trip from the Timesaver to Selonia Reed's front door in under 15 minutes.

On a bulletin board in my office at home, a yellow newspaper clipping commands my attention at least once a day. *The Hammond Daily Star* photo by Steve Petorka shows the Loranger High School homecoming court of 1976. The high school junior smiling second from left is Selonia Smith.

I keep it to remind me that justice for Loni has not yet been served.

Coffee with Victims

With new information from readers and other sources, this chapter evolved from the Bayou Justice column entitled "A monster's victims Converse over coffee," initially published in south Louisiana newspapers on Tuesday, February 5, 2019.

IN A PRESS CONFERENCE last week, Ascension Parish Sheriff Bobby Webre labeled confessed murderer Dakota Theriot a monster. Last Friday night, that description dominated my thoughts as two Tangipahoa Parish women described another monster — one they believe has escaped justice for more than three decades.

The staff and customers at Joe Muggs Coffee Shop in Hammond Square Mall likely wondered what I kept saying to these ladies to bring them to tears, again and again, the four hours we sat there, but I merely arranged the reunion, drank my coffee and listened — and at times, my stomach turned.

These two women worked for the same Hammond business in the 1980s, along with one of the women's sisters. I would have loved to have invited that woman as well, but she — I will call her Tina — was murdered a year after leaving that company for another job.

Tina's sister described how the monster would arrive at their workplace on payday, upsetting Tina and leaving with her paycheck. Following those paydays — and a few other days — Tina reported for work in dark glasses and refused to let anyone see her eyes.

Tina's sister said Tina did not yet own a car in those days. Tina's husband would pick her up from work — often hours after her shift had ended. Her sister would offer her a ride, but Tina always refused, saying it might anger her husband.

"And he would have been angry too," the second woman said. "I should know. He's my brother — and I've been afraid of him all of my life."

The monster's sister then described in detail how her brother had raped her as a child. The first time, she said, she was 11-years-old. He made his last attempt while he was still married to Tina.

"I was a senior at Hammond High," she said. "I expected my mom to pick me up after school, but my brother picked me up instead, and he refused to take me home. He drove until almost dark, saying he wanted to show me something. Then he pulled the car over and showed me something I didn't want to see, saying 'make me feel good like you used to.'"

The two sisters stared silently at each other for five minutes or more, and then the monster's sister took the other woman's hand.

"I should have told you, but I didn't know how," she said.

"What do you mean?" Tina's sister asked.

"I heard you on tape." The monster's sister said. "My brother tapped the house phone line and recorded all of Tina's calls. Most of them were with you."

"Remember all those times that he sent flowers to her work. You talked about it on the phone. Tina said she knew it was him because she didn't have a secret admirer."

"I do remember that," Tina's sister said. "She was so scared."

"Not long after the baby was born," the monster's sister said. "I was at their house. Tina had lost weight so fast. I was asking her how she did it. She got on the floor to show me, doing sit-ups, and my brother came in. He said she was losing weight for her boyfriend and stomped her in the stomach."

"My God. Why?" I asked.

"Oh," Tina's sister said. "He was extremely jealous."

"Yes," the monster's sister confirmed. "He tried to make people think she was seeing a Hammond lawyer, but I listened to those tapes. She loved him. She wanted to have another child by him — she was just deathly afraid of him."

"How did you hear the tapes?" Tina's sister asked.

"Right before their house fire," the monster's sister said. "He moved a bunch of boxes into my mother's garage. I was a nosy teenager, so I found the tapes and played them."

"Oh, that fire," Tina's sister said. "He sent Tina to stay with our mother the week it happened. I called there and told her the house was burning. Tina said that she suspected something would happen. [Her husband] had increased their home owner's insurance a few weeks before."

Both sisters told me that shortly before someone murdered Tina, the monster increased her life insurance policy and then purchased a second policy. Because of the brutality of her murder, they said, the husband collected double indemnity.

The monster's sister said she had held her tongue all her life out of fear.

"In 1985, my brother took Tina and me to see the movie, *the Jagged Edge*. We hated that movie, but he loved it. It was about a man who murdered his wife for the money."

"And a few months after Tina died, my brother got my husband to help him take a heavy bag from his shed and lower it into a dumpster on Airline Highway near LaPlace. When they were loading it in our truck, I heard my brother mention something about 'Sloppy HPD' — that was what he always called Hammond Police."

"Sometime after that," she said, "my brother tried to convince me to increase my husband's life insurance. I refused and told him he was crazy, but he got someone to draw up the paperwork anyway."

She opened a leather binder, allowing me to read the unregistered insurance policy. The agent listed the payout at one million dollars.

I asked the monster's sister why she was telling her truth today.

"My perspective changed," she said, "when my daughter told me how many times my brother had raped her."

Willie Jones

With new information from readers and other sources, this chapter evolved from the Bayou Justice column entitled "Link considered in Reed, Jones murders," initially published in south Louisiana newspapers on Tuesday, February 12, 2019.

TWO WEEKS AGO, I RECOUNTED the brutality of Selonia Reed's unsolved murder. Several readers responded, asking about a connection between Selonia Reed and Willie A. Jones — a man found murdered one week after the Reed slaying.

My grandmother, Margaret Courtney, retired from the Hammond State School after 30 years in state service. There, she supervised the facility's telephone switchboard operators. Through my grandmother and two aunts who worked there, I knew several of the employees at the school, and I spoke with many in the weeks following Selonia Reed's death. Primarily, they wanted to tell me about two Hammond State School co-workers, Willie Jones and his roommate, Michael Morris — the man who later confessed to shooting Jones in the face.

Both Jones and Morris worked the 2: PM to 10: PM shift at the school. Jones worked in the residential area, while Morris worked the infirmary at the onsite hospital. For two days following the Reed murder, Willie Jones failed to report to work.

Phoning his supervisor, he said he had known Selonia Reed and that her husband, Reginald, had stood in his wedding. Jones said he was too upset to focus on work.

On the third night, according to co-workers, Jones did return to work, but without his usual friendly demeanor. With bags under bloodshot eyes, he shook visibly and mumbled when he spoke.

Forty-eight hours before Jones died, a nursing supervisor witnessed an intense argument between Jones and Morris outside the hospital infirmary. From their heated discussion, she overheard one name clearly — "Reed."

Hammond Resident Reginald Reed reported his wife missing at 8:30 on a Sunday morning, August 23, 1987. Hammond Police Chief Roddy Devall told the *Daily Star* that Reed said his wife had left their Apple Street residence the night before, saying she was "going out" and had not returned. Reed also provided police with the license plate number of his wife's car.

Approximately one hour later, a Hammond police officer who knew the 26-year-old bank teller, found her car in the parking lot of John's Curb Market on Highway 190 East. Inside, he discovered her partially nude body drenched in blood.

Tangipahoa Parish Coroner Vincent Cefalu told the *Daily Star* that someone had raped and stabbed her. He said she was "beaten around the head and suffered other bad acts," including being sexually assaulted with an umbrella.

Following the autopsy at Earl K. Long Hospital in Baton Rouge, Cefalu said Reed died from four stab wounds, three in the right middle lobe of her lungs, and one in the right atrium of her heart. Her attacker had stabbed her more than a dozen times around her breasts and neck with an instrument "larger than an ice pick but smaller than a kitchen knife." Cefalu said he did not believe the tip of the umbrella had caused the stab wounds.

Relatives of the victim later recalled detectives mentioning the discovery of a screwdriver they believed to be the murder weapon. Still, officially, police have made no public disclosure of this information.

The coroner did say that someone had drawn lines on the body in a "distinct pattern" using what he initially believed to be shaving cream. He later altered that opinion, saying the substance had an off-white color that hardened in the sun instead of melting, as shaving cream would have done. Asked whether the "distinct pattern" meant the killer had written actual words on the corpse, Cefalu refused to comment, saying the "particulars" were still under investigation.

According to Assistant Police Chief Jim Richardson, that investigation involved converting their main squad room into an interrogation facility, where Hammond and Tangipahoa Parish detectives teamed to question potential witnesses, informants, and suspects around the clock over multiple weeks.

Richardson said that by August 31 — the day Willie Jones died — he and Chief Devall had not slept for at least two days.

That night, a Mississippi man, traveling south from McComb, took the Tickfaw exit off Interstate 55. As he did so, the right tire of his van ran over a man's head. After confirming the man was dead, he drove to a nearby service station and flagged down Tangipahoa Parish Sheriff's Deputy Robert Roberts, who followed him back to the scene of the accident.

Roberts radioed his office, reporting that different vehicles may have hit the victim multiple times and that one had crushed his skull.

A driver's license identified the victim as 28-year-old Willie A. Jones of 131 Honeysuckle Drive, Hammond. Dispatchers sent additional deputies to that address, where Jones' roommate confessed to Murder.

Detectives Larry Westmoreland, Mike Sticker, and Kerry Dangerfield questioned 26-year-old Michael Morris at the sheriff's substation on South Morrison Boulevard for hours before charging him with second-degree murder.

The detectives told reporters that Morris and Jones had been traveling on the interstate around 10:15 PM and arguing. When Morris stopped the vehicle, and Jones stepped out, Morris shot him in the face with a .357 Magnum and left the scene with Jones lying in the roadway.

When Vincent Cefalu sent Jones' badly damaged remains to the Orleans Parish Coroner's office, the examiner there determined that Jones had been alive when something crushed his skull. Cefalu said they found a bullet had entered his left cheek and exited through his nose or mouth, knocking out teeth, and grazing his forearm. A microscopic examination found gunpowder residue in all three areas, he said.

"This type of wound is excruciating, and there was heavy blood loss, but not enough to kill him." Weakened and in such pain, Cefalu said, Jones could have passed out or was ran-over attempting to crawl off the roadway.

Norman Davidson, TPSO's Chief of Detectives, said he considered this new information irrelevant. Morris, he said, confessed to killing Jones, and therefore a jury would make the final decision.

The following year, Michael Morris pled guilty to a manslaughter charge in a 21st Judicial District Court before Judge Edward Brent Dufreche, who sentenced him to 15 years in prison. Because of the plea, Morris never publicly explained what he argued with Jones about — or answered the question of whether the argument and subsequent murder had anything to do with the death of Selonia Reed.

Michael Morris completed his sentence more than a decade ago, but I have been unable to locate him today. I want to ask him these questions. If you know him, please have him call me. I believe we are all anxious to hear his side of this story.

Following the initial release of this column, relatives of Willie Jones contacted me with an exciting recounting. According to Willie's aunt, he was at home and on the phone with her near the time of his murder.

On his house phone, Willie told his aunt to hold on a moment. He had a call coming in on another line. Moments later, Willie told his aunt, "That was Michael. He and Reginald broke down on the road. I've got to go help them out."

Henry Forrest

With new information from readers and other sources, this chapter evolved from the Bayou Justice column entitled "Bridegroom murdered after a visit to betrothed," initially published in south Louisiana newspapers on Tuesday, February 19, 2019.

LOCAL HISTORIANS DR. Sam Hyde and Clark Forrest, Jr. prompted this week's investigation into a 1925 murder of a Springfield farm supervisor killed on the road between Springfield and Ponchatoula.

The victim, 28-year-old Henry Dalton Forrest — an ancestor of Clark's — died violently on the eve of his wedding less than three hours after visiting his betrothed. The list of suspects includes former suitors of the bride-to-be, random bandits, and relatives of both the future bride and bridegroom, but oddly enough, the man arrested seemed to have no motive whatsoever.

In an Amite courtroom on a Saturday morning, June 25, 1927, Judge Columbus Reid sentenced Roy McCrory to life in prison for killing Forrest. McCrory's wife fainted when the bailiff read the verdict, leaving Judge Reid to manage the McCrory's crying children — all 12 of them.

But I am getting ahead of myself.

If we have learned anything from our little real crime adventures, it is the inescapable fact that all great murder mysteries begin at the scene of the crime.

Marion Forrest discovered his brother's body "in a thicket" a half-mile from his home at 11 a.m. on a Saturday, July 11, 1925 — the day Henry Forrest planned to be married. The dead man's .32 caliber pistol lay near his hand, and a bullet appeared to have gone through his skull at close range.

Sheriff Lem Bowden told reporters the next day that Forrest's gun had been loaded would steel-jacketed bullets, whereas the shot that killed him appeared to be lead only. He said he had sent the gun to the Bertillon Fingerprint Lab in New Orleans for further study. Bowden said he felt police could rule out suicide as the cause of death and that his deputies were pursuing other leads.

The night before his death, Forrest had walked to visit his fiancée at her father's home on the Ponchatoula-Springfield Highway. Miss Lillian Fontenot said he left her near midnight and was in good spirits. She said that her father suspected a former suitor of killing Forrest, but insisted that she had not seen or spoken to that man in over a year. She also said that the New Orleans man had not entered Tangipahoa or Livingston Parish in over a year.

A neighbor told police that Fontenot's former suitor told him two years prior "if he couldn't marry her, no one else would."

Lillian Fontenot remained in bed all weekend and did not attend her fiancée's funeral, Saturday afternoon.

Witnesses saw Henry Forrest the Friday night before his death before and after his visit with Fontenot. One saw him walking down the Ponchatoula-Springfield Highway after midnight.

Earlier that evening, over a dozen people saw him buy a handkerchief at a country store near her home. At the store, he discussed wedding plans and displayed a leather wallet and a large stack of bills — estimated by various witnesses as between $100 and $500 — which he described as his honeymoon nest egg.

One witness said he left the store with four men, but police thought that unlikely since he saw Fontenot soon afterward.

When police examined the body, they found a single dollar bill and seven pennies. Forrest's wallet could not be located.

At the crowded funeral, the deceased man's father, C. H. Forrest, offered a $1000 reward for information, which C. E. Forrest, a relative from Beaumont, Texas, subsequently doubled. By the funeral's end, the premium totaled $5,500. The Tangipahoa Parish Police Jury donated the last $500.

In the weeks that followed, Sheriff Bowden interviewed several men, including Luther Mixon, Fontenot's former suitor in New Orleans, and each of the men Forrest supervised at the Chief Thomas Stock Farm in Springfield. Still, no one seemed to know who killed Henry Forrest.

A Springfield woman did step forward, saying she saw Forrest inside the cab of a car traveling east on the Ponchatoula-Springfield Highway. She said there were two other men and a young girl in the car and that Forrest was in the back seat. She said she saw them around 1:00 AM and recognized Forrest when one of the men lit a cigarette in the vehicle.

At a press conference one week later, Sheriff Bowden said the fingerprint lab's report came back inconclusive and would be of no help. He noted that Coroner Ricks had ruled out suicide and that after interviewing Mixon, he had ruled out the jealous suitor theory.

"We don't have a clue," he said. "This case is the most baffling I've entertained since taking office. We're dumbfounded."

Clueless, Sheriff Bowden let the case grow cold, but the Forrest family maintained the reward. In 1927, a private detective employed by C. H. Forrest announced that he knew who killed Henry Forrest and insisted that police arrest Roy McCrory of Ponchatoula.

Roy McCrory

With *new information from readers and other sources, this chapter evolved from the Bayou Justice column entitled "McCrory found guilty, Jury votes for hanging," initially published in south Louisiana newspapers on Tuesday, February 26, 2019.*

AT 4:50 AM ON A COLD Monday morning in the 1980s, I sat in the newsroom at 200 East Thomas Street, preparing for the morning's broadcast. WFPR Program Director Steve Chauvin called me in when News Director Mary Pirosko contracted bronchitis. As usual, I started 30 minutes early, ripping stories from the news-wire and rewriting local bits from *The Advocate, The Times-Picayune, and The Daily Star* — prioritizing them all for the morning's hourly newscasts and phoning local newsmakers as they awoke to record soundbites.

On this particular morning, I had Tangipahoa Parish Sheriff's spokesperson Deputy Chuck Reed on the line, when a woman started screaming four-letter unmentionables outside my door. I apologized, told Chuck I would call him back, and then opened the door to hell.

Sports Director Robin Roberts held another woman back from scratching the eyes out of the AM morning show host. Everyone's hair and clothing looked in disarray, and the AM jock's left eye was beginning to swell.

He yelled at me. "Did you let this woman in here?"

"Well, yea," I said. "She said you were friends, and it's freezing outside."

With more screaming and some kicking, we managed to escort the cursing intruder from the building. The AM host had stood her up for some date the night before — and in the process, she discovered he was married.

By now, you are wondering where I am going with this and what it has to do with the bridegroom murder that we started reviewing last week. Bear with me. Clarity is only three paragraphs away.

Terrel Cotham "Foots" McCrory directed Sales at WFPR, but he started at the station the day Big John Chauvin opened the doors. At one time or another, Foots did everything one could do at a radio station from playing music and hosting Swap Shop to sports commentating and scrubbing floors. Foots knew almost everyone in town and could tell you a story or two about anyone you could name. Collecting these humorous tales was somewhat of a hobby of his.

When I finished my last newscast that morning, Foots met me outside the control room, chewing on an unlit cigar — and snickering. "Okay," he said. "Give me the play-by-play."

The morning host had not left the building, so I waved Foots down the stairs, and we walked to the Fountain Café. Over coffee, I recounted every syllable uttered by the scorned radio groupie, and Foots laughed until his face turned red. For the next hour, we swapped stories about the various Casanova's we had known, and somewhere in that discussion, Foots McCrory told me about his uncle.

"I had a relative once who made a woman so angry; she got him life in prison. Somebody fingered him for murder, but he was innocent. The woman was his alibi, but she wouldn't agree to tell the sheriff where he was that night unless he would agree to leave his wife and marry her."

"What happened?" I asked.

"He didn't have to marry her; got out on appeal. The judge had a better punishment — leaving him to face his angry wife and the 12 kids he was going to pay child support for if he didn't straighten up."

Any story Foots told was funny, but my retelling suffers without Foots' facial expressions and trademark mumbling. Most of his stories rang true but sounded hard to believe. Over 30 years passed before I discovered the trial of Mr. Royal Jackson McCrory took place.

On a Saturday morning, June 25, 1927, an Amite jury found Roy McCrory of Ponchatoula guilty of murder. The jury deliberated all night following the two-day trial and ultimately voted 11-2 for hanging. Since capital punishment in Louisiana required a unanimous verdict at the time, Judge Columbus Reid sentenced the defendant instead to life in Angola prison.

On June 25, 1927, the New Orleans States recounted the story this way:

"In a special session of the grand jury, the courtroom filled to standing room capacity. The presentation of evidence took more than two days, but Roy McCrory was ultimately found guilty of murdering Springfield foreman Henry D. Forrest."

"McCrory shot Forrest in July 1925, as Forrest returned from the home of the woman he was to marry the next day. He carried with him the money to buy all of their household furnishings."

"All efforts to resolve the crime proved fruitless until the deceased's family brought in Captain A. R. Osborne, a noted detective from Chicago."

SLU History Professor Sam Hyde believes the news story is wrong regarding who contacted Osborne. "This murder would have remained a mystery if Amite Newspaperman Lee Lanier hadn't expressed outrage that so little had been done to solve the crime. He sought A. R. Osborne's help after hearing of the detective's success with the infamous Leopold and Loeb case."

From the *Times-Picayune*, June 24, 1927:

"Osborne found the chief witness for the state, Mrs. Randolph Struble of Albany, who testified that at midnight, returning from Ponchatoula, she met a car on the night of the murder and recognized Henry Forrest riding in the backseat between two men. Forrest was leaning forward with his body limp. Struble identified the driver of the car as Roy McCrory."

Returning to the New Orleans States account:

"Warren Comish and Shelby Reid, McCrory's attorneys, worked to break down the woman's testimony to no avail. Amos L. Ponder, Jr. prosecuted the case, assisted by Amos L. Ponder, Sr, but in the end, the attending crowd seemed satisfied with the verdict and life term sentence."

I became involved in this case when local historian Clark Forrest, Jr. asked the question: why is there no record of Roy McCrory incarcerated at Angola, and why does the census for 1920, 1930, and 1940 all denote Roy McCrory still living in Ponchatoula?

Searching digital archives and the dusty microfilm of newspapers across South Louisiana, I have found no better answer than the tale provided by Foots McCrory regarding his ancestors and their 12 children. I have discovered evidence that corroborates his little anecdote.

Five months before the McCrory trial, at a doctor's office in Hammond, McCrory's wife, Mary "Minnie" Causey McCrory, gave birth to their youngest son, Loy, naming him after one of Roy McCrory's brothers.

Loy "Sonny" McCrory died 85 years later on August 30, 2012. The Albany resident lived near Hungarian Settlement and was a veteran of the Merchant Marines, Army Transportation Command, and the U.S. Navy. He was also an active Mason and union president, presiding over all carpenters in Louisiana.

According to his obituary, Loy McCrory's parents preceded him in death, along with five older brothers and six older sisters.

Charles Ray Spears

With new information from readers and other sources, this chapter evolved from the Bayou Justice column entitled "Goodyear Killer escapes justice multiple times," initially published in south Louisiana newspapers on Tuesday, March 5, 2019.

BEFORE NEWSPAPERS ACROSS the state labeled him the Goodyear Killer, 23-year-old Charles Ray Spears escaped from the Jackson Barracks work-release center ran by the Louisiana Department of Corrections, where he served time for petty theft.

That was July 29, 1975.

Eleven days later, he landed in Hammond, where he handcuffed two employees of the Goodyear Tire Center back-to-back and shot them in the head.

Three days after that, an armed robber shot a Slidell police officer in the head and critically injured a jewelry store clerk. Police in Hammond said the gunman's description matched that of the Goodyear Killer.

New Orleans police apprehended Charles Ray Spears the following spring and charged him with the death of a 33-year-old named Ernest Smith. Co-workers found the body of the restaurant chef in his apartment on February 23, 1976, with a .22 caliber bullet in his head.

Police did not charge Spears with the death of the police officer, and a New Orleans District Attorney eventually dropped the charges against him related to the Smith murder — and after being convicted of the Goodyear slaying, an appeals court overturned the conviction.

This week and next, we will consider whether Charles Ray Spears was the luckiest murderer in the history of armed robbery or whether he just had a damned good lawyer.

The killing rampage began after 5:30: PM on August 8, 1975, as the Hammond Goodyear Tire and Appliance Service Center closed for the day. With the doors still unlocked, the store's manager and assistant manager balanced the day's books, as a black man walked in asking about cassette players. Producing a snub-nosed .22 caliber handgun, the intruder handcuffed the men together, and — as his captives begged for their lives — he shot both in the back of the head.

Store manager John Reid, 47, later died in the Ochsner Foundation Hospital in New Orleans. Assistant Manager Roy Walters, 26, lived in critical condition at Ochsner for several months. Although Walters could not see after the shooting, he managed to drag Reid's body to the phone and dial the operator after his assailant left the store.

The South-Central Bell operator then transferred the call to the Hammond Police Department. Lieutenant Ed White responded, finding the victims, Walters unconscious and Reid dead. The manacles attached to their wrists looked different. Manufactured in Spain, White said he felt lucky the keys still fit them.

Before losing consciousness, Walters described his assailant as a black man with a medium length afro, 6 feet 2 inches tall, weighing about 180 pounds, wearing a brown shirt, green trousers, and black shoes.

A second man joined the gunman after Walters lost his sight. Both men fled with a small amount of cash and no merchandise.

The Hammond Police Department, assisted by the Tangipahoa Parish Sheriff's Office, closed all streets and highways leading from the city, searching anyone attempting to leave, but to no avail; the assailants escaped.

Less than one week later, Sergeant Earl Alfred, a 31-year-old Slidell police officer, stopped a gunman running out the back door of a jewelry store. That gunman shot him in the head with a .22 caliber handgun.

Minutes earlier, the officer's assailant stabbed a 20-year-old jewelry store clerk, Betty Hodge Graves, multiple times with a pair of scissors, leaving her in critical condition. Sergeant Alfred, a five-year veteran whom police described as the most loved cop on the force, died instantly.

Police said clerk Graves triggered the silent alarm at the Champagne Jewelry Store. When it sounded at the Slidell police station, Alfred responded. The holdup man shot Alfred at the back door, then stole the officer's handgun and ran.

Wounded, Betty Hodge Graves crawled to the officer's patrol car and attempted to radio the station for help, but lost consciousness trying.

Witnesses reported a black and white 1964 Chevrolet truck sped from the scene, and as they did in Hammond, police set up roadblocks throughout the city, but once again, the gunman escaped.

The following February, Hammond police arrested Larry Donahue, 24, charging him with purse snatching. Following the arrest, police questioned Donahue's cousin, Clay Spears, who told him that Donahue discussed robbing and killing a man in New Orleans — along with two other cousins, Leroy Donahue, 24, and Charles Ray Spears.

During his four-hour interrogation, Donahue confessed to robbing Ernest Smith, a drug dealer, of his money and his supply, but he named Charles Ray Spears as Smith's killer.

Hearing his cousin had confessed, Leroy Donahue did the same, also tagging Spears as the murderer.

The case seemed cut-and-dried until Larry Donahue's attorney, William R. Ary, argued that his client had been "constantly interrogated" by Hammond authorities, as well as homicide and robbery detectives from the New Orleans Police Department. Ary contended his client's statements had been "tainted" and cited the so-called doctrine of "the fruit of the poison tree," demanding that the district attorney drop charges against his client.

New Orleans Judge Alvin Oser agreed, as did New Orleans Assistant District Attorney Joseph Meyer. Meyer said that since Leroy Donahue and Charles Ray Spears confessed as outgrowths of Larry Donahue's coerced confession, the doctrine of the fruit of the poison tree prevailed.

He dropped charges against all three defendants.

Police then transported Charles Ray Spears back to Tangipahoa Parish, where he faced one last first-degree murder charge — and another get-out-of-jail-free card called "a writ of habeas corpus."

The Goodyear Killer

With new information from readers and other sources, this chapter evolved from the Bayou Justice column entitled "Justice catches up with Goodyear Killer," initially published in south Louisiana newspapers on Tuesday, March 12, 2019.

LAST WEEK, WE RECOUNTED the multiple crimes of the Goodyear Killer, 23-year-old Charles Ray Spears of Greensburg, and the multitude of times he escaped Justice. After a defense attorney used police collaboration to build a case for coercion, the New Orleans District Attorney dropped all charges in the murder of Ernest Smith. In Slidell, Judge Wallace Edwards sentenced David E. Lewis to die following the robbery of the Champagne Jewelry Store, the near-death of store clerk Betty Hodge Graves, and the execution of Sergeant Earl Alfred, the first black officer to serve with the Slidell police department.

Three days before Alfred's murder, a holdup man shot two Hammond store clerks in the head during the robbery of the Goodyear Tire and Appliance Service Center. Initially, police suspected prison escapee Charles Ray Spears in all three crimes, but he only stood trial for one.

Shortly after 5:30: PM August 8, 1975, store managers began to close the Hammond Goodyear on South Cate Street. With the doors still unlocked, they balanced the day's books, as a black man walked in asking about cassette players. Producing a snub-nosed .22 caliber handgun, the intruder handcuffed the men together, and — as his captives begged for their lives — he shot both in the back of the head.

Store manager John Reid, 47, died in the Ochsner Foundation Hospital in New Orleans, but 26-year-old Assistant Manager Roy Walters, Jr. lived to serve as the state's star witness identifying Charles Ray Spears as the Goodyear Killer.

Walters testified Spears entered the store, purchased a radio from Reid, and then asked about a tape recorder. Walters said, as Reid reached for one, Spears pulled the gun, handcuffed the two, and searched the safe and cashboxes before shooting both men in the back of the head. When he regained consciousness, he dragged himself and Reid to telephone and called the Hammond Police Department.

Dennis Taylor, 20, testified he was in a jail cell with Spears and Spears confessed the story to him.

Prosecutors Joseph Simpson and William Quin said Taylor knew none of the particulars of the crime at the time police placed him with Spears.

Spears, testifying in his defense, said he was serving time for a burglary conviction and assigned to the Jackson Barracks. He said that he and his cousin escaped on July 29, 1975, and fled to Chicago, where he got employment. Spears testified that he was working in Illinois on August 8, the day of the Goodyear invasion.

In March of 1976, a grand jury indicted Spears on charges of first-degree murder, attempted murder, and two counts of armed robbery. The following July, those charges became null when the United States Supreme Court threw out Louisiana's death penalty law. This forced the grand jury to reconvene — this time, indicting Spears on second-degree murder instead.

One month later, an Amite jury deliberated less than 35 minutes before finding Spears guilty of all four charges. In 1977 and 1982, Spears appealed the convictions and lost.

Twenty-first Judicial District Court Judge Gordon E. "Buddy" Causey sentenced Spears to life for the murder of Reid and 20 years for the attempted murder of Walters. Causey also gave him two 99-year sentences for the armed robbery of each victim, with all penalties running concurrently.

While serving time in the Tangipahoa Parish Prison, Spears sued the sheriff's office for mistreatment and won. After Judge Causey moved him to Angola State Penitentiary, he filed the same motions there.

In 1986, a federal court magistrate granted Spears a new trial citing concerns about the original testimony. District Attorney Duncan Kemp had three months to retry Spears or set him free.

"I'm concerned about this," Kemp told reporters. "But if there's any way possible, we will retry him."

Kemp said a judge ruled the testimony of Angola inmate Dennis Taylor admissible. "Taylor was illegally released after [after the Spears trial] and subsequently held up a Mini-Mart in Independence and then killed an elderly ticket taker at the Joy Drive-In in Hammond," Kemp said.

Shortly after the news from the federal court in New Orleans, Judge Causey suffered a massive heart attack and ultimately retired from the bench.

In September of 1986, justice prevailed. A new jury deliberated under 40 minutes, and Judge Brent Dufreche upheld the original sentencing. Roy Walters was again the star witness. If he had died from the 1975 gunshot to the head, Charles Ray Spears would be a free man today, but Assistant District Attorney Charles Genco said Walters' testimony was not the only reason Spears would remain behind bars.

Genco presented the case and spoke to reporters afterward. "I'd like to express my deepest gratitude to the police officers who investigated," he said. "This was the second time around, and we saw cooperation from all departments involved. We would not have succeeded without them."

The Axe-man of Tangipahoa

With new information from readers and other sources, this chapter evolved from the Bayou Justice column entitled "Confessed Axe-man dies in Tangipahoa Parish Jail," initially published in south Louisiana newspapers on Tuesday, March 19, 2019.

ONE-HUNDRED YEARS AGO this month, someone claiming to be the Axe-man of New Orleans sent a letter to the *Times-Picayune* newspaper. The note said the serial killer would leave the city for good if everyone played or listened to jazz the following Tuesday night during the traditional Feast of St. Joseph. Shortly after, the city complied, and the killings stopped, leaving unsolved more than one dozen murders attributed to America's most notorious serial killer.

A century later, historians still cannot prove the identity of the Axe-man, but one Tangipahoa Parish police officer may have taken the answer to his grave. Former Tangipahoa Parish Sheriff John A. Ballard told a newspaper editor that a man he arrested in 1920 confessed to those crimes. That man, Tickfaw Grocer Frank DiPrima, died as an inmate at the Tangipahoa Parish Prison in 1931.

Miriam C. Davis, the author of "The Axe-man of New Orleans: The True Story," summarized the killer's reign of terror this way: "Although the attacks began in the fall of 1910, it was not until June 1911 that one of them was fatal and Joe Davi died. Then the Axe-man (or the "Cleaver" as he was known in 1910—1911) disappeared for six years. It was when he returned — beginning with his murder of the Maggios in May 1918 and culminating with his brutal attack on Charlie and Rose Cortimiglia and death of their little daughter Mary in March of 1919 — that the Axe-man had New Orleanians thoroughly terrorized."

She described how the Axe-man grew more violent over time.

"The first Axe-man attack seemed almost tentative. The second attack was more violent, but it took the killer three tries before he managed to kill someone. Joe Davi's murder, though, was certainly cruel. He beat Davi's face with a weapon consistent with a butcher's cleaver. His brains dripped out of his skull. The attack was so brutal that the force of the blows knocked a 15-degree angle into the mattress. When he returned after a six-year absence, the Axe-man slaughtered the Maggios in May 1918."

According to Davis, multiple attacks came in 1918 and 1919, but the last three killings traditionally attributed to the Axe-man, she said, are more likely acts of organized crime.

"There were vendettas between different groups of Italians reluctant to talk to the police. I think the murder of Tony Sciambra and his wife, and that of Mike Pepitone, fit that category. Sometimes verifying details, especially if the newspaper accounts did not agree, is nearly impossible, but I believe historians have misunderstood those attacks. They do not belong in the Axe-man chronology."

I asked the author what she thought of the attack on Sarah Laumann. She said that was an unfamiliar name, but she promised to look into it before the second edition of her book went to press.

On a Sunday morning, August 3, 1919, at around 3:15 AM, 19-year-old Sarah Laumann awoke in her bedroom at 2123 Second Street in New Orleans to find a man standing over her, both arms raised over his head. He swung something that struck down hard against her pillow and gashed the side of her head just above her left ear.

Reacting to their daughter's screams, Mr. and Mrs. John Laumann burst through the door, as Sarah's attacker escaped through a window.

Mrs. Laumann told *The New Orleans Item*, "The first thing the police did was ask my husband where he kept his ax. That's when we found out it had been taken from its place in the woodshed."

New Orleans Police later located the Laumann ax under the St. Francis de Sales school next door to the Laumann home.

Sergeant. Fred Smith of the New Orleans Police Department told a *New Orleans Item* reporter, "the method of entry parallels the Axe-man attacks; entry made by removing a panel from the back door."

Police Superintendent Frank T. Mooney told the New Orleans States: "The person making such an attack with robbery or revenge as a motive certainly would not carry such a heavy ax and leave with it, only to drop it next door. This man, to my mind, is a sadist or pervert. The man's mental condition is far below normal."

The Item reported that the New Orleans Police Department had long supposed that the Axe-man was a black man. However, Sarah Laumann described him differently: 5 foot 8 inches tall, weighing about 165, wearing a brown suit and white shirt with no tie, and a dark cap pulled over his eyes.

She described the Axe-man of New Orleans as a white man with a dark olive complexion.

In 1920, Sheriff John A. Ballard told reporters he locked Italian-born Frank DiPrima up for his protection. DiPrima, he said, had "lost his balance" and "ran amuck," after discovering his Tickfaw neighbors, the Congalero family, bloody and unconscious at their dinner table.

Ballard said DiPrima joined the search party for Rosaria Restiva, the suspected shooter, carrying a cane knife and a straight razor.

On May 25, 1920, Rosaria Restiva appeared at the Tickfaw home of Bernard Caldorera with a shotgun and fired on the family at their dinner table. The 22-year-old Restiva had asked Caldorera for his 16-year-old daughter's hand in marriage the week before. Caldorera had refused, citing her age, and suggesting that the rival farmers discuss the matter further at the end of strawberry season.

After the attack, Rosaria Restiva escaped via a pre-cut trail into the swamp. The sheriff's office contracted bloodhounds from Mississippi, but Restiva vanished, never standing trial.

Frank DiPrima was Bernard Caldorera's closest friend and one of the first neighbors to arrive after the massacre.

In an article from May 27, 1920, newly appointed Hammond Police Chief John E. Morgan described DiPrima as violent, saying the grocer lived in a "semi-demented state" for some time, but police never considered him dangerous. "His actions this week, however," said Morgan, "made his incarceration imperative."

In 1931, *Louisiana Progress* Editor John D. Klorer asked Ballard why DiPrima remained behind bars for so long.

"We considered sending him to the insane asylum in Pineville," the former sheriff said, "but they couldn't handle him. He turned violent when he found that bloody baby."

Klorer asked if it was true that DiPrima confessed to being the infamous Axeman of New Orleans.

"Well, yes," the sheriff replied. "He kept saying that, but we never took him seriously."

Sheriff Ballard apprehended Frank DiPrima on May 26, 1920. The last known Axeman murder occurred in August of 1919 — six months before Frank DiPrima opened his grocery store three miles outside Tickfaw.

The Kentwood Shoot-out

With *new information from readers and other sources, this chapter evolved from the Bayou Justice column entitled "Unanswered questions in Kentwood police shoot-out," initially published in south Louisiana newspapers on Tuesday, March 26, 2019.*

AFTER JUDGE KENNETH Fogg described a 1986 murder trial as "hopelessly deadlocked," he declared a mistrial. He moved the state's plight for justice to Covington, where a second jury — in 1987 — found Gregory Griffin, 25, guilty in the shotgun death of Tangipahoa Parish Sheriff Deputy R. A. Kent, III.

For many, this case left questions unanswered, those regarding motive, an alleged tri-parish drug-smuggling operation, and the accusation that an Assistant District Attorney covertly swore allegiance to the Ku Klux Klan.

On a Friday night, November 1, 1985, shortly after 8:00 PM, grocer Marty Guy locked up Guy's Quick Stop near Kentwood. Outside the store, he followed a noise and found Griffin attempting to pounding on his soft drink machine.

As Griffin drove away, Guy unlocked the store and stepped back inside to call the Tangipahoa Parish Sheriff's Office.

On patrol, Kentwood Police Captain James Rimes heard the radio call over the parish channel and drove to Guy's Quick Stop to assist. Marty Guy climbed into the front seat of the squad car, and the two left to find Griffin.

Captain Rimes knew the accused. Griffin had worked as an informant for the city of Kentwood on two occasions. Rimes found Griffin at home and convinced him to drive back to the store, where Sheriff's Deputy R. A. Kent, III, of Fluker, stood, waiting.

Rimes walked Griffin without handcuffs to Kent's car, where Griffin found himself once again locked in a caged backseat. Both police officers joined Guy inside the convenience store, where Kent began to write his report.

Soon after, Rimes departed back to his jurisdiction, the city of Kentwood, leaving Kent and Guy, inspecting Gregory Griffin's car.

At approximately 8:30 PM, Gregory Griffin yelled from the backseat of that patrol car. Although his exact words changed later, during the first trial, quoted Griffin as saying, "Hey, did you know there was a shotgun in here?"

Kent then stepped closer to his unit, and Guy heard gunshots. When the smoke from the shotgun blasts cleared, Guy saw Kent laying in the gravel, while a wounded Gregory Griffin ran to his car and drove away.

Curiously, in the court transcripts, I found no one asking how Griffin's car got back to the store. The court focused instead on a bigger question: who shot first?

Deputy R. A. Kent, III, died in a Hammond hospital after pellets from three shotgun blasts hit his body. Still, long before the coroner pronounced him dead, every law enforcement agency in three parishes searched for Griffin, including those across the Louisiana-Mississippi state line.

Gregory Griffin's cousin, Monroe James of Osyka, Mississippi, later testified that a group of unnamed Louisiana police officers came to his home searching for Griffin. "They held me like I was some prisoner." He said they harassed his wife. "They wanted to kill Gregory. They said if they found him in our home, they'd kill me, too," James said.

Police initially charged Monroe James and his wife as accessories after the fact in the murder. Still, District Attorney Duncan Kemp dropped those charges the day before James testified for the Prosecution.

On November 2, 1987, 33-year-old Thado Gordon sat in bed watching cartoons at the Lover's Lane Motel in Pike County, Mississippi, when — according to Gordon's testimony in court — officers from Tangipahoa Parish, Pike County, and the city of Amite burst into his room "without probable cause or warrant." Gordon said the officers mistook him for Griffin and drug him into the parking lot where they beat him severely, ultimately causing permanent injury and forcing him to abandon his lifelong career as a truck driver and day laborer.

A federal court judge later awarded Gordon $120,000 for his experience.

During Gregory Griffin's second trial, the state's star witness, Marty Guy, described what happened the night Kent died. He said he and Kent were standing outside the patrol car talking when Griffin stuck his head out the window and said, "Let me out of here," and then he fired a shotgun at the deputy.

According to Guy's report, Kent did not pull his handgun until after the first shotgun blast. "I saw the blast, but I didn't see the shotgun," he said. "I got burned across my forehead."

Guy said he was standing behind Kent, watching him write Griffin a ticket for an expired inspection sticker when Kent's body blew back against his. Guy said he then ran around the corner of the store, looking for a place to hide.

"I thought he had already killed R. A. and was coming after me," Guy said. He said he heard rapid-fire pistol shots as he ran, followed by two louder shotgun blasts.

The prosecution said Griffin pried the shotgun from a rack in the front seat and shot Kent. Griffin said he found the weapon on the floor of the car, raised it to the window, and yelled, "hey, shotgun." According to Griffin, Kent panicked and fired once or twice into the car door.

"I ducked into the seat," Griffin testified. "All I could see was a shadow, but when he started shooting, I shot back."

One of Griffin's lawyers, Gerard "Gerry" Rault, a professor working pro-bono from the Loyola New Orleans School of Law, made several unusual charges against members of the prosecution team. Rault said that Griffin knew Assistant District Attorney William Quin's family and that Quin was "a KKK type person," insinuating that he hated black people.

Griffin testified that he sold marijuana to a member of Quin's family on several occasions. He said the last time he called the house, Quin called him a racist epitaph and told him never to contact his family again.

Quin took the stand and admitted to knowing Griffin, but insisted that he hated the klan and never called anyone that name.

District Attorney Duncan Kemp told the court that Gerry Rault threatened to schedule a press conference and distribute a handbill making allegations involving "150 pounds of marijuana, both of which Marty Guy and R. A. Kent (allegedly) had an interest in."

In 2019, Griffin told me Kemp misspoke. He said Kent had nothing to do with the sale. Marty Guy sold the drugs in his store, he said and used the soft drink machine as the pickup location. Griffin said Guy wanted him jailed to eliminate the competition.

During the trial, Kemp said Griffin's "marijuana conspiracy" allegations were unfounded and that his attorney should be disbarred, calling Rault "a disgrace to the legal profession."

In the end, Judge John Greene sentenced Gregory Griffin to only 21 years, noting that before the shotgun incident, the Kentwood native had a prior record of non-violence. In 1979, the judge said, police arrested Griffin for petty larceny, in 1982 for receiving stolen property, in 1983 for disturbing the peace, and in 1984 for theft of a lawnmower and a record player.

Judge Greene noted that, during the trial, in a there-but-for-the-grace-of-God-go-I moment, Independence sales executive Gus Guzzardo testified that he had lost money in and repeatedly slapped the same vending machine Guy reported Griffin for vandalizing.

"We know this deputy was shot by you, but the court understands you felt you were being attacked," Greene said. "The jury found that you did not fire first, but you were running, and you did turn to shoot the victim twice after he had fallen to the ground."

After exhausting all appeals, Gregory Griffin served 15 years of a 21-year sentence in state prison for manslaughter. Following parole, he left the state of Louisiana and currently lives in Mississippi.

I asked him if the parole board released him early due to good behavior. He replied, "No. This is Louisiana. I just knew somebody who knew somebody."

Edward Toefield, Jr.

With new information from readers and other sources, this chapter evolved from the Bayou Justice column entitled "Edward Toefield, Jr. A hero's death remembered," initially published in south Louisiana newspapers on Tuesday, April 2, 2019.

LAST WEEK, I RECOUNTED the final hours of Tangipahoa Parish Sheriff's Deputy R. A. Kent, III. His son, Rusty, called me when the papers hit the street, asking, "Why would you bring up such painful memories after all these years?"

My answer to him was a simple one: "Because your father died serving us. He died a hero's death, and we should remember that day at every opportunity."

We can say the same of Sheriff's Deputy Edward Toefield, Jr. He died serving the people on February 2, 1984.

Gone are the days when police walked a beat — the days when "we, the people" knew our neighborhood patrol officer. Today, budgets stretch officers too thin. An officer patrolling Kentwood today may be assisting south of Ponchatoula tomorrow, but — just like those beat cops of old — he or she risk their lives for you and me all the same.

It does not matter whether the officer is a dedicated rising star in the department, or a seasoned detective, or a doughnut-eating cliché barely keeping gas in a squad car. If that officer awakes every day and pins a badge to his or her chest, that officer is painting a target on their back that says, "Shoot me first."

Like the soldier abroad, those officers have volunteered to take a bullet for you or me. That makes them superheroes in my book, and Officer Toefield's case is an excellent example of this. The call he answered was routine. When he left for work that day, his family had no idea they would never speak to him again.

According to court testimony, witnesses saw 34-year-old Thomas Sparks, Jr. shoot Ed Toefield, 41, in front of a Hi-Ho restaurant on Highway 51 outside Amite. Toefield had just put handcuffs on Spark's left wrist when Sparks pulled a pistol from the front of his trousers and shot his arresting officer.

Two witnesses saw Sparks shoot Toefield once in the chest, and then twice more near his face as the deputy fell. Pathologist Dr. Richard Tracy testified that the shots hit his head, neck, and chest.

The assailant fled the scene, but the Sheriff's Office caught up with him 24 hours later in the woods near Natalbany. Thomas Sparks surrendered after one of his pursuers shot him in the shoulder.

He confessed to the murder the next day.

Two years later, Sparks stood trial in a Livingston Parish court, and a jury of 12 found him guilty of first-degree murder. Judge Kenneth Fogg had Clerk of Court Lucius Patterson confirm the verdict before handing it to a deputy to read aloud.

Twelve officers then led Sparks away, shackled hand and foot. The trial helped his family and fellow officers get some closure, but truly, the case was only a formality. Another judge in another courtroom had sentenced Sparks to 99 years for bank robbery. A warrant related to that case is what brought Sparks and Toefield together in 1984.

District Attorney Duncan Kemp and Assistant District Attorney Billy Quin prosecuted the case. Kemp told the jury that Louisiana allowed capital punishment only when "aggravated circumstances" are present in the commission of the crime.

One of those aggravated circumstances, he said, was the killing of a police officer in the commission of his duties.

"We need to send a clear message that a police officer's life must be protected, both by law and by society. If we cannot impose the death penalty here, today, then we can impose it nowhere."

"What do you say when you're begging for a man's life?" Defense Attorney Wayne Stewart asked. "I don't know what to say. My client acted out of haste, fear, perhaps stupidity, but he did not plan this act. It was not premeditated."

In his closing arguments, Billy Quin handed the jury a portrait of Officer Ed Toefield in uniform, and when he presented them with a photograph of the officer's bullet-riddled body after the autopsy.

"This is what is left of him," Quin told the jury. "If you get in a merciful mood when you're back there in that jury room, remember these photos and give to Sparks what he gave to Ed Toefield."

The jury's verdict gave Sparks the death penalty, a fitting prize for murdering one of our heroes.

The Lynchings

With new information from readers and other sources, this chapter evolved from the Bayou Justice column entitled "Should Tangipahoa Parish apologize for racist lynchings?" initially published in south Louisiana newspapers on Tuesday, April 9, 2019.

ON APRIL 12, 2019, in a public ceremony, the mayor of New Orleans will formally apologize to Italian Americans nationwide. This apology is for what many consider one of our country's most violent acts — the mob lynching of 11 Italian immigrants following their acquittals in the murder of the New Orleans police chief on March 14, 1891.

In 1892, the United States government paid $25,000 in reparations to victims' families, but according to Michael Santo of the Order Sons and Daughters of Italy, that monetary compensation fell short.

"This has been a longstanding wound," he said. And when we asked the city earlier this year for an apology, Mayor LaToya Cantrell embraced the idea.

Author Michael J. Pfeifer told me that the New Orleans massacre "was a horrific act of collective violence inspired by ethnic prejudice, but it was hardly the largest act of collective violence in Louisiana history."

"Someone," he said, "should be talking about Bloody Tangipahoa."

In the years before the civil rights movement, residents of Tangipahoa Parish illegally executed 22 black men — 18 more than St. Helena and Livingston Parish combined. Of course, these numbers account only for those deaths reported in local newspapers. There were likely many more, said Pfeifer, that went unreported.

Pfeifer's statements caused me to research the matter and to consider the question: Should Tangipahoa Parish apologize to anyone?

Before answering, consider just a few of the reported cases:

- On January 27, 1887, the St. Helena Parish Echo said that police brought John Johnson — "the black boy who so unmercifully slaughtered the Cotton family in Tickfaw, Louisiana" — to Amite to stand trial, but "the court was relieved of this pleasure" by a mob of 250 hooded men who raided the jail after dark. The crowd hung Gus Williams — a man who allegedly killed his wife — at a nearby church, but they took Johnson and Arch Joiner — a man accused of assisting Johnson — to the Cotton farmhouse near Tickfaw. When the authorities arrived later than night, they found no mob; only Johnson and Joiner's bullet-riddled bodies swinging from a tree.

- In January of 1893, the *Times-Picayune* said a jury verdict for acquittal against Merethe Lewis "was not favorably received" by a citizen committee who decided to "administer justice" themselves.

- In May of 1898, a mob from Kentwood executed William Bell after he pled "not guilty" to an assault charge. *The New Orleans Item* started their report with "The armed citizens of Bloody Tangipahoa took the life of another negro this week."

- On September 19, 1900, *The Baton Rouge Daily Advocate* reported the hanging of four men in Ponchatoula: Isaiah Rollins, 18, Charles Elliot and George Bickham, 20, and Nathaniel Bowman, 47, who left behind a wife and seven children. Following the robbery and deadly assault of Louise Hatfielder, Sheriff Frank P. Mix picked up a total of 18 men for questioning. A witness saw one black man leave her house, but that witness could not identify which of the jailed men — if any — was the assailant. After police released 14 of the men, 15 masked men dismantled the jail door with axes and overpowered the sheriff. The mob hung the men from a tree two blocks North of Ponchatoula. After the bodies fell to the ground, George Bickham still breathed until two men strangled him by hand. A news reporter asked a witness later why the mob killed all four men. The witness answered, "They took no chances. They made sure they got the guilty party."

- On December 12, 1905, a mob in the town of Tangipahoa lynched Monsie Williams for "connection to the attempted assault" of an elderly farmer's wife. Williams, *The New Iberia Enterprise* reported, confessed to "standing watch for the principal in the affair under compulsion." A deputy was transporting Williams by horse and buggy when the crowd attacked and hung Williams near a church. One of the participants told the deputy, "We needed to make an example of him."

- In October of 1909, another angry mob — this one in Greensburg — hung Aps Ard for "shooting at and missing" Judge B. T. Young. Young later told a grand jury that Ard had not been the shooter. He had identified the wrong man.

- On October 27, 1912, *The Times-Democrat* reported that Deputy Sheriff W. R. Mullins transported Dock Bell, "the negro who stabbed and almost seriously wounded two young white men in Natalbany" to the parish jail, where a dozen men overtook the deputy and hanged Bell. Days before, the news reporter interviewing Bell said he appeared frightened. "He was so nervous that his teeth chattered when he talked. He admitted to cutting both men, but he said he did not realize what he had done until it was all over."

- On March 3, 1917, a special session of the grand jury met to discuss the lynching of Emma Hooper, a Hammond woman accused of shooting Hammond Police constable Fred Carlton. According to the New Orleans States, following the officer's shooting, "a crowd of Hammond citizens went to Hooper's home and demanded her surrender. Instead, the woman leveled a shotgun at the Hammond police chief and fired." When the gun jammed, several men broke through the door and apprehended the woman. Later, the chief walked home to change his clothes, leaving two deputized citizens guarding Hooper. When he returned, he found all three gone. He then discovered Hooper's naked body "hanged just outside Hammond's city limits." In the grand jury hearing, jurors said they were concerned because the accused had been a woman but ultimately decided that they did not have enough information to identify the hangmen.

- On July 31, 1917, Judge Robert S. Ellis called another Tangipahoa Parish grand jury, this one to investigate the double lynching of Dan and Jerry Route of Amite. In 1996, I spoke with a man who saw their bodies.

I met Bishop Willie K. Gordon, Sr., during my days at WFPR radio. When he died in 2007, Bishop Gordon was 97 years old and had served as pastor of Reimer-Gordon Temple Church in Hammond for almost 70 years.

As an eight-year-old boy playing in the streets of Amite, he watched two undertakers load the bodies of Dan and Jerry Route into pine boxes.

Bishop Gordon said he was also on the courthouse grounds in Amite when Tangipahoa parish authorities hung the five Italians charged with robbing the bank in Independence and shooting bank president Dallas Calmes.

Bishop Gordon also recalled meeting one of these armed mobs in his pre-teens.

"I was walking east and crossed paths with another black boy walking south." He said. "There were some cows on the sidewalk, and the other boy began to curse them in a loud manner. A little white girl nearby started crying and told a horse trader that a black boy had offended her. I had walked away by then, but when I got to the next block, several white men lifted me over their shoulders. One had a rope ready to hang me when the white girl told them I wasn't the right one and made them release me."

Eric Walber

With new information from readers and other sources, this chapter evolved from the Bayou Justice column entitled "Eric Walber's killers may go free," initially published in south Louisiana newspapers on Tuesday, April 16, 2019.

WHEN THE 21st Judicial Court convicted six men for the 1998 robbery and brutal murder of 16-year-old Eric Walber, the victim's friends and family in Albany expected those found guilty to either die by lethal injection or spend the remainder of their lives behind bars. Those expectations grew stronger each year as jury after jury denied each of the convicted's appeals.

Then, three years ago, those expectations began to die.

Since 2016, the homicide case the United States Supreme Court said resembled "a house of cards" has continued to collapse, and in time, all of those convicted in the case may be set free.

Last week, a state district judge ruled that James Skinner and Darrell Hampton — two of the six jailed in the case — could seek new trials following events of 2016, when the high court overturned the first-degree murder conviction of Michael Wearry, the accused instigator of the crime.

Skinner and Hampton are serving life, along with Shadrick Reed, each convicted of second-degree murder. Two others, Sam Scott and Randy Hutchinson, earlier pled guilty to manslaughter in exchange for reduced sentences and release dates.

Back in 2000, the state's case against the six hinged primarily on the testimony of a convicted cocaine dealer and a 10-year-old boy. The 2016 court saw this as a flimsy case and cited the state for not sharing all they knew with the Defense. The drug dealer had changed his story multiple times. In his earliest interviews with detectives, he named the wrong location for the attack on Walber and stated that Walber's red car was gray.

In May of 2018, the Roderick and Solange MacArthur Justice Center, a nonprofit civil rights law firm in New Orleans, filed a federal lawsuit on Wearry's behalf accusing investigators of coercing the 10-year-old, Jeffrey Ashton of Springfield, into giving false testimony.

The prior November, Ashton, then 30-years-old, testified that a now-retired detective with the Livingston Parish Sheriff's Office coached him to lie, insisting that he witnessed the murder in Springfield at a time when he and his family were attending the Ponchatoula Strawberry Festival. Ashton's attorneys also claimed that investigators bounced him from jail to jail to prevent him from meeting with Wearry's attorneys.

Wearry's lawsuit remains active today and accuses investigators of having "intentionally and deliberately coerced and intimidated Ashton, a minor, into fabricating false evidence implicating Wearry in the Walber murder."

To understand how the case got to this state, we must reexamine the crime scene and the events of that fatal evening.

The horrible news broke at approximately 9:30 p.m. on April 4, 1998, when police found the body of a teenage boy lying face down alongside a dark gravel road in Tangipahoa Parish, Louisiana.

Police searched the area surrounding Crisp Road, but they could find no vehicle, only the victim's corpse covered in blood. A short distance away, a large puddle of blood formed the imprint of a body in the gravel, and near the imprint, police found a receipt for a pizza delivered that night to a woman named Mary Ann Davis.

The autopsy of the 5'11", the 190-pound victim, found substantial injuries to most of the body's surfaces with investigators finding the worst injuries on the victim's head and face. The pathologist logged multiple lacerations on the victim's scalp and the facial area extending down to the skull, including a palpable skull fracture. The pathologist also noted brush burns on the victim's face, cheeks, and on the point of his chin with additional lacerations found inside the victim's lips. Extensive cuts and abrasions covered the body, including the victim's arms and shoulders.

The examiner initially believed the body resembled someone who had sustained a motor vehicle accident, ejected from the car onto asphalt, concrete, or gravel. However, a closer examination of the head proved that a homicide had occurred. Pathologists found no broken bones beyond the victim's skull and determined that the victim died at the crime scene.

In the early morning hours of April 5, 1998, Cherie Walber identified the body as that of her son, Eric Walber. Eric was a 16-year old honor student at Albany High School, who worked part-time as a delivery boy at Pizza Express in Albany, delivering food part-time in his red Ford Escort.

Walber worked the night of April 4, 1998, making his last pizza delivery to Mary Ann Davis on Blahut Road in Albany. Davis said Walber arrived sometime around 8:15 p.m. and left six minutes later.

Cherie Walber said her son had been wearing an Albany High School class ring and a watch. She also described his car and its contents. She told investigators that Eric did not wear a uniform while working and that his vehicle had no decal or other identifying features that would have indicated he was delivering pizza.

She said Eric had intended to leave on a ski trip the next day with friends and that his wallet had approximately $200 in cash for the trip.

In his car, the high school football player kept a policeman's nightstick for protection. He had just bought a new set of car speakers still in their packing box on the backseat. For his ski trip, he brought with him a backpack and a smaller fanny pack.

The Tangipahoa Parish Sheriff's Office's initial investigation of the location discovered long skid marks in the gravel of Crisp Road and blood where the skid marks terminated, along with blemishes in other areas.

A grid search located Eric Walber's car on April 8, 1998, behind an abandoned school between Albany and Springfield in Livingston Parish, and the Livingston Parish Sheriff's Office sent the vehicle to the crime lab for processing.

The lab technicians found a sizeable blood-stained area in the vehicle's hatchback and more droplets throughout the car. DNA testing matched all of the blood samples to Eric Walber. They also identified several partial fingerprints or smears but none suitable for identification.

The Tangipahoa Parish and Livingston Parish Sheriff's Offices both collected leads and information from several persons. Following one of those leads, detectives questioned Michael Wearry as a possible suspect, but multiple witnesses saw him at a wedding reception in Baton Rouge the night of the murder.

By the year 2000, police had no leads left to investigate. Even with Crime Stoppers offering a significant reward and three nationally televised crime shows spotlighting the unsolved homicide, the tips stopped coming in, and the case grew cold.

Then, in the Fall of 2000, police developed two new leads. A Springfield school teacher phoned the Livingston Parish Sheriff's office to say she had overheard one of her students discussing the case. Also, Sam Scott, a prison informant at Elayn Hunt Correctional Center, recounted for detectives the night he participated in the attack on Eric Walber.

Michael Wearry

With new information from readers and other sources, this chapter evolved from the Bayou Justice column entitled "Witness says Walber tortured repeatedly before his murder," initially published in south Louisiana newspapers on Tuesday, April 23, 2019.

TWO YEARS AFTER THE incident, an inmate at the Elayn Hunt Correctional Center told authorities he watched Randy Hutchinson torture the 16-year-old car-jacking victim, beating him five times before James Skinner repeatedly drove over the teenager with his car.

Serving a 5-year sentence for distributing cocaine, Sam Scott was in the center's "boot camp" program, and in April of 2000, he told his boot camp coordinator that his conscience bothered him. After seeing Eric Walber's murder featured on the television shows America's Most Wanted and Psychic Detective, Scott said he could neither eat nor sleep and needed to speak to someone with the sheriff's office in Livingston Parish.

Scott later testified at Michael Wearry's trial. As the state's star witness, he recounted every detail of that horrible night for a crowded courtroom.

Sometime after dark on April 4, 1998, Sam Scott, Michael Wearry, Darrell Hampton, Shadrick Reed, Randy Hutchinson, and others stood, shooting dice, in the front yard of a home on McCarroll Street, not far from Hutchinson's residence.

According to Scott, when Wearry — wearing an unusually formal pink shirt and slacks — lost all of his money, he said he wanted to find someone to rob. At that moment, a red Ford Escort pulled onto McCarroll Street from Highway 43. Wearry pointed at the car, telling the group if the vehicle passed again, they would rob the driver.

Approximately 15 minutes later, 16-year-old Eric Walber, returning from another Pizza Express delivery, drove back by the group. Randy Hutchinson flagged him down by standing in the street. As Eric Walber lowered his driver's side window, Wearry ran up and hit him three times in the face through the open driver's side window.

Wearry and Hutchinson opened the driver's door, pulled Walber out, and began beating him in the head. Wearry took Walber's black tri-fold wallet from the pocket of Walber's jeans and his class ring from his finger.

Climbing into the driver seat of Eric Walber's car, Wearry ordered Scott, Reed, and Hampton to join him on a drive to buy marijuana. Hutchinson pushed Walber through the passenger door and into the hatchback of the car, Scott climbed into the passenger seat next to him, and Hampton, Hutchinson, and Reed slid into the back seat.

Inside the car, Scott saw a Scrabble board game, a hand-held electronic poker game, a deck of cards, and a portable compact disc player. He saw new car speakers, a school backpack, and a smaller travel bag. Inside the pack, he saw Girbaud brand blue jeans and a Tommy Hilfiger shirt.

Wearry drove approximately 3 minutes before Walber started talking, and Wearry turned down a gravel drive, somewhere off Presbyterian Road in Springfield. He parked the car near a church graveyard and ordered the group out of the vehicle.

Hutchinson drug Walber from the hatchback and up the gravel road, leaving him in a kneeling position in front of the car's headlights. Wearry stepped up and began punching Walber in the face while Hutchinson beat him with a black, shiny stick for 20 minutes or more.

Here is where the story takes an even stranger turn.

According to Scott, the crew then climbed back into the car, seated in their same positions with Eric Walber, wounded and moaning in the hatchback. They drove to an abandoned house near the location of their dice game and again pulled Walber from the car for another stick beating.

After another 20 minutes, they climbed back into the car a third time, sitting in the same position with Walber again moaning in the hatchback.

This time, Walber drove further down Highway 43 toward Albany. Near a convenience store called Potluck Too, where he recognized a passing car and flashed his headlights to flag the driver down. Both vehicles pulled into the store parking lot, and Wearry asked the driver of the second vehicle, Eric Charles Brown, if he had any weed for sale.

Beyond the range of Scott's hearing, Wearry spoke to Brown's passenger, James Skinner, who then joined them in the red Escort.

This time, Skinner drove. They found another location, pulled Walber to the front of the car, and the group again watched Hutchinson beat Walber with a nightstick under the high beams of the car's headlights.

After another 20 minutes, the crew loaded up for the fifth time and drove across the Tangipahoa Parish line to Crisp Road, where Walber's final beating took place.

According to Scott, this time, Hutchinson and Wearry stood Walber in the middle of the gravel road, with each holding him up by one of his shoulders. Skinner jumped back into the car and drove into the darkness. Soon, they heard the revving of the engine as the vehicle accelerated toward the group at top speed. Wearry and Hutchinson let go of Walber's shoulders, just as the frontend struck his chest.

As the group watched, Skinner drove the vehicle back and forth multiple times over Walber's now silent body.

Later, Wearry and Skinner drug Eric Walber to the side of the road, and the group rode away, leaving Walber's corpse face down in the dirt.

Scott said he saw Wearry driving Eric's car the following day and again the day after. Police found the red Ford Escort behind the school on April 8, 1998, four days after the murder.

Sam Scott did not explain the multiple stops to multiple locations or the repeated beatings. Still, another witness, 10-year-old Jeffrey Ashton of Springfield, told the court that he also saw Wearry and Hutchinson in Eric Walber's car that night.

According to his court testimony, at approximately 11:20 p.m., little Ashton was walking home from a music program at the church across the street from his residence when he heard footsteps and men arguing.

He ran and hid under his family's mobile home. From there, he saw Michael Wearry, Randy Hutchinson, and Darrell Hampton throw something into a roadside ditch before climbing back into the red Ford Escort and driving away.

Sam Scott and Jeffrey Ashton both told the court they saw Michael Wearry driving Eric Walber's car that night, but that is not all the two have in common. The families of both witnesses insist their family member committed perjury on the stand when each testified, together insisting Sam Scott and Jeffrey Ashton were not in Springfield or Albany on the night of Walber's death. These relatives claim that throughout the timetable described in their testimonies, their family members were 20 miles away, attending the Ponchatoula Strawberry Festival with their respective families.

The Cazan Crime-fighters

With new information from readers and other sources, this chapter evolved from the Bayou Justice column entitled "Crime fighting amateurs assist police with cold cases," initially published in south Louisiana newspapers on Tuesday, April 30, 2019.

LAST YEAR, I LAUNCHED this column to assist southeast Louisiana's overloaded police agencies in collecting more leads on cold cases and in moving closer to providing closure for families of missing persons and homicide victims. In southwest Louisiana, a group calling themselves the "Cazan Crime-fighters" has found another way to support these goals.

Last weekend, I delivered the keynote address at the group's monthly true-crime conference in Mamou, Louisiana. Other speakers included active and retired law enforcement personnel, local librarians, private investigators, schoolteachers, bail bondsmen, elected officials, bounty hunters, and most importantly, the families of missing persons and homicide victims from all over south Louisiana.

I left the two-day event inspired, wondering if the Florida Parishes are ready for their amateur crime-fighting association. Cazan Crime-fighters invited me to discuss the Bayou Justice column and the two true-crime books I have coming out later this year. Still, I left their facility — the historic Hotel Cazan, originally opening as a brothel in 1911 — humbled and thankful for the knowledge I had gained from these folks who like to call themselves "Prairie Cajuns."

At their conference, the family members of cold case victims said they are still seeking answers and expressed their gratitude for the group for keeping the stories of their loved ones alive. One-by-one each attendee updated all in attendance on their cold cases, beginning with anything that transpired since their meeting last month, and finishing by answering questions from newcomers. As each family member or armchair sleuth recounted their progress, the good this conference is doing became increasingly apparent.

Among the topics discussed at this month's conference:

- The murders of Russell Foote, A. J. Breaux and David Matte
- The St. Landry Church Fires
- The "Cajun Mafia" and their connections to New Orleans, Carlos Marcello, and the assassination of John F. Kennedy
- The strange disappearances of Alice Marie Reeves, David Matthew Martin, and Alton Lowe

The Cazan Crime-fighters gained national notoriety earlier this year when the television show America's Most Wanted spotlighted the group's investigation into the death of Melissa Perritt's mother. Before this year, Perrit, a police officer, had worked her mother's case alone for 36 years.

"The crime-fighters have helped me find more information this year than I found in the previous 35 years combined. I'm more grateful to them than they will ever know," Perritt said.

Perritt is the daughter of Alice Marie Reeves, who disappeared from the Mamou-Ville Platte area in May 1967. Perritt was four months old when her mother vanished. Alice Marie Reeves dropped her infant daughter off at a babysitter's house on her way to work at a local beauty shop. Her family never saw her again.

The state placed Perritt with her mother's cousin. She discovered the facts about her mother's disappearance at age 15 and set out to find the truth for her well-being, as well as that of her grandmother and two siblings.

Perritt learned some about her mother's life through the babysitter, a member of her father's extended family. She told Perritt that her parents never married and of her father's rumored association with organized crime.

Her mother, Alice Marie Reeves, danced in local men's clubs, including a place called the Purple Peacock, and she may have witnessed a murder in Lake Charles in 1965.

Regardless of her mother's lifestyle or the people she associated with, Perritt says Alice Reeves was a victim and deserves justice. "She was still my mother, still my grandmother's daughter, and she didn't deserve what she got," she said.

Much of the details Perritt has found, she discovered this year with the help of the Cazan Crime-fighters, she said.

Cazan Crime-fighters organizer, Valerie Cahill, said seeing progress like that in Reeves' case is why she and the other Cazan Crime-fighters do what they do. They strive to provide closure to family members, and digging into unsolved cases is a way of caring for your neighbor and community, she said.

At this month's conference — where the stated theme was "Hate Crimes, Cold Cases, and Hot Topics" — attendee Jan Baone said, "These events are exciting, like watching an episode of 48 Hours unfolding before our eyes."

Sandy Ashurst, a first-time attendee from Breaux Bridge, agreed. "Groups like these are essential to bridging the gap between society and law enforcement," she said. "There are no secrets in small towns. When something happens, someone somewhere always knows who done it. It's just a matter of getting them to trust you enough to share what they know."

Phil Lemoine, a former mayor and a candidate running for state office, said he plans to champion legislation to fund crime-fighting groups like the Cazan Crime-fighters. He described them as an extension of law enforcement, a tool that agencies can use similar to Crime Stoppers or the Neighborhood Watch programs.

Valerie Cahill also stressed the importance of community members playing a role in finding this justice and closure. "The more a case is discussed," she said, "the more likely new details will shake loose, or someone will pick up on a tip that's been overlooked."

"The police can't do everything. New cases come in every day, so it is tough to focus resources on cold cases. Our objective is to make those cold cases hot again by getting people talking," Cahill said. "With every unsolved mystery, there is potentially someone out there who saw or knows something that can help law enforcement. Sometimes it's a tip; sometimes it's a word; sometimes it's as small as a facial expression someone observed."

Conference Outreach Coordinator Camile Fontenot added, "Community awareness is key to getting justice and ultimately giving these families a sense of closure. That's what we're here for."

Before I left Mamou, the Cazan Crime-fighters presented me with a Cajun Country gift basket — a metal washtub filled with creole mixes and seasonings, but they gave me a gift even grander than that without realizing it.

I walked away from this conference feeling energized, anxious to inspire like-minded individuals to follow their lead and perhaps duplicate their success in southeast Louisiana. As you read these words today, if you are interested in helping make the Florida Parish Crime-fighters a reality, find some friends who may want to help, email me, and together we can make this happen.

Hermina Reed

With new information from readers and other sources, this chapter evolved from the Bayou Justice column entitled "Husband indicted in Hermina Reed murder," initially published in south Louisiana newspapers on Tuesday, May 4, 2019.

NEWSPAPERS DESCRIBED Hermina Reed, 26, as a "perfectly-shaped pretty young woman" and her murder as "the most ghoulish South Louisiana has ever witnessed."

Police charged her husband, Leroy Reed — a 40-year-old carpenter and part-time taxi driver from Amite — with "disfiguring his wife's face beyond recognition" using a "ship's hammer" found at the scene.

Reed told police he only discovered the body and that his wife feared a former suitor in town from El Paso, Texas.

This investigation began near Madisonville shortly before midnight on March 14, 1919, when a drunken Reed stumbled into a barroom and announced he had just found his wife murdered. Those in the crowded bar that heard him laughed, thinking he had made a joke. Nothing like that ever happened in St. Tammany Parish. However, the bartender had listened, and when he closed the saloon three hours later, Deputy Sheriff Guy A. Smith apprehended Reed in the parking lot.

In tears, Reed told police how he found the body and led them to his home to see for themselves. At the house, they found three doors locked: the front and side doors secured with padlocks on the outside and the rear door held by a latch on the inside. Reed told Deputy Smith he lost his keys to the padlocks weeks before and usually used a knife to open the backdoor.

Inside, a reporter from *The New Orleans States-Item* saw it this way:

"Lying on her bed in one of the four rooms of a wooden house situated in what is usually called the District, in the block opposite Addison Grocery, the finely shaped body of Mrs. Reed presented the appearance of one sleeping. Her small feet protruded from the covers and hung inches from the floor, but when police uncovered her face, the ghastly sight caused all in the home to shudder at the horror."

"The open breast beneath a black and white checked dress revealed silk embroidered underwear. Mrs. Reed had diamond rings on her fingers and diamond earrings in her ears. The exotic fittings of the bed appeared more expensive than the other furnishings in the room. The mattress was saturated with blood, as was a fancy pillow beside her head."

"When the coroner lifted what remained of her head, all gasped at the horrible work of a monster. Her eyes were closed in clotted blood. Her forehead and the back of her skull had been smashed as one would crush a bag of ice by pounding on it with a hammer."

"Near the bed, police found the bloody weapon, an automobile hammer, which must have been wielded in a frenzy to cause such damage, blow after blow until the wire-wound handle of the hammer broke rendering the tool useless."

"The coroner also found wound on the side of her face, clean-cut by a sharp instrument, something other than the hammer. One of these wounds severed an artery and would have caused the woman to bleed to death without the follow-up blows from the hammer."

Bulloch signed an affidavit later that morning before Judge Pichon Carter, and Deputies Smith and Devereaux took Reed to jail where he would await trial.

Huey Long

With new information from readers and other sources, this chapter evolved from the Bayou Justice column entitled "Huey Long killed by gambling syndicate," initially published in south Louisiana newspapers on Tuesday, May 14, 2019.

JUST BEFORE DUSK ON a Wednesday evening, July 11, 1935, Hammond Police Chief George F. Smith called a press conference to discuss rumors that Louisiana Governor Oscar K. Allen had fired him.

"There has been some misunderstanding — by myself and others — as to whether or not I am still employed here," he said. "And I would like to assure everyone that I most certainly am."

"Chief Smith?" Hodding Carter, Jr. of the Hammond Daily Courier raised his pencil. "Can you tell us why the governor summoned you to the state capitol this morning and whether it's true that Senator Huey Long is pushing you out?"

Carter — like the editors of most Louisiana dailies in 1935 — opposed Huey Long because of his Share-the-Wealth program. Long wanted wealthy newspaper advertisers to give more back to their communities.

"Junior," Chief Smith answered. "My service to Hammond is subject solely to the pleasure of the city council until such time that the council decides to appoint my successor."

"Actually, Chief," interrupted Huey Long supporter George B. Furbos, editor of *The Hammond Vindicator*, a weekly newspaper serving primarily poor farmers, "I heard the governor called you to Baton Rouge about what happened in Ponchatoula last week. Is that true?"

"George," the chief answered. "The 25 slot machines destroyed by state police last week in Ponchatoula have no relevance here. However, let me say this: From now on, I intend to enforce all city ordinances and laws, hoping the affluent citizens of Hammond will cooperate. I am going to stand against and will drive out all slot machines and gambling from our city. Let this be a warning to all violators. I will enforce the law against friend or foe, and I will not discriminate."

Two weeks later, a civil service commission approved the removal of Chief Smith for "incompetence, inefficiency, and negligence." Commission Chairman Lorris M. Wimberly told reporters the inquiry began after residents of Hammond filed civil service complaints with the state. Still, he refused to disclose the details of those complaints. "If you require more information," he said. "You must consult the Hammond City Council."

Nine months earlier, on August 7, 1934, *The American Progress* — a Huey Long owned newspaper produced in the offices of *The Hammond Vindicator* — reported:

"Political officials in New Orleans collect $13,000,000 annually in graft from the red-light district and gambling houses in Orleans, St. Bernard, and Jefferson Parishes."

The newspaper itemized the list of vices generating money as racing handbooks, prostitution, slot machines, lotteries, blackjack, keno, roulette, and "lesser gambling games, such as punch-boards, marbles, and dice."

In today's dollars, that 13 million equates to nearly 250 million annually.

Two weeks later, Governor Allen sent the order to the police chiefs of every city and the sheriffs of every parish demanding the closing of all casinos, private gambling houses, and brothels in the state — and he demanded the destruction of all slot machines in Louisiana.

Shortly after Christmas that year, Governor Allen realized law enforcement had ignored his order, so he delivered a fresh ultimatum. Law enforcement agencies statewide had until New Year's Eve to comply with his original order and destroy all slot machines, or the state police would begin doing it for them.

Initially, this plan seemed to work. By June 1935, Hammond and Ponchatoula were among the few towns left with working slot machines. By the end of July, if any remained, their owners hid them somewhere outside of public view.

But that had all changed by mid-August 1935.

In under two weeks, shiny new "Chief" brand slot machines appeared in the lobbies of almost every business in Baton Rouge and New Orleans, as well as most restaurants and grocery stores along the Mississippi River on the route between the two cities.

According to *The New Orleans States*, the appearance of these new "Chiefs" was just the beginning. On August 17, the newspaper reported:

"Several poker games reopened this week, and resorts are beginning to install dice, blackjack, and other gambling games. This started when some favored gamblers started operating boldly without police molestation. They explained they had 'an understanding' with a New York syndicate that provided both the slots and the protection for the other games."

New Orleans Superintendent of Police George Reyer told *The States* that he knew nothing of any slot machine violations in the city. "If there are any violations of the law," he said, "I'll see to it that those slot machines are immediately seized and destroyed."

The article went on to say:

"Side doors which had been closed to prevent surprise raids by police in recent days have swung wide open. With the peephole no longer needed, the syndicate offers customers free and uninterrupted access to their favorite illegal games."

The last week in August 1935, Senator Huey Pierce Long telegraphed Governor Allen from Washington, telling him that he would be back in Baton Rouge for a special legislative session the first week in September. The telegram also asked the governor to thank General Louis F. Guerre of the state police for finally dismantling gambling in the state.

Within 24 hours, according to three daily newspapers, every slot machine in Baton Rouge and New Orleans vanished.

An armed assassin shot Senator Huey P. Long in the Louisiana State Capitol on September 8, 1935 — 12 minutes after he introduced a bill regulating at the state level the installation of "any and all mechanical devices."

Two days later, Huey Long died in a Baton Rouge hospital.

On September 19, 1935, *The Times-Picayune* reported that all Chief slot machines had returned to Baton Rouge and New Orleans as mysteriously as they had vanished two weeks earlier.

Uncle Jerry

With new information from readers and other sources, this chapter evolved from the Bayou Justice column entitled "Alleged serial rapist presumed innocent," initially published in south Louisiana newspapers on Tuesday, May 21, 2019.

HAMMOND POLICE ARRESTED Jerome Hills, 45, on September 17, 1996, charging him with the rape and murder of Laquinta Mercedes "Sadie" Henderson — a 5-year-old girl who called him "Uncle Jerry."

A grand jury indicted Jerry Hills the following month. Still, in 2004, the District Attorney's Office for the 21st Judicial Court discovered that DNA from a hair found on the preschooler's body belonged to someone other than Hill.

Soon after, DA Scott Perrilloux returned the case to the grand jury. After reviewing the 9-year-old case, the new grand jury found the evidence against Hills insufficient for trial and set him free.

Hills walked out of the Tangipahoa Parish Jail on January 26, 2005, escorted by his New Orleans attorney, Martin Regan, Jr., who told reporters, "He was always adamant he didn't commit this crime. Back when they offered a plea deal, he could have gone home on probation, but he said no. He said he wouldn't plead guilty to something he didn't do."

The Baton Rouge Advocate ran photos of Hills leaving jail with a grin on his face, seemingly just another falsely accused black man, exonerated by DNA evidence after spending nearly a decade, imprisoned improperly.

However, the newspapers of the day may not have reported the complete story. The rape and murder of Sadie Henderson were not the only crimes women had accused Hills of committing without standing trial.

At a Prieur hearing on March 4, 1998, the State presented evidence of three earlier alleged rapes, and one alleged attempted rape, all attributed to Hills.

In arguments, the State claimed these incidents showed Hills' modus operandi; that he picks his victims up in his car, transports them to another location, and commits a crime against them. This MO, according to the State, also matched the modus operandi of Sadie's murderer.

During a pretrial Prieur hearing, HPD Sergeant. Melissa Spurling described the reported rape of a 15-year-old on January 3, 1994. Spurling said that the victim told her that she obtained a ride from Hills around midnight, wanting to visit her mother at the North Oaks Hospital. Instead of taking her to the hospital, the victim told Spurling, Hills drove down Highway 51 near Manchac and told her to have sex with him, or he would abandon her on the dark road.

Afraid, the victim said she submitted, and Hills drove her to the hospital to visit her mother. She saw her mother while Hills waited to take her home. Entering his truck for the second time that night, she said, Hills told her they were not going straight home. Fearing another assault, she jumped out of the vehicle and ran. Later that night, a friend took her back to the hospital, where she reported the rape.

Spurling testified that the doctor found inactive spermatozoa in the victim's vaginal area, but no other trauma. The Hammond Police Department issued a warrant for Hills without executing it for another two years — after he became a suspect in Sadie Henderson's murder.

Another alleged rape victim, a 43-year-old, testified that on December 10, 1990, she caught a ride with Hills from Hammond to Kentwood. En route, she said, Hills told her something was wrong with his truck. When they stopped, she said, Hills hit her with a hammer and raped her multiple times.

The third alleged victim, a 44-year-old, testified that she caught a ride from Hills early one morning in 1993. Instead of taking her home, she said he took her to an isolated area near the airport and forced her to have sex with him.

She testified that afterward when Hills took her home, she broke his nose with a beer bottle from the floorboard of the truck. She said this action (together with the crack she smoked) gave her satisfaction, so she did not report the rape.

The final witness, recently arrested for the attempted murder of her husband, entered the court in handcuffs. The 25-year-old testified that on April 15, 1992, she accepted a ride from Hills outside a bar. She said Hills drove her down Coonville Road, pulled a knife, and told her she was going to have sex with him. The two struggled, she said, but she escaped and did not file charges.

The 1st Circuit Court of Appeal agreed with the DA that these incidents demonstrated "evidence of a method of operation and system," saying they found all of the witnesses highly credible and would allow the introduction of this new evidence in Hills' eventual murder trial.

However, a higher court overturned this finding. It ultimately denied the state's request to call these witnesses at trial — the hearing later canceled when the grand jury ruled the DA did not have enough evidence to prosecute.

Today — since no court has found anyone guilty of these crimes — the Hammond Police Department considers each of these alleged rape cases unsolved. Like the rape and murder of Sadie Henderson, these are cold cases still under investigation.

If you or someone you know has information that may bring the perpetrator or perpetrators to justice, please contact the Hammond Police Department today.

Regarding the murder of 5-year-old Laquinta Mercedes "Sadie" Henderson, this is what we know today:

On March 2, 1996, Shiela Henderson, left her daughter, Sadie, and her 4-year-old brother playing and eating candy in their grandmother's backyard, both children excited to be spending the night at grandmother's. The 4-year-old went inside at approximately 4:00 p.m., but Sadie never did.

Fishers found her body over a week later, on March 11, 1996, floating face down in a pond adjacent to Yokum Road, near Hammond, south of Interstate 12 — less than three miles from the grandmother's home.

Tangipahoa Parish Coroner James G. Traylor, Jr. — based on the remains of undigested pickles in Sadie's stomach — fixed the time of death somewhere between 4:00 p.m. and 6:15 p.m. on March 2, 1996.

The coroner found no outward signs of rape but noted both anal and vaginal trauma. Sadie's body had begun to decompose, making cause-of-death tough to determine, but Traylor said he believed the girl's death came from a blunt strike to the head.

The Naked Hitch-hiker

With new information from readers and other sources, this chapter evolved from the Bayou Justice column entitled "Livingston parish investigators say stripper faked kidnapping, vanished," initially published in south Louisiana newspapers on Tuesday, May 27, 2019.

ON A WEDNESDAY NIGHT, October 9, 1962, Sheriff Taft Faust of the Livingston Parish Sheriff's Office got a call from Trooper Frank E. Miller of the Louisiana State Police. Miller had picked up a half-naked girl walking down a gravel road near Watson, Louisiana, with her hands tied behind her back.

State Police had set up roadblocks to trap two Italian men who Sandra Manente, 23, said abducted and raped her an hour earlier. Miller called Faust, requesting that LPSO take over the investigation.

Deputies Odom Graves and James Lott met Miller and Trooper Ralph B. Powers with the victim at the Baton Rouge General Hospital. Manente, a native of Jackson, Mississippi, told the deputies she had started classes at LSU in the spring, but quit in July to take a job in New Orleans. She said the business where she worked had since closed.

She was driving East on Highway 190 en route to visit a friend in Denham Springs, she said, when two men ran her off the road.

"They drove alongside me, flirting," she said. "I ignored them and turned right towards Watson. After a few miles, I got scared and tried to turn around on a gravel road when the driver laid on his car horn. Somehow I lost control and hit a sign."

With her face badly bruised and briar-like abrasions all over her body, Manente told the officers the two men chased her into the woods. There, they tackled her and tied her hands with fishing cord, before cutting off her clothes and sexually molesting her.

Deputy James Lott interviewed a man in Denham Springs who admitted to meeting Manente in New Orleans and inviting her to visit, but he said he knew little about her. He had no idea, he said, who the assailants were or why they accosted her.

The following Saturday afternoon, October 14, Deputy Odom Graves interviewed Manente again. This time, she told a different story. "I lied," she said. "Just trying to get attention."

Deputy Graves asked how she got the bruises and scratches. Manente told him she checked into a motel in Denham Springs and used curlers and razor blades on her body. Graves asked why she left the motel and wrecked the car, and then he asked how she tied her hands behind her back and why she cut her clothes. Manente replied, saying she could not remember. "I had a big drink of whiskey," she said. "Anything's possible."

In 1962, the Livingston Parish Sheriff's Office did not have the luxury of being able to search newspaper archives as investigators can today. If they could have done so, they would have known the rest of the story.

On July 19, 1962, Sandra Manente worked as a burlesque dancer at 225 Bourbon Street, in a club called the Blue Angel. That night, New Orleans police arrested 23-year-old bartender Milton Rafael for shooting and killing stripper Jane Hernandez, 22, in the back as she left the club walking down Bourbon Street.

Rafael told Police that Hernandez was walking down Bourbon Street in the direction of Bienville Street when his .22 caliber semi-automatic accidentally discharged, killing the dancer. Police found the body lying face down approximately 28 feet from the front door of the Blue Angel Lounge.

Police Sergeant. Cornelius Drumm told patrol officer James Webb of Homicide Division that he suspected club-owner Vito J. Sortino shot Hernandez, so they collected both men, leaving stripper Sandra Manente to close up the bar.

Drumm had arrested Sortino two years earlier for wounding bar customer Wilbert Batiste using the same .22 rifle, but the District Attorney's office refused to prosecute him.

Manente told investigators that she was on stage when she heard the shot and did not witness the crime.

Two months later, the office of District Attorney James "Big Jim" Garrison raided the Blue Angel Lounge and arrested Sandra Manente, charging her with "B-drinking" — convincing bar patrons to buy bottles of cheap champagne at premium prices.

The following week, the DA's office led a total assault on Bourbon Street vice. From *The Times-Picayune*, August 14, 1962:

"The crackdown on Bourbon Street continued at full steam Monday night with the arrests of 14 on charges ranging from improper lighting to conspiracy to commit prostitution. Undercover agents of the NOPD vice squad and the district attorney's staff, working separately, combed the blocks known as 'stripper's paradise' in the new DA's effort to rid the French Quarter of vice. Jim Garrison added emphasis to the drive-by personally leading the inspections of each club."

Judge Paul Garofalo set Sandra Manente's trial for October 25, 1962 — two weeks after her reported assault in Livingston Parish.

At the New Orleans court, she failed to appear, forfeiting her fifty-dollar bail. The judge said he would not issue an attachment for her arrest "since there would be no point to it if she has left town," he said. "But if she comes back and I hear about it, I will send the police after her."

On October 20, 1962, East Baton Rouge Sheriff Bryan Clemmons and Livingston Parish Sheriff Taft Faust jointly asked the East Baton Rouge Parish coroner to sign forms transferring Sandra Manente to a hospital in Whitfield, Mississippi — the Mississippi State Mental Hospital for the Criminally Insane.

One week earlier, Manente told Deputy James Lott she wanted to remain in police custody for her protection. She said someone would kill her if doctors released her from the hospital too soon.

When interviewed by the coroner, Manente said, "I think I need to go back to Mississippi, but some strange things have been going through my mind. I wonder if driving home and killing my parents might convince you doctors to keep me locked up."

Modern-day Bonnie and Clyde

With new information from readers and other sources, this chapter evolved from the Bayou Justice column entitled "Alleged drug-dealer murdered by modern-day Bonnie and Clyde," initially published in south Louisiana newspapers on Tuesday, June 11, 2019.

IN 1987, A HAMMOND woman and a man living in Pennsylvania testified before a seven-woman, five-person jury in Amite. While the jury, the press, and Ad Hoc Judge Cleveland Marcel listened intensively, Barbara Rogers Dickerson Hebert and Jesse Lord collectively recounted the following events:

On April 24, 1981 — according to both testimonies — Barbara's former lover dropped by her mobile home in Hammond. Lord said the couple sat reminiscing about old times and wishing they had money. The conversation, he said, soon turned to consider potential targets they might find to rob.

Barbara, according to Lord, suggested they phone Walter Tally, Jr., whom she described as a traveling drug dealer making his rounds from the Bogalusa area. When her friend agreed, Barbara called Tally and invited him over, telling him they were interested in buying some marijuana.

Inside the mobile home, Lord said, Tally opened a briefcase containing $10,000 in cash along with a $20,000 cache of cocaine. Lord said he had gotten the story from Barbara's former lover and that he could have been mistaken about the value of the briefcase contents. It may have been $20,000 in cash and only $10,000 in cocaine, he said.

Viewing the contents of the briefcase, according to both witnesses, Barbara's former lover pulled a .38 caliber handgun from his pocket and taped Tally's mouth and limbs with Duct tape before forcing him from the mobile home and into his car.

With Barbara in the passenger seat and Tally laying across the backseat, according to both testimonies, they drove from Hammond until they came to an overpass near Bayou Manchac. There, both said, on the road beneath the Interstate 55 twin-span bridge, Barbara's former lover pulled Tally from the backseat and drug him near the back bumper of the car.

The prosecutor, Assistant District Attorney Charles Genco, added, "[Tally's] attempts to plead for his life were muffled by the tape pulled over his mouth."

Barbara testified that while Tally and her former lover stood outside the car, she heard a single gunshot. Moments later, her former lover got back into the vehicle without Tally and drove the two of them back to Hammond.

Lord testified that Barbara's former lover considered killing her and leaving her body on that dark road along with Tally's, but something Barbara said caused him to change his mind.

The coroner's report said Tally died from a close-range shot to the back of his head.

Four police officers also testified in court that day, describing how law enforcement had discovered Tally's burned car in nearby Livingston Parish and how the murder weapon — the .38 caliber handgun — had never been found.

The 21st Judicial District Court had granted Barbara Rogers Dickerson Hebert immunity from prosecution before the trial began. At that time, she was on probation for a drug conviction.

The biggest question in the case involved identifying Barbara's former lover. The prosecution (and Barbara, their star witness) identified the killer as Johnny Dickerson, Barbara's ex-husband. The defense team — and at least four witnesses — contended that, instead of Dickerson, a federal inmate named Brian Foret accompanied Barbara that night.

In his closing arguments, Baton Rouge defense attorney Mike Walsh said Barbara Hebert testified falsely against Dickerson. He did so, they said, out of jealousy and revenge related to his relationships since their divorce, and he recounted witness testimony saying Barbara had said she lied to police and that Foret robbed and shot Tally.

Willie Johnson, chief criminal deputy for the Tangipahoa Parish Sheriff's Office, said investigators had not heard about Foret's potential involvement in the case before the trial opened.

Brian Foret's father testified that his son died of cancer in 1983 and that, at the time of Tally's murder, his son could barely walk.

Asked about witness Jesse Lord's testimony regarding Dickerson's confession to him and about Lord's life sentence for kidnapping, Charles Genco said, "Like relatives, you can't pick your witnesses in a murder investigation. You've got to take the people who know the information."

On June 3, 1987, a jury of 12 voted 11-1, finding Johnny Dickerson guilty of second-degree murder, aggravated kidnapping, and armed robbery. The mandatory sentence for both second-degree murder and aggravated kidnapping is life without parole.

Genco praised investigators from the Tangipahoa Parish Sheriff's Office, along with DA investigator Murphy Richardson for locating witnesses vital to the investigation.

"Tally should not have been involved in narcotics," Genco said. "But he was a human being who had a heart and walked and talked just like us. He had a right to live. It was hard-fought, but I am glad the jury accepted our case."

This story also has a sad footnote. Two years before the Tally murder, Independence Police Department investigators found Johnny Dickerson's older brother, David Dickerson, 35, along with David Dickerson's 20-year-old wife, Tina Leto Dickerson, both dead from gunshot wounds to the chest. Investigators discovered no note but officially recorded both deaths as suicides.

The Poultry Pioneer

With new information from readers and other sources, this chapter evolved from the Bayou Justice column entitled "Poultry pioneer's suicide questioned," initially published in south Louisiana newspapers on Tuesday, June 18, 2019.

RAISING CHICKENS ON a commercial scale fast became one of Southeast Louisiana's most vital industries in the 1950s, primarily due to the vision of one man, 32-year-old Leo Luke Lea, an instructor with the Veterans Farm Training Program.

According to a March 22, 1953, multi-page feature in *The Advocate* newspaper, poultry breeders from across the state flocked to hear lectures from Luke Lea, hoping to take home with them the secrets of his success.

The Associated Press picked up the feature and distributed Lea's story nationwide. Two months later, *The State Times* celebrated news of Luke and Beatrice Lea's newborn son.

No one imagined that eight months later, Luke Lea would be dead.

Luke Lea grew up in Pride, Louisiana, a star athlete; he graduated high school in 1939. After college, he started work as a high school basketball referee and moved to Denham Springs.

Returning home to Louisiana after World War II, Lea got assistance from the GI Bill and started a program to assist farmers when the income from truck crops became slim.

In November of 1948, Lea married Beatrice Mildred Hoover and moved to her hometown of Albany. There, Lea insisted farmers learn from past problems and adapt. When the chickens from the fields ate the strawberry crop, Lea had them build a poultry house large enough for the flock to both lay and live indoors. When the egg market grew over-saturated, Lea instructed breeders to supply the hatcheries.

Lea traveled the state lecturing against the traditional one-crop system of farming, insisting that local farmers needed a supplemental crop to survive. At first, Lea considered dairy and beef but soon realized the small acreage of the average south Louisiana truck farmer would not support large herds of cattle.

Eventually, Lea proved that only poultry could save the parish's dying farms. He had identified the right supplement but still needed someone interested enough to help him launch the project. He found that someone in Travis Lobell of Springfield, initially the only Livingston Parish farmer he could convince to invest in poultry on a commercial scale.

One of the most significant objections the truck farmers had to the poultry business was the fact that free-range chickens were extremely destructive to farm crops. Still, Lea proposed a radical solution to the problem. He suggested that from the time of their arrival as chicks until the day they went to market, growers would keep the chickens confined. Lea proposed a new type of hen house, one large enough for chickens to live in continually, going open-range only when fields had no crops.

Because of the mildness of Louisiana winters, the biggest problem, he said, was one of space rather than one of material. For that reason, he proposed an open hen house, merely a roof with a supporting framework and wire stretched around the braces rather than expensive lumber for walling.

Breeders would keep part of this house closed off to serve as a brooder room for hatchlings, enlarging the area around the brooder room as the chickens grew, providing more space until the birds filled the whole structure, where they would live until sold.

Lea instructed farmers to allow four square feet per bird. He said a poultry house built following his plan, with the dimensions of 40 x 100 feet, would be large enough to accommodate 1,000 laying hens — from the time of their arrival until the day they went to market.

He also proposed the cycling of manure to the fields instead of purchasing expensive fertilizers. He eventually replaced the old type farm brooders (kerosene heated) with those heated by gas or electricity, and his water systems became automatic.

While working as a traveling fertilizer sales clerk, Lea started his flock back in Denham Springs in 1946 by ordering 250 New Hampshire Red baby chicks.

By 1953, he and his partners no longer ordered chicks by the 100; they ordered them by the 1,000.

On arrival, Lea instructed farmers to cull the chicks rigidly, vaccinating each bird as they entered the brooders. He provided them with a detailed feeding, vaccination, and culling regiment that ultimately provided each grower with self-sustaining farms, hatching their chicks, and leveraging moneymaking flocks, by selling eggs, baby chicks, and meat.

Eggs candled, weighed, cleaned, and packed in cases of 30 dozen eggs per case were either transported weekly by truck or shipped by express to incubators across the country. Some eggs went to large packinghouses in New Orleans and other large cities. Others shipped as far as Havana, Cuba, by air.

By 1954, Luke Lea and his partner, Travis Lobell, were on the fast track to becoming wealthy men when — according to the Livingston Parish Sheriff's Office — Luke Lea committed suicide with a shotgun.

On July 31, 1954, Livingston Parish coroner Dr. Montgomery Williams presided over a coroner's inquest at the Hollabaugh-Seale funeral home in Baton Rouge. Lea had been missing from his home since Monday, July 26.

Hunting a lost calf in the area one mile north of Centerville, cattleman Reid Martin and his sons discovered a body the following Thursday morning. The corpse — wearing the same green shirt and khaki trousers newspapers described Luke Lea as wearing when he disappeared — lay on a partially overgrown cow path approximately 309 feet from Red Oak Road.

Livingston Parish Sheriff Taft Faust, his deputies, and state police had been combing the parish, looking for Lea since his disappearance. When Reid Martin phoned the sheriff's office, state trooper Ivan Foster responded to the call. Luke Lea's brother, Lawrence Lea, arrived with Foster and identified the body. The state police plane flew overhead, searching the area, and identified Lea's car at nearly the same moment.

Both the sheriff and the coroner drove to the scene, but a hard rain prevented Dr. Williams from holding the inquest on site.

In Baton Rouge, Sheriff Faust told the jury he found a suicide note in Lea's papers shortly before the inquest began. Friends and relatives also testified that Lea had been "melancholy."

Faust testified that Foster found Lea's body eight feet from his 1952 green Dodge coupe, parked in a small clearing in the woods. Foster, he said, described seeing a 16-gauge shotgun near the dead man's outstretched hand. Sheriff Faust said investigators found one fired shell inside the gun and the cash Lea collected for the Mathew's Feed Company inside the car's glove box.

The coroner's jury returned an official verdict of "Death by a self-inflicted gunshot wound," but a relative of the deceased phoned me recently, asking that I research the case.

The relative — who asked that I not use his name — wonders why Sheriff Faust elected not to present the alleged suicide note to the jury. He also wonders why Trooper Foster did not attend the inquest, and generally, he wonders why Luke Lea, a local celebrity with an infant child at home, took his own life and chose such an awkward weapon to accomplish the deed.

After reviewing the case, I now also wonder.

Reginald Reed

The following is from a news story written by the author of the Bayou Justice column entitled "Reginald Reed indicted in wife's murder," published in the Hammond Daily Star on June 21, 2019.

DISTRICT ATTORNEY SCOTT M. Perrilloux reported today that a Tangipahoa Parish Grand Jury returned a true bill of indictment in the 1987 homicide of 26-year-old Selonia Reed.

Indicted for second-degree murder and conspiracy to commit second-degree murder were Reginald Reed Sr., age 59, and Jimmy Ray Barnes, age 60. Hammond Police booked Reed Friday afternoon, June 21, 2019, at 2:44 PM, minutes before the district attorney's office distributed a press release announcing the indictment. Police arrested Barnes Friday evening in Atlanta, Georgia.

On August 23, 1987, police found the body of Selonia Reed inside of her vehicle in the parking lot of John's Curb Market on East Thomas Street in Hammond.

"Recent developments and additional investigative work by law enforcement and further review of the case by the District Attorney's Office resulted in the case being presented to the grand jury. We felt there was sufficient evidence for consideration, and I am pleased with the indictments," Perrilloux said. "We will continue the work to bring those responsible for the killing of Mrs. Reed to justice."

Honorable Judge Charlotte Foster returned the indictments, issuing warrants for both Reed and Barnes and setting bond at $250,000 for Reed and $200,000 for Barnes.

A true bill is a type of indictment handed down by a grand jury after it has convened in a criminal matter. Most cases don't go before a grand jury; these proceedings are reserved for more severe crimes. A grand jury decides whether the defendant should be tried for the crime. Its decision doesn't result in a conviction; it determines whether the defendant should go to trial. The trial jury will decide whether he should be convicted.

According to the DA, arraignment for both Reed and Barnes will be scheduled at a later date. However, the court will summon Reed on July 18, 2019, for rape charges from another incident. He may be arraigned on all charges at that time.

Homicide charges are the most severe charges a person can face in Louisiana, a state which supports capital punishment.

The Louisiana State Legislature defines first-degree murder as the killing of another person with intent while committing another specified felony — or the planned execution of a police officer or public official.

In order words, the main difference between a first-degree murder conviction and a second-degree murder conviction in Louisiana is that a sentence for first-degree murder can lead to the death penalty should the jury decide it is an appropriate punishment. Otherwise, both offenses will lead to life imprisonment with hard labor and without the benefit of having the sentence suspended.

Jimmy Ray Barnes

With new information from readers and other sources, this chapter evolved from the Bayou Justice column entitled "Homeless murder suspect found in Atlanta," initially published in south Louisiana newspapers on Tuesday, June 25, 2019.

LAST FRIDAY, 21ST JUDICIAL District Judge Charlotte Foster issued arrest warrants for Reginald Lathan Reed, 59, and Jimmy Ray Barnes, 60. She did so after a Tangipahoa Parish Grand Jury charged both men with second-degree murder and conspiracy to commit murder in a 1987 homicide — the butchering of Reginald Reed's 26-year-old wife, Selonia Ophelia Smith Reed.

Hammond residents know Reginald Reed as a former city mayoral candidate, but few knew the name Jimmy Ray Barnes before last week.

Jacqueline Smith, however, was Selonia Reed's younger sister, and she will never forget that name.

On August 20, 1987, shortly after 10:30 pm, "Jackie" stepped outside her sister's Apple Street home for a smoke. As she approached the edge of the porch, a shadow moved near the front steps, startling her, causing her to scream, and bringing Selonia from inside the house.

"Leave us alone," Selonia said to the shadow. "Why are you here?"

Jimmy Ray Barnes, a neighbor and local handyman, stepped into the light emanating from the door. Grinning, he claimed he had taken his dog for a walk and that the dog had gotten away.

Selonia pulled Jackie back into the house and locked the door behind them. Her son, six-year-old Reggie, Jr., stood outside his bedroom door, concerned about the commotion.

"Loni, that guy outside," Jackie said, "Is he the reason you asked Dad to buy you a gun?"

"It's late," Selonia replied. "Let's just go to bed."

Three days later — on a rainy Sunday morning, August 23, 1987 — police found Selonia Smith Reed's car parked near John's Curb Market, a convenience store on East Thomas Street. The vehicle sat three blocks from the police station and within walking distance of 1314 Apple Street — the house where Jackie met Jimmy Ray Barnes.

Inside the car, police found Selonia's body slumped in the passenger seat, the handle of an umbrella visible between her legs.

Before or after sexually assaulting her with the umbrella, her assailant beat her face profusely and stabbed her chest and neck a dozen times or more, wielding an instrument slightly larger than a Phillips screwdriver.

Before exiting the car, the monster drew or wrote something in the victim's blood, squirting a white substance that Coroner Dr. Vincent Cefalu said refused to melt in the August heat.

Selonia Reed died, the coroner said, from three stab wounds in the right middle lobe of her lungs and one in the right atrium of her heart.

Investigators questioned Jimmy Ray Barnes days after the murder, along with Reginald Reed and nearly 100 other people, including Selonia's friends and family and her co-workers at Citizen's National Bank. Working 24-hour shifts, investigators would not close the case that week. The brutal murder remained unsolved for nearly 32 years.

A decade after the murder, Reginald Reed announced his candidacy for mayor of Hammond. By then, Jimmy Ray Barnes had fled the state, and the Hammond Police Department had seemingly forgotten the cold case.

In October 2018, Hammond Police Chief James Stewart told me how recently retired investigators had closed the case on their way out. They marked the case "cleared by exceptional means" — meaning investigators had identified the likely perpetrators, but would never find the evidence to win a conviction in court.

That all changed in January of 2019.

That month, Hammond Mayor Pete Panepinto dismissed Chief Stewart. Assistant Chief Thomas Corkern then notified me that the Selonia Reed case was active again, this time with the District Attorney's Office, the Tangipahoa Parish Sheriff's Office, and the Louisiana State Police all involved in the investigation.

District Attorney Scott Perrilloux told the *Daily Star* last week that relatively new developments in DNA matching allowed investigators to reconsider the case. "I was able to assign this to someone who went back and reviewed all of the prior investigative materials," he said. "And we felt like it was now a prosecutable case."

Questioned by investigators in January, Claudette Matthews — Reginald Reed's sister — explained why she believed Jimmy Ray Barnes had left the state, and in an interview this week, she recounted that information.

"As I understood it, Jimmy Ray Barnes left Louisiana in the 90s, just before my brother announced he was running for mayor," she said. "Before that, Reginald had shot Barnes in the back of his neck, supposedly on accident, after inviting him on a fishing trip to Bayou Manchac. I believe Reginald threatened to kill him and feed him to the alligators if he broke his silence about Selonia."

"Jimmy Ray Barnes' mother took him to Big Charity when he was shot," Claudette said, "And she made him leave town when he got out."

On June 3, 2004, the Fulton County Sheriff's Office in Atlanta, Georgia, booked Jimmy Ray Barnes into the Fulton County jail, charging him with possession and attempting to sell cocaine. Two weeks later, their local drug court released him with time served, and Jimmy Ray Barnes fell off the grid.

"Last thing I heard," Claudette Matthews said, "His family said Jimmy Ray was homeless, living under a bridge somewhere."

In January 2019, church volunteers in Atlanta, Georgia, complained to television station PBS-Atlanta about local police officers rousting the homeless and questioning vigorously anyone living under bridges within the city limits.

"This is what I've heard," camp resident Tony Hines told PBS. "I heard if you get caught living under a bridge, you are going to jail."

Interviewed on the National Public Radio network, Pastor Monica Mainwaring told the interviewer that Atlanta's mayor wanted all homeless encampments cleared out before the Super Bowl in February. Still, in an interview with WABE radio, Mayor Keisha Bottoms denied that accusation.

"This has absolutely nothing to do with the Super Bowl," the mayor told the listening audience. "If it did, I would say so."

In the end, neither the Atlanta Police Department nor the Fulton County Sheriff's office dismantled any vagrant camps. Instead, they merely interviewed camp residents, asking questions, as if they were looking for someone.

Today, I cannot verify that the Atlanta raids on vagrant camps are in any way related to the search for Jimmy Ray Barnes. However, on Saturday, June 22, Assistant District Attorney Taylor Anthony confirmed for Jackie Smith that Jimmy Ray Barnes had been located, homeless, living under a bridge in Atlanta, Georgia.

The Tangipahoa Parish Sheriff's Office booked Reed in Hammond on June 21 — Friday afternoon at 2:44 and transferred him to the parish jail in Amite Friday night shortly before 10: pm.

Judge Foster set bond at $250,000 for Reed and $200,000 for Barnes.

According to Taylor Anthony, Barnes should be booked into the Tangipahoa Parish Jail in Amite by Wednesday, June 26.

Taylor Anthony joined Scott Perrilloux's team last fall. He is a Tangipahoa Parish native, who has earned praise from the FBI for his recent prosecution of a child pornography case. Today, Anthony is the lead prosecutor in the second-degree murder case against Reginald Reed and Jimmy Ray Barnes.

The Louisiana State Legislature defines first-degree murder as the killing of another person with intent while committing another specified felony — or the planned execution of a police officer or public official. Second-degree removes the additional felony requirement, but both demand a sentence of life in prison doing hard labor without any option for parole.

The indictments against the two men came Friday afternoon, June 21. That night, Jackie Smith's phone rang. News of the Grand Jury and Reginald Reed's arrest had reached her nephew's home in San Antonio, Texas.

Reggie, Jr. asked Jackie, "Why now, Auntie, after 32 years?"

Jackie replied, "Baby, you were only six-years-old when you lost your momma. You didn't need to lose your daddy, too. I think God's been waiting all this time, just waiting until you were strong enough to handle what comes next."

Pleading the Reed murder

T*he following is from a news story written by the author of the Bayou Justice column entitled "Suspects plead not guilty in Reed murder," published in the Hammond Daily Star on July 4, 2019, and a follow-up article on July 18, 2019.*

FORMER HAMMOND MAYORAL candidate Reginald Reed, and a homeless man, Jimmy Ray Barnes, pleaded not guilty Wednesday to charges of second-degree murder and conspiracy to commit murder in the 1987 death of Reed's wife, 29-year-old Selonia Ophelia Smith Reed. Their next court date is August 28.

Wednesday, July 3, at 9:20 a.m., jailers escorted two groups of inmates into Courtroom Number 1 at the Tangipahoa Parish Courthouse in Amite. All eight men shuffled in with manacled hands and feet, wearing orange jumpsuits stamped TPSO. Reginald Reed, 59, walked in the center of the first group. Jimmy Ray Barnes, 60, stood last in the second group.

Throughout the morning, Reed sat with his head bowed, while Barnes stared at the ceiling, wearing what appeared to be new spectacles.

A public defender represented Reed. Barnes also requested counsel, which Judge Charlotte Foster appointed during the court session. Both suspects, now following the advice of their new lawyers, then pled not guilty.

The defendants will appear in court again, August 28, for criminal pre-trial motions. This hearing will allow prosecutors and defense attorneys to request Trial Judge Beth Wolfe's decision on various issues before criminal proceedings begin.

Motions applied for in this session can affect the trial itself, the venue, defendants, evidence, or testimony. This is also the session where the process of discovery — the exchange of evidence and alibis — begins.

On the day before Independence Day, the courtroom was unusually bare, filled only with less than a dozen court personnel, the defendants, Assistant District Attorney Taylor Anthony, State Trooper Barry Ward, a columnist from the *Daily Star*, and the family of Selonia Smith Reed.

Gwen Smith, the victim's sister, said afterward that these last few weeks have been bittersweet for her and her two sisters.

"We have much ahead of us," she said, "but we appreciate everyone involved. Without the different investigators over the years, the District Attorney's office, and the newspaper, we might not be here today, but I thank God that we are."

In August 1987, Hammond Police found Selonia Reed's body inside her car parked near a wooded area on East Thomas Street next to John's Curb Market, a convenience store not far from city hall and within walking distance — through the woods — to the couple's home on Apple Street in north Hammond.

In other 21st Judicial District Court business, Judge Foster granted the extradition of two fugitives back to Mississippi and set bonds in four domestic cases involving inmates with active protection orders.

Jesse Brooks, a crime reporter for the *Daily Star* in Hammond, reported that a trial date of October 15 was set on July 17 for Reginald Reed, 59, of Hammond for the aggravated rape charge he faces.

Brooks writes:

"In shackles, Reed was brought into the courtroom with a group of inmates also awaiting trial dates to be set by Judge Beth Wolfe. He appeared thin and with much longer hair and an unkempt beard as compared to his previous appearance in court."

"Though Reed looked detached as he slumped in his seat, he smiled as he was called up before the judge."

"A pre-trial date of August 28 has been set for Reed on the charges of second-degree murder and conspiracy to commit murder."

Clay Bertrand 2019

With new information from readers and other sources, this chapter evolved from the Bayou Justice column entitled "Clay Bertrand dead at 80," initially published in south Louisiana newspapers on Tuesday, July 1, 2019.

TUESDAY, JUNE 25, 2019, eighty-year-old Claiborne Roy Bertrand died in a nursing home in Opelousas, Louisiana. "Clay" Bertrand's death came nine months after I met him and fifty-two years after New Orleans District Attorney Jim Garrison assured the world that he never existed.

On Tuesday, May 11, 1965 — less than two years before Garrison arrested a Tangipahoa Parish native and accused him of being Clay Bertrand — Clay Laverne Shaw spoke to the Amite chapter of the Louisiana Colonials. As a keynote presenter at their spring tea party, Shaw described his investment strategy and his vision for the revitalization of the Florida parishes.

Among the group of 24 at the meeting, Clay Shaw's parents drove up from Hammond. United States Marshall Glaris Lenora Shaw and his wife, Alice, rode with them, to attend the presentation at Loma Linda, the Spanish style home of Mrs. J. H. McClendon, and so did celebrity Cajun chef and humorist Justin Wilson.

Dr. J. H. McClendon, Jr., along with his brother, Robert McClendon, and their fiancés, catered the event. Still, it was the organization's president, Mrs. Sam Claiborne Hyde, who had invited Shaw to speak.

Shaw began his talk not by describing his position as director of the International Trade Mart, but by focusing instead on his philanthropic work to restore the French Quarter. He expressed his belief that historical places should not be museums, but places where people could live, work, and interact with history.

After recounting a brief history of New Orleans and the Vieux Carré, he described fourteen homes he had purchased and restored in the French Quarter, including the home of John James Audubon. His primary objective, he said, was to prevent modern builders from destroying history. He wanted to prove that such restorations could prove profitable.

The fifty-two-year-old executive spoke of his upcoming August retirement and his goal of returning to Tangipahoa Parish, describing plans to invest in the restoration of downtown landmarks in Kentwood, Amite, Independence, Hammond, and Ponchatoula.

"Every day, Louisiana's food and wildlife attract more tourists," he said. "As your markets for local agriculture dwindles, Tangipahoa Parish will need to find alternatives. Becoming a bedroom community to New Orleans tourists and business travelers can be that alternative, but only if we give them a reason to come here."

Shaw, born in Kentwood, Louisiana, was the son of a United States Marshal and the namesake of another Clay Shaw, his grandfather, a favorite Tangipahoa Parish sheriff during prohibition.

As a teenager, the younger Clay Shaw became an accomplished playwright. He and co-author H. Stuart Cottman sold the play, Submerged, published in 1929, before either student graduated Warren Easton High School in New Orleans.

At the Amite presentation, Justin Wilson, a fellow veteran, asked Shaw about his service during World War II. An officer in the United States Army, Shaw served as secretary to the General Staff and later fought in Europe. Three nations decorated Shaw. The United States awarded him with the Legion of Merit and the Bronze Star, France with the Croix de Guerre, and Belgium named him Chevalier of the Order of the Crown.

Honorably discharged with the rank of major after the war ended, Shaw helped launch the New Orleans International Trade Mart to facilitate sales exchanges of domestic and imported goods with other countries.

Becoming Trade Mart Director in 1947, he traveled the United States and abroad, describing the work of the Trade Mart, promoting open markets at home and lower tariffs with trading nations.

In January of 1965, he told an audience in Jackson, Mississippi, that world nations would eventually use trade as a weapon. "The major task of this generation," he said, "is to show the world that the free enterprise system represents a better way of life than the Marxist system."

In 1949, the United States Central Intelligence Agency granted Shaw a five-agency security clearance. In 1979, former CIA Director Richard Helms explained under oath how Shaw used his position as Trade Mart Director to serve his country. As a part-time contact of the Domestic Contact Service of the CIA, he collected information during his travels abroad, mostly from Latin American countries, including Cuba and others in the Caribbean.

On March 1, 1967, New Orleans District Attorney Jim Garrison arrested Shaw, charging that he — using the alias "Clay Bertrand" — conspired with Lee Harvey Oswald, a pilot named David Ferrie, and others to assassinate President John F. Kennedy in 1963.

On January 29, 1969, Shaw stood trial in Orleans Parish Criminal Court, and on March 1 of that year, a jury took less than an hour to find Shaw not guilty. By then, attorney fees and medical bills had brought him to financial ruin, and despite the acquittal, Shaw's reputation and public image never recovered.

Lung cancer took his life five years later.

In 1988, New Orleans news commentator Bill Elder told me that he informed the Federal Bureau of Investigation where they could find Clay Bertrand in 1967, two weeks before Clay Shaw's arrest.

Elder said that Aaron Kohn of the New Orleans Metropolitan Crime Commission also made a similar report.

In 1981, working for *The Hammond Vindicator*, I interviewed then Judge Jim Garrison at his office in New Orleans. He told me that he still believed Clay Bertrand never existed. He said the man who called a New Orleans attorney, looking to hire someone to represent Kennedy's alleged assassin, must have been Clay Shaw.

"Who else could he have been?" he asked.

In 2018, working for the *Daily Star* in Hammond, I found 79-year-old Claiborne Roy Bertrand at the Senior Village Nursing and Rehabilitation Center on Harry Guilbeau Road in Opelousas, Louisiana.

Clay Bertrand 1967

With new information from readers and other sources, this chapter evolved from the Bayou Justice column entitled "FBI, DA's office found Bertrand in 1967," initially published in south Louisiana newspapers on Tuesday, July 8, 2019.

LAST WEEK, READERS of this column recalled Kentwood native Clay Shaw and his lecture to an Amite congregation, detailing his vision for revitalizing Tangipahoa Parish. Soon after that speech, New Orleans District Attorney Jim Garrison charged Shaw with using the alias Clay Bertrand and conspiring to kill President John F. Kennedy.

This week, we peek into the life of the real Clay Bertrand, but before we do, I feel I must respond to the messages I have received asking about the integrity of Jim Garrison. Let me make this clear. Having met Garrison, I do not believe he intentionally misled the public regarding the identity of Clay Bertrand. I have come to think that Garrison's team may have misled him.

In the fall of 1981, I asked Judge Garrison how he could be confident that his investigators had not manufactured evidence or bribed witnesses.

Shaking his head negatively, he responded.

"When the [Shaw] trial began," he said, "I did not know who on my staff had not been compromised. Several volunteers proved to be CIA, and others, the opposition easily offered more financially. But how do you address — or even consider — sabotage with a press that labels you paranoid and delusional?"

To understand the importance of Clay Bertrand, and evaluate the integrity of Garrison's staff, a review of the events of February 1967 is required.

February 17, 1967: A front-page story in *The New Orleans States-Item* revealed that Garrison was investigating the assassination of President John F. Kennedy.

Feb 18: *The States-Item* published an interview with David Ferrie confirming that Garrison's staff had interviewed him regarding the assassination and his association with Lee Harvey Oswald and some anti-Castro Cubans.

Feb 19: According to author Edward Jay Epstein, Garrison assigned Assistant DA Andrew "Moo-Moo" Sciambra with questioning French Quarter workers and patrons, attempting to locate a man named Clay Bertrand.

Feb 20: WWL-TV commentator Bill Elder told Sciambra and investigator Lou Ivon that Bertrand had worked on Bourbon Street at the Sho-bar, but had since graduated from Tulane and moved to Lafayette.

Feb 21: An FBI report says, "*The New Orleans States-Item* reported that Dean Andrews, Jr., Assistant Jefferson Parish District Attorney, said he was contacted by a man named Clay Bertrand shortly after the [Kennedy] assassination and he asked him to defend Oswald. The Warren Commission was unable to identify anyone as Bertrand."

The report then describes Bill Elder stopping an FBI Agent on the street, reporting that Clay Bertrand, approximately 30-years-old, lived in New Orleans in 1963, but now worked in Lafayette as a real estate agent. Elder described Bertrand as a radical with a violent temper, a man who once punched a Louisiana Sheriff.

Feb 22: Police find David Ferrie dead in his apartment.

Feb 23: Dr. Ronald A. Welsh, following Ferrie's autopsy, reported that Ferrie died when a blood vessel ruptured in his brain.

Feb 24: Orleans Parish Coroner Nicholas J. Chetta initially declines to classify David Ferrie's death as natural.

Feb 25: In a memo to Garrison, investigator Lou Ivon stated that he could not locate any Clay Bertrand despite numerous inquiries and contacts. He also reported that an employee of the Fountainbleu Hotel said Dean Andrews told him that Clay Bertrand never existed.

The following March, Garrison charged Tangipahoa Parish native Clay Shaw with conspiring to kill President Kennedy. That week, Shaw told *The Hammond Vindicator* that he did not understand why.

"Last December," he said, "I was questioned by an assistant DA who told me that Lee Harvey Oswald had known someone named Clay Bertrand when he was in New Orleans. They had gone over a list of Clays, thought about me, and wanted to know if I had known Oswald. I told them I never met Oswald and that I did not know any Clay Bertrand."

I met Bill Elder in 1987 and considered him a friend until his death in 2003.

A respected news-anchor and award-winning investigative reporter at WWL television for 34 years, Bill Elder held the George Foster Peabody Award for investigative reporting, the Edward R. Murrow Award from the Radio-Television News Directors Association, and numerous awards from the Press Club of New Orleans.

His career began in newspapers at *The Opelousas Daily World*.

From there, his career took him to *The Lafayette Advertiser, The New Orleans States-Item*, and KATC television in Lafayette. While working at KATC-TV, he also worked as a technician and camera operator for CBS News. That position took him routinely to Baton Rouge and New Orleans.

Covering Jim Garrison's 1962 raids on French Quarter gambling and B-drinking — the soliciting of drinks with the promise of prostitution, Elder paid an insider to feed him information, a friend from high school named Clay Bertrand. At the time, Bertrand worked as a bouncer and sometimes bartender at the Sho-bar on Bourbon Street.

In 1963, Elder paid Bertrand again for insider information on the Ku Klux Klan, while Bertrand worked as a bodyguard for Judge Leander Perez. That same year, according to Sho-bar burlesque headliner Joy "TNT Red" Murphy Pelletier, David Ferrie met with Bertrand at the bar along with "a Mexican, two Cubans, and a Marine called Lee."

Bill Elder first met Bertrand in a high school boxing ring in 1953. Elder represented Cathedral High School in Lafayette. Bertrand fought for Opelousas High School. Bertrand won the bout.

In October of 2018, I visited 79-year-old Clay Bertrand at the Senior Village Nursing and Rehabilitation Center on Harry Guilbeau Road in Opelousas, Louisiana.

I asked him about his high school boxing team, and he reminded me that he also played football for the Opelousas Tigers. I then asked him what he did after high school, and almost indignantly, he said, "I went to college."

Next, I asked him where he went to college, and he seemed to get agitated.

I said, "I know from various news stories that you were a math teacher and a school board member in St. Landry Parish for 30 years. I know you sold real estate for Joe Anzalone in Lafayette and cars and mobile homes in the 1970s, and that you were heavily involved in local politics."

As I rambled, a scowl on his face told me he did not remember.

I walked away, thinking about my dad's last days and the suffering he had endured with dementia. I drove home from Opelousas, broken-hearted, sad that I could not get answers to my questions and embarrassed that I had disturbed the man at all.

Claiborne Roy Bertrand died, Tuesday, June 25, 2019.

Donna Lynn Bahm

W*ith new information from readers and other sources, this chapter evolved from the Bayou Justice column entitled "Daniels only exploited Bahm murder," initially published in south Louisiana newspapers on Tuesday, July 16, 2019.*

AROUND 2:30 P.M., SATURDAY, January 23, 1988, the St. Helena Parish Sheriff's Office responded to a call on the Tickfaw River. Swimmers discovered the body of Donna Lynn Bahm, a 31-year-old Amite attorney missing two days and found under a bridge on Louisiana Highway 1045 near Hillsdale.

According to St. Helena Coroner Dr. L.E. Stringer, after striking her twice in the head with a tire iron and fracturing her skull, someone shot her twice in the chest with a .22 caliber handgun. Her murderer then used a 30-foot logging chain to tie her partially clothed body to a 15-inch tire rim, tossing it over the bridge like an anchor. The water was 3-feet higher on Thursday and dropped on Saturday, exposing the body.

In August of 1988, Tangipahoa Parish Sheriff Ed Layrisson announced the arrest of 38-year-old Alvin "Bubba" Daniels, charging him with two counts of extortion.

On July 28, 1988, Donna Bahm's father, Edward Bahm, received letters from someone, who police later determined to be Daniels, claiming to have evidence identifying Donna Bahm's killer.

Initially, Daniels requested $30,000 for the information, instructing Ed Bahm not to inform the sheriff's office, and to follow his orders. Otherwise, Daniels would not release the evidence.

After one failed attempt to deliver the money, Daniels contacted Bahm again, informing Bahm that he avoided the money drop because he knew someone had notified the sheriff's office. This time, he said, Bahm would have to give him $50,000 in exchange for his information.

Detectives arrested Daniels during his second attempt to pick up the money. After his arrest, he told police he made the phone calls and sent the letters to Bahm to obtain cash, but insisted that he knew nothing about Donna Bahm's murder.

To understand why a man who thinks this way, consider his history.

In February of 1975, an armed bandit stopped a vehicle at an intersection in Amite and then forced his way inside the car. He locked the driver, a local insurance agent, in the trunk of the car and drove to a wooded area near Arcola, where he pulled the driver from the vehicle, shot him in the eye, and then left him for dead.

Soon after, investigators matched a fingerprint on the car to suspect Eddie Charles Griffin, 23, of Amite. When the attending physician released the driver from Hood Memorial Hospital in Amite, detectives asked him to identify his assailant from a lineup of four men.

He selected Eddie Charles Griffin, who the District Attorney subsequently charged with attempted murder, aggravated kidnapping, and armed robbery.

At Griffin's trial, defense attorneys insisted their client had not committed these crimes, claiming that the defendant had left his fingerprint on the car window 24 hours earlier, when the driver, a homosexual, propositioned him for sex.

To support this claim, the Defense called a Fluker resident, Alvin "Bubba" Daniels, to the stand.

Judge Burrell Carter and a 12-member jury watched intently, while Daniels, dressed in his Sunday best, described, ever so eloquently, how he had stayed in the area for the last year and that the driver of the car had propositioned him for what he called "homosexual activity." Daniels described in detail how the driver often stalked pedestrians, stopping his car and offering unsuspecting males a ride in exchange for sex.

When the pedestrian walked over to the car, Daniels said, the driver would roll down his window halfway, causing the pedestrian to touch the glass as he listened to the driver's pitch.

"If you look at that window close enough," said Daniels, "you may find my prints on that glass, along with several other innocent men this sexual predator stopped last week."

The jury appeared moved by the testimony, at least before the prosecution's cross-examination.

"Mr. Daniels," the prosecutor began, "Can you tell the jury where you slept last night?"

The Defense objected, but Judge Carter allowed the prosecutor to continue.

"And Mr. Daniels," the persecutor continued, "perhaps you can also tell the court where you were last week when the car-jacking occurred?"

"Isn't it a fact, Mr. Daniels," he said, "that you have been sleeping upstairs in this very building, a prisoner of the Tangipahoa Parish Sheriff's Office?"

Once again, the Defense objected. This time, correctly, citing Section 495 of Title 15 of the Revised Statutes. "No witness, whether he be a defendant or not, can be asked on cross-examination whether or not he has ever been indicted or arrested, and can only be questioned as to conviction."

However, the prosecutor had never mentioned anyone indicting or arresting Daniels for an armed robbery of his own.

Just days before the robbery that the 21st Judicial District Court accused Eddie Charles Griffin of committing, at 7:59 on the morning of February 3, 1975, Flo Bankston reported to the Tangipahoa Parish Sheriff's Office that a bandit had robbed her grocery store three miles east of the town of Arcola. The robber, she said, drew a snub-nosed revolver from a lunch pail and demanded all the cash, a little over $400, from her cash register.

A week later, investigators asked Flo Bankston to attend a line-up at the courthouse, where she identified Alvin "Bubba" Daniels as the robber of her store.

The jury found Eddie Charles Griffin guilty, and Judge Carter sentenced him to 99 years with the Department of Corrections.

The following July, after another jury convicted Alvin Daniels, District Judge Leon Ford III committed him to 30 years in the Tangipahoa Parish Prison. He served ten years before his release for good behavior.

Two years later, while working as a private investigator for an Amite attorney, Daniels claimed to uncover information on Donna Bahm's murder. A jury later convicted him of trying to sell that information to Donna Bahm's father, winning Daniels yet another 30-year conviction that he would not fulfill.

Al Daniels, Private Eye

With new information from readers and other sources, this chapter evolved from the Bayou Justice column entitled "Meet Al Daniels, private eye," initially published in south Louisiana newspapers on Tuesday, July 23, 2019.

AFTER SERVING TEN YEARS in prison, 35-year-old Alvin "Bubba" Daniels walked out of the gates of Angola determined never to return. No more armed robberies. No more confidence games. No more baring false witness against thy neighbor of any sort. From that day forward, "Bubba, the con man" would push up daisies.

Long live Al Daniels, Private Investigator.

After all, it worked for James Rockford, except Jim got out of Leavenworth without half the things that Al had going for him. Inside, Al had devoted every waking hour to studying law, those of God, and the criminal justice system. He read a book on forensic science, and he watched twice every episode of Magnum, P. I.

Al's newfound dedication impressed Tangipahoa Parish Sheriff Ed Layrisson enough to vouch for him at his parole hearing. Layrisson also allowed him to serve his last year as a cook in the Tangipahoa Parish prison, and to convince a Hammond attorney to hire him after his release.

Al began work with Jack Hoffstadt & Associates in 1985, tasked primarily with shadowing unfaithful spouses and insurance cheats, taking the occasional photograph, and testifying in court when necessary. Al never came close to Jim Rockford's "$200-a-day plus expenses," but his pay more than warranted the daily drive from Bay Street in Amite.

In 1987, Jack Hoffstadt & Associates branched out from their Defense specialty by advertising in the state's largest daily newspapers and promoting Al's skills to a broader market. The ad read "Divorce, Separation, Child Custody, and Support. A marriage ending is stressful enough without making unprepared decisions that affect you, your children, and your property. For confidential assistance, call for a free consultation. Evening appointments available."

By winter 1987, Al was the real deal, a genuine, certifiable detective for hire.

On days when he was not photographing strangers or digging through files at the courthouse, Al propped his feet up near the law firm's coffee machine at the office on North Cherry and read the newspaper. It was there, in that position, that Alvin Daniels first met Amite attorney Donna Bahm.

Then only 29-years-old, Donna Bahm, thin but athletic, stood 5'4" with olive-colored skin and brown eyes and hair, usually wearing a broad smile. Judge Brenda Ricks said Donna Bahm never met a stranger and would talk to anybody about anything.

"I talked to Donna a lot of time about a lot of things," Al Daniels told detectives Larry Westmoreland and Oliver Jackson in 1988. "She used to come by the office all the time down in Hammond."

"She drank a lot of coffee. Anytime I went to the Sheriff's Department and she was there, she would be at that little coffee stand downstairs. She said it took two or three cups of coffee for her to get started in the mornings. Going to night school, she studied some days at the law library in Hammond, and she tried to set up something with Jack for them to work together, so she came by a lot — but, most times, she stopped by to get coffee."

"I knew some about her personal life because she talked about everything." He said. "She used to jog somewhere in Amite, and since I lived up there, she always tried to get me to go jogging with her."

"I told Jack I wasn't going jogging with her, and Jack said if I did and there were white folks around, I'd better make sure I ran ahead of her," Al told the police.

"So, no, I never went jogging; we just talked about jogging a lot." He said, "One time, I told her how I do long-distance jogging. I said I hated how my socks get wet and drip, and I said my underwear does the same thing."

Daniels said Donna Bahm then told him, "That's why I don't wear underwear."

In the two years that Daniels knew Bahm, he also learned that her father still paid for her continuing education and that she carried and often used her father's checkbook.

Someone abducted and murdered Donna Bahm in January of 1988.

By July of that year, Jack Hoffstadt had opened an office in Mandeville and was spending more time there than Hammond. As a result, he began accepting clients and hiring private investigators from St. Tammany, Orleans, and Jefferson Parishes, leaving Al to fend for himself in Tangipahoa Parish. There, he offered his services to other attorneys, but more often than not, he bought groceries with "love offerings" he received after preaching at local churches.

A deputy with the sheriff's office stopped Al one afternoon at the courthouse. "You hear anything on the street about this murder, Al?"

When Al told him no, the deputy told him Edward Bahm, Donna Bahm's father, had grown frustrated with the Sheriff Department's investigation. He asked Al, "Why don't you go to Mr. Bahm, tell him you can work the streets, see if he will hire you to investigate his daughter's murder?"

Al told him he felt indebted to the sheriff for helping him out of Angola, and that if he did find out something, he would turn it over to the sheriff rather than Bahm.

Days later, Al drove out to the bridge where someone had dumped Donna Bahm's body six months earlier.

There are three bridges on Highway 1045 in Hillsdale, each only feet from one another. Driving east from Amite, the first two bridges stretch over lowland creeks with little to no water. The third bridge crosses the river, which was at crest state the night someone tossed Donna Bahm's body over the rail.

Standing on that bridge, Private Eye Al must have realized that only a local would know which bridge to toss the body from, as the roadway included no lights to see the water. For days, Al hung out at the Greensburg Chicken Hut, six miles from the bridge, absorbing any information he could from the people of St. Helena Parish.

One fried chicken eater said the police first saw Donna Bahm as a rape victim because someone ripped the crotch of her pantyhose. Al almost discarded the gossip until Chicken-eater mentioned the corpse wore no panties.

Weeks later, Al refocused on Tangipahoa Parish, where he camped out in the emergency room at Lallie Kemp Hospital, a few miles from Donna Bahm's home in Independence, Louisiana. There, Private Eye Al again sat and listened to anyone speaking, collecting any information he could on the Donna Bahm murder.

After weeks of investigating this way, Private Eye Al confessed he did not have enough information to aid the Sheriff in his investigation, nor did he have enough information to convince Ed Bahm to employ him.

However, Al decided, he did have enough information to convince Ed Bahm that he knew more than he did, and that information should be worth something.

At that moment, Private Investigator Al Daniels ceased to exist, and "Bubba, the con man" returned.

Ed Bahm and the Extortionist

*W*ith *new information from readers and other sources, this chapter evolved from the Bayou Justice column entitled "Ed Bahm meets his extortionist," initially published in south Louisiana newspapers on Tuesday, July 30, 2019.*

ON A FRIDAY EVENING, August 26, 1988, 58-year-old Edward Elton Bahm, a lifelong resident of Independence, pulled a note from a gatepost at the front entrance of Hammond's Zemurray Park. Scanning the squiggly ink and hand-drawn map, he imagined the note's author hiding somewhere inside the park watching.

The squiggly words instructed Ed to enter the park and look for a plastic bag held in place by a bottle of bleach. He was to drop $50,000 into the bag while pouring the bottle's contents over the cash. According to the note, the solution in the bottle would nullify any alarm, radio-controlled incendiary device, or exploding dye packs the FBI may have hidden between the greenbacks.

A state police helicopter buzzed overhead, and Ed wondered if the man extorting him had heard it. The detectives told him an FBI plane was up there, too, and on the ground, 12 marked and unmarked police units circled the area.

Would any of them accidentally alert the blackmailer?

Probably not.

In the weeks leading up to the drop, the blackmailer had proven himself just a little bit on the incompetent side. Two days earlier, Ed had left $30,000 in a trashcan at a Schwegmann's supermarket in Hammond. Soon after, the blackmailer appeared, searched fruitlessly inside the wrong trashcan, and then drove away empty-handed.

Moreover, the incompetence did not begin at Schwegmann's.

The first week in August, the blackmailer composed an intricately detailed extortion letter, filling it with minute facts he had gathered about the January 1988 murder of Ed's daughter, a 31-year-old lawyer named Donna.

In his letter, the blackmailer included unique details not reported in the newspapers; details he believed would convince Ed that he knew who killed his daughter. The blackmailer's letter described the torn panty-hose found on the body, Donna Bahm's missing panties, and her lost pocketbook with Ed Bahm's checkbook inside.

The letter described the discarded business card found near the body, and how the autopsy would show that the young attorney drank coffee shortly before two .22 caliber bullets pierced her skull.

The letter insisted the blackmailer had nothing to do with her murder, but knew who killed her, and had all of the evidence needed to convict the murderer. It said he would sell all to Ed Bahm for a negotiated price, warning him that if he did not pay-up quickly, the evidence would disappear forever.

After completing this manifesto, the blackmailer half-buried it in the gravel at the end of Ed Bahm's driveway, and the next morning, exactly as the blackmailer had planned, Ed spotted the note as he backed down his driveway.

Picking it up, Ed pondered why someone had handwritten such a manuscript, and he wondered what the writings had said before the overnight rain stuck the pages together and rendered the words illegible.

Days later, mowing his grass, Ed discovered a second manifesto, this one tacked to the utility pole in his yard. This one had fewer pages but told Ed when and where to answer a payphone for further instructions. Ed followed orders, after working with the Tangipahoa Parish Sheriff's Office and South-Central Bell to trace and record the call.

Between August 5 and August 26, Ed's blackmailer sent him four legible letters, following each with a phone call recorded by law enforcement. The account below condenses the phone conversation following the failed ransom drop at Schwegmann's supermarket:

"Who's speaking?" the voice said after Ed Bahm answered the phone.

"This is Ed, Ed Bahm."

"You understand what just happened?" the voice said.

"Yea," Ed replied. "You playing some game with me."

"I know you had people with you."

"You just getting paranoid," Ed said.

"Did you get your money out the can?"

"Yea," Ed replied. "Now, let's get this done today. My nerves can't take it."

"This weekend."

"Today. I am willing to pay for your information. Just meet me at the bank."

"No," the voice insisted. "And now the price is going up from 30 to 50."

"Look," Ed yelled. "I think you're just trying to get money. You ain't got nothing."

"If I didn't have anything, you wouldn't keep coming to the phone like you coming. You don't want to go through with it, hang up now. Tapes of the kidnappers, the rifle that shot your daughter, ballistic tests. I got all that, but it's gone if that's what you want."

"I can't do this anymore unless you prove you got something," Ed said. "At least tell me why they killed her."

"The letter you buying explains all that."

"You're asking for a lot of money, and you can't tell me anything? How about where they killed her? Did they kill her in Amite?"

"No. Outside of Amite."

"What about her jewelry?" Ed asked.

"What about it?"

"What was she wearing?" Ed asked again.

"Rings. A watch."

"What about her shoes?" Ed kept asking. "I haven't been able to find her purse."

"You get all that after you drop off the money. I'm calling you the same place tomorrow at 10:30. Be ready for the drop, and don't bring no people with you this time."

"Stop being paranoid. I'll be here at 10:30."

The next day, Ed answered the payphone in Amite, and the blackmailer told him to drive to a payphone in Natalbany. At the payphone in Natalbany, a note told him to drive to the front gates of Zemurray Park in Hammond and look for another note.

As Ed walked from the park, a black man passed him riding a bicycle.

When Ed unlocked his car door, he heard a siren squawk, and the sound of the helicopter grew louder while a voice on a bullhorn, said, "Drop the bag, and raise your hands over your head."

No Justice for Donna

W*ith new information from readers and other sources, this chapter evolved from the Bayou Justice column entitled "Daniels charged, suspects mount," initially published in south Louisiana newspapers on Tuesday, August 6, 2019.*

ON A THURSDAY, SEPTEMBER 1, 1988, Tangipahoa Parish Sheriff J. Edward Layrisson called a press conference. He announced that his office had charged Alvin "Bubba" Daniels with first-degree murder, aggravated kidnapping, and armed robbery related to the January 21 death of Amite attorney Donna Lynn Bahm.

Less than two months later, a grand jury refused to indict on any of those charges.

"I can't elaborate on the evidence," Layrisson told reporters at the September press conference, "But I'm confident we have a strong case."

Searching Daniels home, police discovered a photograph of the ex-convict-turned-private-investigator standing near a Ford pickup truck. The wheels on the vehicle resembled the 15-inch rim found chained to Donna Bahm when divers pulled her partially nude body from the Tickfaw River near a bridge in St. Helena Parish. Investigators were unable to identify or locate this truck, but suspected Daniels sold it to someone in another state.

On Monday, August 29, a witness selected Daniels from a lineup, identifying him as the man whose car the 31-year-old lawyer boarded the morning of her disappearance. However, the grand jury expressed concerns with this testimony:

(1) The witness described the vehicle as a car — a four-door gray or green Chevrolet Celebrity — not the pickup truck prosecutors wanted to show Daniels owned.

(2) The week of Bahm's disappearance, a forensic sketch artist worked with the same witness and developed a drawing of the suspect that did not resemble Daniels.

(3) Additional witnesses reported seeing Donna Bahm alive and smiling, traveling with another attorney in the afternoon on that same day.

"Ransom was the motive," Layrisson told the September press conference. "[Daniels] knew [Donna Bahm] because he worked [as a private investigator] for other attorneys."

Six days before the press conference convened, a five-agency taskforce arrested Daniels at Zemurray Park in Hammond. Investigators charged him with two counts of extortion following his bungled attempt to sell the identity of Donna Bahm's murderer to Edward Bahm, the victim's father, for $50,000 cash.

On October 27, 1988, after interviewing 22 witnesses, including Daniels, the grand jury upheld the extortion charges but refused to indict on the homicide, kidnapping, and robbery charges, calling the evidence presented "circumstantial and inconclusive."

Back in September, the sheriff told the press, "Daniels has given statements to investigators [regarding the extortion], but no [murder] confession."

In his voluntary statement to Detectives Larry Westmoreland and Oliver Jackson two days before that press conference, Daniels insisted he did not kill Bahm. However, he described in detail the extortion plan he developed to fool Ed Bahm into thinking he knew facts about the homicide not yet reported in the press.

"I was in a bad financial situation, so I come up with this idea to con Mr. Bahm out some money," Daniels told the detectives. "Ninety percent of the stuff I had in the [extortion] letters, I knew from talking with Donna when I worked for Jack Hoffstadt's Law Firm. The other ten percent's just stuff I found out talking to people."

"While I was in Angola, I was, you know, studying law," he said. "I knew Donna always drank coffee, and I did this autopsy with Dr. Charles Cefalu, where I learned it takes a considerable amount of time for gastric acids to get coffee out the stomach."

"Also, Donna told me she didn't wear no underwear and that her mama did her laundry. That gave me one of the clearest parts of the scheme," he said. "With that and the coffee, I figured I could make a little money off of this thing."

At the press conference, Sheriff Layrisson said, "Since January, we have interviewed more than 300 people in this investigation, and, as recent as July, we didn't have the right suspect. We looked at spouses of divorce clients; one guy had made some threats, but his alibi checked out."

Shortly after the arrest of Alvin Daniels, the five-agency task force disbanded, effectively abandoning all other leads in the case, including potential links between Donna Bahm's death and the following homicides:

Two weeks before Donna Bahm died, someone murdered her neighbor on Old Independence Highway. John Albanese fell dead, unloading groceries, like Bahm, shot with a .22 caliber weapon.

Two years before Donna Bahm's death, someone killed a friend of hers, former Assistant District Attorney Margaret Coon, like Bahm, a family law attorney who loved to jog, found with jewelry still on the body and not sexually assaulted.

St. Tammany Parish investigators have long considered connections between Margaret Coon's murder and the shooting of another assistant district attorney, Vincent Marinello; like Bahm, a lawyer killed with two .22 caliber slugs to the head and found with money and jewelry still intact.

Margaret Coon's best friend, Lynn Nunez, had also worked with Donna Bahm and Vincent Marinello. Nunez worked as a court reporter in St. Tammany Parish for over 30 years. Like Bahm and Marinello, shot in the head with a .22 caliber.

Coincidentally, each of these victims — excluding John Albanese — likely knew or worked with attorney Jack Hoffstadt, Alvin Daniel's former employer. Shortly after Bahm's death, Hoffstadt moved his law practice from

Tangipahoa to St. Tammany Parish. Daniels told investigators his employer relocating was the reason for his financial difficulties and the reason he turned to extortion.

Alvin Daniels also told investigators that he had his suspects.

"I put a listening ear out there, you know, to find out what the streets was saying," he said. "[Donna Bahm] had a boyfriend in Texas, and she worked with a couple of black fellows in this drug-related thing; some in the sheriff's department say she got killed about a domestic case she was doing. I also heard she was killed because of family problems, over a land dispute, or something."

In the weeks ahead, I plan to revisit these cold trails and others.

Sheriff Layrisson concluded the 1988 press conference saying, "I'm very happy for the people of Amite. This was probably the most exhaustive case we have ever worked. I'm glad it's over, and I think we have time for questions."

At that point, a young reporter raised his hand and asked the sheriff why he had barred WWL-TV news anchor Bill Elder from attending the press conference.

For the first time that afternoon, Eddie Layrisson grinned, revealing the trademark gap between two front teeth.

Shaking his head, he said, "Once again, allegations of connections with devil worship raised by a New Orleans television station in the middle of an investigation have made our job very difficult. And just like last time, the accusations made are completely unfounded."

Two months before that press conference, Ponchatoula residents Rose Allen and Betty Hebert invited the Channel 4 news magazine, Bill Elder's Journal, to visit their ranch and to film nine cattle that someone slaughtered overnight.

Sheriff Layrisson criticized the television station for covering the story and insisted that wild dogs killed the livestock without explaining the uniform circular incisions or the cattle's missing hearts.

Two months later — and one week before Alvin Daniel's arrest — June Bahm, Donna Bahm's mother, told WWL's southeast Louisiana television viewing audience that reliable sources had convinced her that a demonic cult, comprised partially of prominent Tangipahoa Parish residents, had sacrificed her daughter to Satan and his minions.

Margaret Ann Coon

With new information from readers and other sources, this chapter evolved from the Bayou Justice column entitled "Murdered attorney hunted sex traffickers," initially published in south Louisiana newspapers on Tuesday, August 13, 2019.

LAST WEEK, WE NOTED alleged connections between the murders of attorneys Donna Bahm and Margaret Coon. This week, we dive deeper into Margaret Coon's cold case homicide, recounting the circumstances of her death and placing sex traffickers among those high on the suspect list.

Days after Donna Bahm's murder in January 1988, authorities told the press, it was time to re-examine the 1987 slaying of Margaret Ann Coon, an ex-prosecutor from Mandeville who specialized in prosecuting sex crimes.

February 19, 1987, someone stabbed the attractive 41-year-old blonde out on her nightly 5-mile jog. She fell dead a half-mile from her home inside the exclusive Beau Chene subdivision, a fenced and guarded country-club community near Mandeville. As in the murder of Donna Bahm, her attacker neither robbed nor sexually assaulted her. Both women had expensive jewelry on or near their bodies.

"We are looking into it," St. Tammany Parish Chief Deputy Wallace Laird said at the time. "The only major difference was the weapon used."

Bahm, who was single and lived with her parents, Edward and June, had two small-caliber bullet wounds in her chest, and she had a fractured skull.

In 1998, Webster A. Coon, Margaret Coon's father, told me the two were acquainted. "I wouldn't say they were friends," he said, "But I know Margaret helped a young woman attorney in Amite when she was starting. It had to be her."

After Margaret's death, Webster drove to Mandeville from his 500-acre cattle ranch in Alexandria and photographed every room in her condominium. Using those photos as a guide, he transplanted Margaret's home exactly as it was the day she died to his spacious brick home.

Throughout his house, he kept what some described as small shrines to his daughter. A Polaroid photo sat on a counter in one of his bathrooms with the label "Upstairs bathroom 3-7-87." The arrangement of vases and other decorations on the vanity matched the picture precisely.

Webster lovingly recreated Margaret's Oriental-style living room within his own. On the table, another Polaroid depicted Margaret's den in 1987.

"It's not just about remembering," he said. "I've done all I can to preserve anything that might prove to be evidence. I want to see Margaret's killer found before I join her."

Webster Coon visited St. Tammany Parish twice monthly, interviewing witnesses and following up with investigators and the media until his death in 2004.

"I may go to my grave never knowing who killed her," he said, "but it won't be because I haven't tried. I spent every spare moment trying to piece it together. The answer is related to one of the cases she worked on or looked into. I know it."

"She left the District Attorney's Office the year before she died, but never stopped being involved. Fighting sex abuse and child molesters was her passion."

Webster said the week before Margaret died, he saw a folder in her apartment with papers relating to Human Trafficking. "I didn't even know what that was at the time," he said. "She just picked them all up, saying 'nothing for you to worry about, Daddy.'"

During that same visit, Margaret gave Webster a key to her condominium, saying, "Take it, Daddy. You never know when you may need it." He protested, but she insisted that he leave with it. He never saw his daughter alive again.

At 5:30 a.m., February 20, 1987, a woman out walking her dog found Margaret face down in the damp grass. Margaret's dog, an Afghan hound named Charlene, stood guard over her body.

"At first we thought we had a jogger hit by a car," Detective Ed Baroni told *The Times-Picayune* newspaper in 1987. "There wasn't much blood," he said, "so the stab wound wasn't immediately obvious."

The autopsy noted that the killer's knife went between the 9th and 10th ribs upward 6 inches into the victim's back, puncturing her left lung and her heart. The force of the blow also shattered one of her ribs.

Baroni was one of the first St. Tammany Parish deputies on the scene and the first person to identify Margaret. They had worked cases together when she was a prosecutor in the 22nd Judicial District Attorney's office.

"We ruled out rape and robbery," he said. Police found four-thousand dollars in jewelry, and she still wore her stylish maroon jogging suit, the top tied around her waist.

"When Margaret dressed, she dressed all the way," Webster had said.

He felt sure someone related to one of her cases caused her death and studied her notes nightly, looking for clues. However, Baroni said the sheriff's office identified many suspects, some not directly related to her family law cases or her work as a prosecutor.

Margaret had been married to the mayor of Mandeville and was elected the first woman president of the St. Tammany Bar Association. She had been in private practice 13 months after serving six years as an assistant district attorney.

As a prosecutor, Margaret had made many enemies. She won two first-degree murder convictions in 1981. She specialized in child abuse cases and pioneered the courtroom use of videotaped testimony by young victims.

"If she had a good case, she jumped into it whole-hearted," said St. Tammany detective Earsley Hart. "More often than not, she got a little personal."

Since Beau Chene was a gated community with access limited to residents and their guests, detectives focused part of their investigation on the 3,000 residents. Still, Baroni said the sheriff's office also received a deluge of phone tips.

"I can't tell you the number of calls that came in after the murder, all pointing to different suspects," Baroni said.

Baroni said police quickly downgraded Margaret's ex-husband, former Mandeville Mayor Bernard Smith, as a suspect. Their divorce became final the month she died, and it had been a nasty one, but Smith's alibi looked solid. A Lafayette Piccadilly manager remembered him eating dinner in his restaurant at the time of the murder.

The list of suspects that did not pan out included Margaret's boyfriend, a New Orleans dentist, and his estranged wife. They also had solid alibis, Baroni said.

Detectives even looked at Charles Mule, a former St. Tammany Sheriff's deputy on the lam after being indicted on child molestation charges. Margaret worked the case before she left the DA's office, and according to Baroni, she would have taken the case as a special prosecutor once police caught him.

After the FBI found him in Florida, Mule also provided an alibi the night of Margaret Coon's death.

"Just because they weren't at the condo doesn't mean they are innocent," Webster told me in 1998. "There's such a thing as a hired killer, and that's what makes this so hard to solve."

"I hired a private investigator," he said. "I spent well over $200,000 of my own money. We got tips about the mafia, devil-worshippers, sex parties, drug rings, human trafficking, and God knows what else. Many of the callers were just nuts, but how do you prove one way or the other?"

Next, we recount the story of a police officer who chased two men from the scene minutes before the stabbing of Margaret Coon.

The Jogger

*W*ith new information from readers and other sources, this chapter evolved from the Bayou Justice column entitled "Margaret Coon possibly not killed jogging," initially published in south Louisiana newspapers on Thursday, August 15, 2019.

IN TODAY'S REPORT, Bayou Justice reveals a critical piece of new information in a 30-year-old cold case murder from St. Tammany Parish.

Tuesday night, I interviewed the only law enforcement officer to patrol Beau Chene subdivision the night Margaret Coon died. If this officer's reflection is accurate, the 41-year-old attorney died later in the night than the official report suggests, making it highly unlikely the stabbing occurred during her evening jog as proposed in that official report. This officer's recounting indicates the possibility that someone killed Margaret Coon somewhere else before moving the body and staging the crime scene.

Sergeant Winston Cavendish retired after serving 41 years in law enforcement. A decorated officer, he made national news in the 1980s when President Ronald Reagan shook his hand on national television. The president thanked him for serving his country in the guise of "McGruff, the Crime Dog," a role he helped create and a cartoon character he voiced for 30 years.

On August 26, 2014, in a public forum hosted by the Concerned Citizens of St. Tammany in Lacombe, Winston Cavendish, then a resident of Slidell, stood and addressed all candidates seeking the District Attorney's seat in the 22nd Judicial District election, saying:

"No one tonight has mentioned the murder of Margaret Coon, the Assistant DA murdered in broad daylight, but a boy scout could solve this case. Today, we have more than five [unsolved] political crimes in St.

Tammany Parish. When I ran for Sheriff, my home was shot-up; I lived a living hell. I had a deputy U.S. Marshall at my house for protection after I'd been shot at by an on-duty Deputy Sheriff, and I was beaten severely on top of the high-rise bridge in Slidell."

"Now, I come to you tonight, pleading," he said. "Let's solve the first of those five major crimes. If we cannot solve the most heinous crime in St. Tammany Parish today, I think we ought to pack up our law books and walk into the sunset. It's past time for some justice for Margaret Coon."

To that, then-candidate Warren Montgomery responded, "Thank you for asking about this. Regarding the murder of the assistant DA, sex crimes division, once elected, I will spend whatever resources and time necessary to solve this case."

Now in his second term, I reached out to District Attorney Warren Montgomery requesting a progress report on the case. Lisa Page, his communications director, confirmed that she delivered the message last week, but to date, the DA has not responded.

Retired police officer Joe Freeman told me Tuesday that he was not surprised. "People around here don't talk about Margaret Coon unless they have to. When I run into someone who does, I warn them to be careful and meet in public places. Too many turn up dead otherwise."

"A whistle-blower named Rusty Burns asked questions that upset a lot of people. Then they said he committed suicide." Joe Freeman shook his head. "Believe what you want to, but not me."

A St. Tammany Parish Sheriff's Deputy in 1987, Joe Freeman patrolled Mandeville's upscale, gated community Beau Chene the night Margaret Coon died. "Dispatch sent me in on a 107. Someone called reporting a suspicious person near the clubhouse."

Officer Freeman said he drove slowly through the gates of Beau Chene and circled the grounds before driving back to the clubhouse. Searching diligently, he saw nothing out of the ordinary until he reached the shed the country club used to store golf carts.

"When I got to the golf shed, I saw two young boys, maybe 15 years-old, running across the roof. I exited my patrol unit and ran around to the back of the building to give chase when they jumped down, but the boys had already disappeared into the woods."

The fence, he said, did not surround the facility. It stopped at the tree line. The teenagers, he believed, ran alongside the wall directly into the woods.

"I asked the security guard about his complaint," said Freeman, "He told me he was checking the buildings and saw a man between the golf carts shed and the community building. When the man saw him, he ran into those same woods, back toward Highway 22."

"I went back to that area and walked the fence line until I reached the end of the fence at the woods, then I walked up the highway searching all directions, but I didn't see anything," he said, "I walked all along the wood line after that. Back to Beau Chene Drive. Still no evidence of anyone."

Joe Freeman shook his head as he spoke, obviously wishing he had seen more that night. "I went back and talked to the security guards," he said. "A second guy had joined the first. It was late, they were older, and didn't seem too concerned. I told them about the two I saw on the roof. They just shrugged, saying neighborhood kids always trying to steal a golf cart."

"I left the clubhouse and patrolled inside Beau Chene over an hour, shinning my light in the dark past the sidewalks. When I decided the kids had given up, I left taking Beau Chene Drive to highway 22," Freeman remembered. "On my way out, I passed the clubhouse again and the place where they found Margaret's body that next morning. I never saw her body. Didn't see her dog either. I would have if they'd been there."

According to neighbors, Margaret Coon typically started her nightly jog around 7:30 each evening, running a five-mile circle and finishing back at her condominium. On the morning of February 19, 1987, a neighbor found her body, dressed in jogging gear, face-down in wet grass. Police believed someone stabbed her from behind as she jogged the sidewalk and that she crawled to the grassy knoll where she died.

Charlene, Margaret Coon's Afghan hound, stood near the sidewalk, still leashed to her master.

"The next day, I heard what happened," Freeman said, "So I went to the Sheriff's Department to let them know I'd been in Beau Chene that night. I told the lead investigator. He said he'd get back to me, but he never did."

In 2010, Joe Freeman wrote a book detailing his career in law enforcement, including the events of that night at Beau Chene.

"Well," he said, "I wrote that book from my sickbed. I'd just had a heart attack and thought about the things I'd like people to know if I hadn't survived. They had me on some medication. I should have gone back later, did some editing, and checked my facts, but I got bored with the project quickly once I was able to walk and get out again."

For that reason, he said, the events recorded in the manuscript are not always as accurate or complete as his memory today.

"Well, like I said, you have to watch what you say. There are some people alive today that might still take issue with some information, but there were many more of them still alive when I wrote that book."

In his book, Freeman wrote that dispatch called him to the subdivision between 7:30 and 8:30 p.m., February 18, 1987. Freeman said this week that he was careful then not to write anything that conflicted with official reports.

"I don't know if they still have the dispatch logs from that night," he said, "But somebody should check them. I wasn't called out at 7:30. I got the call sometime after midnight and left there after 1:00 a.m. [on the 19th], and I never saw Margaret or her dog."

If Freeman's testimony proves correct, either Margaret Coon went jogging after 1:00 a.m., or someone fooled investigators into believing she died jogging. It appears more probable that someone killed her elsewhere and staged the murder scene, and if that is the case, then the murderer must have been well known to Margaret Coon's dog.

"The funny thing about this Margaret Coon case," Joe Freeman said. "They kept changing investigators. I do not believe anyone detective stayed on her case for more than a month at a time, and the detectives left her file in a place anyone could get to it. I sure wish I could get to it today. I knew Margaret when I worked as a bailiff. Lynn Nunez, too. Those ladies deserve better than what they got."

Joe Freeman retired from the Covington Police Department following his heart attack. He left the St. Tammany Parish Sheriff's Office in the summer of 1988. Following Freeman's promotion from patrol to Investigations, Tangipahoa Parish Sheriff Ed Layrisson offered him a job. He needed a black investigator unknown in the Amite area who was willing to work undercover. Freeman's assignment: shadowing a conman named Alvin "Bubba" Daniels.

Sandra Davis

With new information from readers and other sources, this chapter evolved from the Bayou Justice column entitled "PI investigated Margaret Coon murder," initially published in south Louisiana newspapers on Tuesday, August 20, 2019.

IN 1991, WEBSTER COON received a letter from an inmate in the Dixon Correctional Institute in Jackson, Louisiana. The inmate wrote saying a man living in his cellblock had confessed to killing Webster's daughter, Margaret, and that, for a price, the inmate would reveal his cellmate's name.

Curious, Webster contacted private investigator Sandra Davis for help.

Sandra Davis was the kind of private investigator who made a living sniffing out worker's compensation and insurance fraud. Years earlier, she left an agency specializing in divorce cases, calling such cases messy and unpleasant.

Sandra opened her office in 1988. Like her boss, she could refuse divorce cases and do something few private investigators ever considered. She dabbled in an open homicide case, occasionally infuriating law enforcement.

Until the inmate's letter arrived, Sandra had been working the Margaret Coon case pro bono with Webster paying only her travel expenses, which sometimes proved significant. Webster and Sandra both lived in Alexandria, and Margaret's murder took place in Mandeville, a three-hour drive the two made at least monthly.

In Alexandria, Webster Coon, president emeritus of the region's largest bank, also managed a 500-acre cattle ranch. Knowing it would be weeks before he had time to travel to Jackson, Webster called Sandra, offering to pay her to investigate in addition to covering the usual expenses.

Sandra told *The Sunday Advocate* in 1991 that she first heard about the Mandeville murder case while visiting her brother in Covington. "It was just irony or fate that brought us together," she said. "Mr. Coon and I both lived in Alexandria at the time, but I never heard about the case back home."

"Eventually," she said, "After following the case for some time, I decided to call Mr. Coon."

Webster invited Sandra over and gave her a tour of the house that was almost a shrine to his murdered daughter. When she died, Webster moved Margaret's things from Mandeville and arranged them just the way they were the day she died.

After the tour, Webster accepted Sandra's offer to help and gave her access to Margaret's correspondence and writings. "He gave me everything the police returned to him," Sandra said. "And that's a lot. Margaret had kept everything, even bags of letters from her grandmother."

Sandra said she did not act as a private investigator initially. "I just went over the material out of human interest at first."

Over time, she got more involved, even obsessed with the case, she said. She helped Webster — whose eyesight was failing — explore St. Tammany Parish, working to uncover leads and interviewing anyone who knew Margaret.

"My business had almost no clients. I had just opened it. Besides nearly starving to death," she said, "I had a lot of free time to help Mr. Coon."

"I'd work on it gung-ho for a week or a month and get discouraged, and then I might go a month or two without thinking about it," she said.

"Sandra Davis worked on the case on her own," Webster told me in 1998. "I just paid some of her phone and gas bills until the guy from prison contacted us."

"That guy turned out to be a con man," Sandra told *The Advocate*.

Webster said, "He was the same crook that extorted money from that man in Amite when his daughter was murdered. I think she was an attorney, too."

Sandra said she never found any connection between the two murders, though. "It was just another attempt to make money by an experienced hustler," she said. "I wish I could remember his name."

Over time, with some mentorship from an unnamed and more experienced investigator, Sandra eventually discovered, she believed, the most likely suspect and motive for Margaret Coon's murder, and she filed a report detailing her conclusions for St. Tammany prosecutors and law enforcement.

Through spokesperson Larry Ciko, Sheriff Pat Canulette told newspapers his office looked into the suspect Davis reported. "We welcome any and all information on the case," the sheriff said. "But we're still looking."

Webster said the St. Tammany Parish Sheriff's detectives saw Sandra as an inexperienced wannabee.

Sandra said her methods clashed with those of Capt. Clark Thomas, who, until his death, was the department's chief of detectives. She said she always fought an uphill battle to get her ideas noticed by the professionals working the case.

Of course, Sandra did not improve relations with the sheriff's office when she circulated a petition asking people to support her effort to get the case turned over to other authorities. Sandra contacted the FBI and later asked the governor to bring in the state police.

On WWL-TV, Ciko called Sandra's charges that they were burying the case "baseless and unfounded," saying his department was keeping the case open and active, adding that the governor had no authority to force them off the case.

Sandra told *The Advocate* she wanted off the case herself, but she needed to be sure someone would follow up on the information she collected.

"After this," she said, "I never want to touch another [homicide case] as long as I live. It's too emotionally draining."

As an investigative reporter, I can relate to Sandra's plight. Two weeks ago, I reached out to the St. Tammany Parish Sheriff's Office and the 22nd Judicial District Attorney's Office, asking for an update on this 32-year-old case.

From Lou Majors at the St. Tammany Parish sheriff's office:

"We have received your email seeking information related to the death of former Assistant District Attorney Margaret Coon in 1987 and processed it as a Public Records Request. Because Ms. Coon's death remains unsolved, and no defendant has been identified or prosecuted, there is no file related to the matter in our electronic case-tracking system. Because we are unable to provide any records that are responsive to your request, we are closing your Public Records Request."

Six years ago, DA Warren Montgomery vowed to spare no expense locating and prosecuting the murderer of Margaret Coon. This week, his office's Communication Director, Lisa Frazier Page, wrote to me to say, "Mr. Montgomery will have no comment about the case, given that it is still an open investigation."

I think it is safe to say, after 32 years, that investigators have done little with the leads provided by Webster Coon, who went to his grave believing they had solved the case, but in 2019, I found Sandra Davis alive and willing to talk.

She told me that Judy Edwards murdered Margaret Coon. Judy, she said, lived near Margaret and married an Appeals Court Judge with whom Margaret once worked. Unfortunately, according to Sandra, justice for Margaret will be delivered only in the hereafter, as both Judy and the judge are now dead.

As for what happened and why, Sandra said, the most vital witness in the case turned out to be Margaret's manicurist. Irma Jean worked as a professional cosmetologist responsible for Margaret's bi-weekly facials, pedicures, and therapy sessions. She was also Margaret's friend and confidant.

Irma Jean and Margaret

With new information from readers and other sources, this chapter evolved from the Bayou Justice column entitled "Neighbor stalked Margaret Coon," initially published in south Louisiana newspapers on Thursday, August 22, 2019.

JUST BEFORE NOON, TUESDAY, February 17, Irma Jean watched Margaret Coon's new 1987 Jaguar turn the corner beneath the Mandeville McDonald's golden arches before bouncing into the parking lot at 2201 11th Street.

At the curb in front of the Beau Monde Hair and Nail Salon, the Jaguar's passenger side window hummed sliding down, and Irma Jean could smell the leather upholstery inside.

Smiling, Irma Jean's buxom blonde friend waved her in, saying, "I hope you're hungry for Nuvolari's," her expensive jewelry glistening in the sunlight. "I've been thinking about their Paglia-e-Fieno all morning."

Irma Jean had no clue that her friend of two and a half years would be dead within 48 hours, a seven-inch blade jabbed up through her back, piercing her heart and lungs.

Margaret had followed Irma Jean to the Beau Monde from Gus Mayer's Lulu Buras Salon, another exclusive salon for the ultra-rich on Lake Ponchatrain's Northshore. The Beau Monde offered better pay for cosmetologists and offered more to customers. They had therapeutic hot waxes for hands and feet, manicures, and pedicures with sculpted or fiberglass nails, electrolysis, bikini waxes, facials, massages, makeup, and hair.

Purchasing the salon's "Day of Beauty" also entitled patrons to lunch with champagne, and Margaret got the works every week. The salon had six hairdressers on staff, five manicurists, a masseuse, and an esthetician, but for Margaret, Irma Jean did everything but hair.

"We talked for hours each week," Irma Jean, now 73, told me. "She shared everything happening in her life, not so much for advice as just needing a sounding board. We were almost the same age, but Margaret came from a different world. She was a beautiful, sweet lady. I still miss her dearly."

Irma Jean left the Beau Monde a year after Margaret's murder, opening her salon. "It was sad working there after Margaret passed, plus I was kind of afraid. I didn't want to end up the same way."

Two months after Margaret's funeral, Eileen Petingil, the owner of Beau Monde, asked Irma Jean to meet with one of Margaret's neighbors. "She's writing a book," Eileen said. "And she'd like to ask you some questions about Margaret Coon."

"That day was the first time I saw Beau Chene," Irma Jean said. "Margaret and I saw each other every week and had lunch together about twice a month, but I had never been to her condo. She said everyone there was about money, who married it, how much they married, and how much they could flaunt."

"Margaret hated that," Irma Jean said. "She had money, lots, but she earned it, and she didn't need all that to be beautiful. She came by it naturally."

"Now, this woman that my boss sent me to see," said Irma Jean, "She was a different story, dressed fit to kill. I'm at this woman's condo three hours, and she gives me the creeps the longer I'm there."

"She started out asking questions as you'd expect: how long had I known Margaret? What kind of person was she?" Irma Jean remembered. "Then she started asking about her husband, whether or not I thought he had been sleeping with Margaret. I told her 'no.' Margaret hated that man's guts. She told me it made her sick when she found out he lived at Beau Chene."

"Besides, Margaret was madly in love with that dentist in Gretna. I told the woman that, and then I changed subjects," Irma Jean said. "A few minutes later, she'd bring up her husband again. She wasn't writing any book. She just wanted to confirm whether Margaret and her husband were having an affair."

"But it gets even weirder," Irma Jean said. "This woman had Charlene, Margaret's dog, there at her house. I didn't know at the time how she got her, but the dog wouldn't leave my side the whole time I was there like she was frightened or wanted to tell me something."

"Finally," Irma Jean said, "I got angry and got up to leave, so she pulls out these pictures of Margaret's body lying bloody in the grass. Horrible pictures. Crime scene photos, I guess. I asked how she got them. She said: I told you I'm writing a book."

"I said, 'you can't put those in a book. How'd you get them?' and she said, 'My husband's got connections. I can get whatever I need,' and then she pulled out copies of police reports. She had everything."

"That's when I left," Irma said. "I couldn't wait to get out of that place."

Before that day, Irma Jean said, she believed that Bernard Smith, Margaret's ex-husband, had killed Margaret. "He was another high-priced lawyer, a mayor one time. Margaret told me stories about his mental and verbal abuse. They had just gone through a nasty divorce. I thought it had to be him, but now, let me tell you, that was all before I met this neighbor."

"Then it dawned on me that Margaret had told me all about her. When my boss sent me to meet her, I didn't realize this was the same woman. Margaret had done told me her neighbor was crazy."

Margaret Coon had told Irma Jean that in the months after she moved into the Beau Chene Subdivision and Country Club, a female living three doors down stalked her. Margaret was an avid jogger, and each time she suited up for her daily 5-mile jog, the neighbor followed, jogging alongside her, talking all the way.

When Margaret changed her routine from evenings to mornings and then to later at night, the neighbor was always there. Margaret had worked with the neighbor's husband at the District Attorney's office, and the neighbor had questions about that working relationship.

Although the neighbor feigned friendship with her, Margaret thought the woman believed Margaret had moved into Beau Chene to be closer to her husband. She even made jokes hinting that Margaret still slept with her husband.

On Valentine's Day, the weekend before Margaret Coon's murder, Margaret flew to Florida with her boyfriend, periodontist Dr. James E. Fagan, to meet his parents. Coincidentally, the husband of Margaret's neighbor also flew to Florida with a friend that same weekend.

Margaret told Irma Jean that the neighbor confronted her the following Monday, accusing her of traveling to Florida with her husband.

A year after Irma Jean's visit with the faux aspiring author, Webster Coon stopped by the Beau Monde salon, asking about his daughter, and shop manager Nancy Jacobs told him about Margaret's friendship with Irma Jean.

"Yes," Webster said. He had read about Irma Jean in Margaret's diary, and that was why he came by. Among other things, Webster wanted to ask Irma Jean whether his daughter knew how much he loved her.

At her new shop on Highway 190, Irma Jean told Webster about the jealous neighbor, and Webster had Sandra Davis, a private investigator, also interview Irma Jean. Afterward, Sandra Davis provided information on the neighbor to the FBI, who confirmed that their agency's psychological profile of Margaret Coon's murderer suggested her killer was a woman.

In 1990, Sandra Davis phoned Irma Jean, saying, "Miss Irma, we can forget about seeing any justice in this case. That neighbor's lawyer-husband just got elected judge."

At that point, the Margaret Coon murder case went dormant and remained that way until court reporter Lynn Nunez decided to talk.

The LSU Murder

With new information from readers and other sources, this chapter evolved from the Bayou Justice column entitled "LSU murder unsolved after 59 years," initially published in south Louisiana newspapers on Tuesday, August 27, 2019.

AT 6:40 ON A MISTY Sunday morning, January 10, 1960, construction workers found the body of Dr. Margaret Rosamond McMillan lying in a pool of blood next to her small foreign car on a shell-covered lane running through an oat field 6 ½ miles south of the LSU campus. She still held her purse, a pack of cigarettes and matches clutched in her left hand. The money in her wallet totaled five dollars and 16 cents.

According to the coroner's report, approximately six hours earlier, the strikingly beautiful, unmarried professor turned from her companion to get in her car. She paused briefly to open a pack of cigarettes, and her companion began viciously and repeatedly striking her about the head, ultimately crushing her skull.

Dr. McMillan, 38, a botany professor, taught biology at LSU's New Orleans branch. However, today, police still consider her death the most sensational murder ever to take place on LSU's Baton Rouge campus, where she studied periodically in a research library.

East Baton Rouge Parish Sheriff Bryan Clemmons discounted robbery and criminal assault as motives. "I think the person who killed her was someone she knew," the sheriff said. "Her clothing wasn't torn, and the only mark of struggle was a broken pearl necklace and a busted pair of eyeglasses."

Four days after the murder, deputies arrested the dean of the LSU Graduate School, 50-year-old Dr. George H. Mickey. Dr. McMillan was a professional associate of the dean.

Investigators found blood spots of the same type as the slain professor on Mickey's car and failed to verify his alibi. They also found correspondence from Mickey to Dr. McMillan in the dead woman's apartment back in New Orleans but never publicly revealed the contents of those letters.

On January 26, 1960, police arrested Earl Hamilton, 43, an unemployed tool sales clerk from Memphis, for attempting to extort $1,000 from Mickey's family.

Police said Hamilton, using the alias Larry Johnston, attempted to sell the "murder weapon" to Don Mickey, the dean's 19-year-old son. Police arrested Hamilton when he accepted a package from Edward O'Donnell, a detective portraying the son.

Hamilton told police he was broke and needed money. He thought of the extortion idea after reading that police never found the murder weapon. Five days before Hamilton's arrest, the con-man initiated telephone conversations with Mickey's son, claiming to have discovered the murder weapon. He said he would surrender it after being paid $1,000 in small bills.

Following Mickey's arrest, an East Baton Rouge Parish grand Jury launched a three-week probe into the case and heard over 30 witnesses, but left the murder charge against Mickey. After the grand jury pretermitted the case, the court released Mickey from his $10,000 bond.

LSU officials allowed Mickey, a zoology professor, to return to campus as a teacher, but University President Troy Middleton refused to reinstate him as Dean.

"I hope this action will not be misinterpreted," said Middleton.

"No judgment of the charge against Dr. Mickey is implied," he said. "A graduate program must be marked by stability and continuity, conditions which obviously could not continue to exist under the present circumstances. This action simply makes it possible for the university to proceed openly with the business of selecting a permanent graduate dean."

The action cut Mickey's salary from $14,000 a year to $10,800 annually.

Mickey resigned and left the state, and District Attorney James St. Clair Favrot withdrew his warrant for murder. Mickey's attorney, Robert Kleinpeter, said he thought the withdrawal of the warrant was "the fair thing for Mr. Favrot to do" and that his action in effect closed the case.

"An unsolved murder case is never closed," said Assistant Chief Deputy George LeBlanc, one of the principal investigators on the case at the East Baton Rouge Parish Sheriff's Office. If investigators uncover new evidence, he said, they would arrest Mickey again on the same charge.

In a follow-up interview in 1962, LeBlanc said Mickey for a private research laboratory in Connecticut studying the effects of radiation on genetics.

By 1967, Mickey had joined the staff at Duke University, where he ultimately retired.

Mickey was an international authority on genetics. His arrest made headlines around the world. Reporters nationwide flocked to Baton Rouge. During the weeks of investigation, over 50 news reporters gathered in the squad room of the sheriff's office each afternoon for a press conference seeking new developments in the case.

Investigators never found the weapon used to club Dr. McMillan to death. Deputies said it might have been a gun butt, tire tool, or some other narrow instrument.

Investigators said Dr. McMillan had met a male friend on Lover's Lane off River Road the night she was murdered. Investigators found her car keys in her coat pocket.

Coroner Chester A. Williams said she suffered several skull fractures from at least 13 blows to the head. He found no other marks or injuries on the body and no evidence of a sexual assault. The fact that there were no signs of a struggle led police to believe that she knew her killer, deputies said.

Dr. McMillan drank a beer with neighbors in New Orleans the Saturday afternoon before her slaying, leaving around 4 p.m., saying she had a date. Deputies said when she left the apartment sometime later, leaving the lights on inside.

Dr. Margaret Rosamond McMillan left an estate valued at $21,584.54, which is approximately $185,216.29 today. Her will made her mother in Wilmette, Illinois, the principal beneficiary.

McMillan graduated from Mundelein College in Chicago and worked as a biology professor at Tift College in Georgia before accepting the position at LSU in 1957.

After 59 years, her brutal murder remains unsolved.

Dr. Mary Sherman

With new information from readers and other sources, this chapter evolved from the Bayou Justice column entitled "Infamous LSU and Tulane murders may be linked," initially published in south Louisiana newspapers on Thursday, August 29, 2019.

LAST TUESDAY, BAYOU Justice reviewed Louisiana State University's most infamous unsolved murder, the 1960 killing of Dr. Margaret Rosamond McMillan. Today, we examine Tulane University's most infamous unsolved mystery, the 1964 death of Dr. Mary Sherman, and consider a possible link between the two homicides.

Tuesday morning, July 21, 1964, children born with bone defects and other crippling illnesses lined up at a clinic in Amite, Louisiana, as they did every 30 days. On the fourth Tuesday of every month, a bone and cancer specialist, 51-year-old Dr. Mary Stults Sherman, drove from New Orleans to study and to treat the children free-of-charge.

However, on that Tuesday morning, the doctor never arrived.

Back in New Orleans, in apartment J at 3101 St. Charles Avenue, a beautifully hand-lettered card on the mailbox read "Mary Sherman, MD." Inside the immaculate home, a single-place setting of china and silver sat untouched on the kitchen bar, a tea bag in a cup, ready for breakfast never served.

Through the entrance into the living room, a painting of a woman stared back into the kitchen, her face frozen in horror, her hands clutching her own throat. Several sketches next to the portrait depicted a Roman soldier stabbing a woman with his sword.

In the bedroom, lying on the floor near the bed, police found Dr. Sherman's nude body, stabbed eight times, half-burned beyond recognition, her right arm missing, burned away.

Police found the lock on a sliding glass door busted and the doctor's wallet empty.

Neighbors told reporters that burglaries often occurred at the Patios Apartments. One string of break-ins two months earlier included Dr. Sherman's apartment while she traveled abroad, according to housekeeper Elmner Peterson.

Peterson, police believe, was the last person to see Dr. Sherman alive, excluding her assailant. Peterson, 55, left the residence around 4:30, Monday afternoon, July 20, 1964. Peterson said Dr. Sherman had recently had a burglar alarm installed, but she usually left it disabled while she was home.

Lieutenant James Kreubbe, chief of the NOPD homicide division, told reporters he believed Dr. Sherman remained inside, never leaving the apartment after Mrs. Peterson's departure.

At 4:13 the following morning, July 21, the New Orleans Police Department responded to a complaint from the victim's neighbor, Juan Valdez, reporting smoke.

The New Orleans Fire Department arrived at 4:25 and began fighting the fire. They discovered the body only after they extinguished the fire, and the smoke cleared.

Mrs. Jake Levy lived below Dr. Sherman's apartment. She said she usually heard Dr. Sherman come in. "I woke up about 3:30 a. m. and didn't hear sounds up-stairs," said Mrs. Levy. "If there had been any loud commotion, I know I would have heard it. The doctor was quiet, but I always heard her come in and take off her shoes, then pad around in her slippers. Sometimes I'd tell my husband, 'Doc's back home.' "

Mrs. Levy said the next time she awoke was 4:30 a. m. and her apartment was full of smoke.

Just after 1:00 that afternoon, police found the orthopedic surgeon's abandoned automobile nine blocks from the crime scene, blocking a driveway at 2625 Chestnut Street. Investigators considered that discovery the first significant break in the investigation and possibly the last.

Immediately after recovery of the victim's vehicle, police found a palm print on the car's fender, but the print matched no one on file.

A neighbor, 17-year-old Stewart McLellan, found the keys to the automobile while trimming the hedges at 1233 Conery Street, just after noon on July 22. The keyring bore a large monogrammed S.

In 1964, Major Alfred Theriot, deputy chief of administration, said investigators questioned all people known to have been associated with Dr. Sherman, including Dr. George H. Mickey at Duke University in North Carolina.

Dr. Mickey, a former dean at Louisiana State University, moved to Connecticut and then later to North Carolina after a Baton Rouge district attorney dropped charges against him related to the murder of Dr. Margaret McMillan in 1960.

"We turned this case inside out and backward to find a solution," Theriot said. "We have questioned her acquaintances in other states and have followed every possible lead with negative results each time."

Theriot emphasized that neighbors first reported the incident as a fire and that the first responders treated the case in that manner, trampling evidence and hindering police in their investigation. "We started at a great disadvantage," he said.

Major Lawrence Casanova said in 1965 that the New Orleans Police Department still treated the investigation as an open homicide case, explaining that an "open homicide case" means that officers work on it when they have time and are not working on something else. He would not comment on the last time an "on the street investigation" took place but said the case is one of several which he would like to bring to a successful conclusion.

"In all cases, nothing is as important as citizen cooperation," he stressed.

Regarding anonymous phone calls reportedly threatening friends of Dr. Sherman immediately following the murder, Casanova said the police department never furnished guards for any persons claiming to have received them. According to Casanova, reports that police protected "a close woman friend" of Dr. Sherman's were false.

Within a year of the murder, the apartment building where Dr. Sherman resided changed hands, and the new owners remodeled. One resident, who preferred to remain anonymous, said that of the 15 apartments occupied at the time of the murder, only five of the same tenants remained at that address.

"Nearly all of them moved out immediately," he said.

"One couple moved two days later, but within three weeks they were all gone but us. Everyone was scared."

Juan Valdez, the neighbor who reported the fire, said in a 1965 interview that when he first smelled smoke, he contacted police. "I always call the police first when I have any trouble," he said. Valdez said the police arrived and then firefighters who entered the smoke-filled apartment with masks through an already open patio gate.

Valdez said the whole apartment was not on fire. He said the flames remained confined to the victim's bedroom.

Fire Chief Arthur J. Hyde released official findings of the investigation by the New Orleans Fire Department's Fire Prevention Division to *The Times-Picayune*. In this report, Inspector Orville Miller listed the cause of the fire as "probable arson to cover a murder." The report estimated the total loss of contents at $175.

Captain Anthony Palermo, acting district chief of the Fourth Fire District at the time Valdez reported the alarm, said he was one of the first to arrive on the scene. He said another engine came almost simultaneously. Palermo said the smoke in the victim's apartment was so thick that firefighters entered it with gas masks. "The fire was confined to the mattress," Palermo said. "The other damage was just from smoke and water." He said the "least amount of water possible was sprayed only on the bed for three or four minutes from a one-inch booster hose commonly used in small places."

Palermo said the mattress was smoking, not blazing, and he estimated that from the amount of fire and the liquid state of the blood, the murder could not have been committed "too far in advance."

The report listed the time of departure from the scene of the fire at 6:30 a. m.

An essential segment in the life of the murdered surgeon was her research and analytic work in the Ochsner Foundation bone pathology laboratory. Dr. Gordon McFarland, appointed acting director following the murder, said told newspaper reporters that he would continue her bone cancer research.

In 2007, Florida advertising agent Edward Haslam wrote a book purporting to detail Dr. Sherman's secret research for the United States Central Intelligence Agency. The book was entitled Dr. Mary's Monkey.

Although Haslam stated his original intention was to identify Dr. Mary Sherman's killer, in the end, he concluded that she most likely died from accidental electrocution while operating an extremely high voltage linear particle accelerator.

Seemingly ignoring the blood spatter on the walls and furniture in crime scene photos, or perhaps unaware that postmortem wounds cannot spatter, Haslam believes the confidential nature of her work for the CIA made it essential to conceal the circumstances of her death and secretly move the body to her apartment.

According to Haslam, Dr. Sherman used the linear accelerator to promote genetic mutations in cell tissue. Officially, the New Orleans Police never considered such a theory nor had any knowledge of the doctor using a linear accelerator or one in any way being involved in her death.

However, perhaps coincidentally, they interviewed Dr. George H. Mickey, who, at that time, happened to be the United States' foremost authority on genetic mutation experiments using a linear accelerator.

A crematorium in Birmingham, Alabama, cremated Dr. Mary Sherman's body less than a week after the death.

Fifty-four years later, police still have no leads.

Dallas Calmes

WITH NEW INFORMATION from readers and other sources, this chapter evolved from the Bayou Justice column entitled "Who killed Dallas Calmes?" initially published in south Louisiana newspapers on Thursday, September 5, 2019.

ON MAY 9, 1924, FOR the first time in Louisiana history, the state hung six men for the murder of one. Almost a century later, historians still wonder who killed Dallas Calmes.

The events leading up to the murder began shortly after midnight, May 8, 1921. A noise at the rear of his home aroused Dallas Calmes, an Independence restaurant operator. As he investigated, a man barely discernible in the darkness shot him dead.

Six men, who came to Independence to rob the bank, boarded their automobile and fled. The Tangipahoa parish sheriff's office summoned bloodhounds from Crystal Springs, Mississippi, and telephoned the New Orleans Police Department.

Detectives in New Orleans, following a tip from detectives in Amite, went to the home of a wealthy Italian resident in New Orleans, a home Tangipahoa Parish police believed might be a refuge for the bandits. They found the house empty with evidence indicating someone had deserted it hurriedly.

In an automobile parked outside the house, they found the bodies of Guiseppe Gaeto and another Italian named Dominick DiGiovanni, who someone had shot dead a few-hour earlier. It took over a decade to solve that part of the mystery.

With the bloodhounds, the sheriff's posse followed a highway out of Independence and found the would-be bandits' deserted getaway car. In the backseat, they discovered one pistol, a large quantity of ammunition, and a case of dynamite.

The dogs followed a trail into a thicket where the posse arrested Joseph Giglio and Roy Lenoa of Brooklyn, New York, Joseph Bocchio, and Andrea Lemantia of Chicago, with Natale Deamore and Joseph Rini of New Orleans.

Along the way, police arrested two other Italians as possible suspects, but later, a grand jury exonerated both men.

Surrounded by police, the six prisoners protested their innocence, insisting they were on a camping trip, but ultimately a jury convicted them all of murder.

An appeal to the State Supreme Court resulted in a re-trial followed by a second conviction, which the higher court sustained. The counsel for the condemned men then appealed to the Supreme Court of the United States, which refused to review the case citing a lack of jurisdiction.

Throughout the three-year legal battle, Italian-American organizations and individuals throughout the country supplied the men with ample funds for their defense, and Governor John M. Parker received thousands of letters, telegrams, and petitions protesting the conviction of innocent men and asking for leniency.

According to experts presented by the prosecution, only one man, or at the most, two, had fired at Calmes. For three years, attorneys and investigators made efforts to determine the guilty man. He would not admit his guilt, and none of his companions would disclose his identity.

The Saturday before Easter, Leona requested that Father Raymond Carra of St. Patrick's Roman Catholic Church in New Orleans, visit him, and perform his "Easter duties." Leona, in his confession to the priest, said he fired the shot, which killed Calmes.

Father Carra told him he could not hope for forgiveness from his maker if he did not make a public confession and clear his five companions. Leone agreed to do so. On Easter Monday, in the presence of the superintendent of the Orleans parish prison, where the authorities held the men for their protection, Father Carra, and three newspaper reporters, he dictated a confession and signed it.

In his statement, Leona said he and Giglio came to New Orleans in late April 1921, to make and sell whiskey. Vito Georgio, who a hitman later killed in Chicago, had told him that he could quickly get startup capital robbing a usually unguarded bank in Independence.

Leona thought well of the suggestion and asked Giglio to Join him. He met Lemantia in New Orleans and broached the subject to him. Lemantia agreed to participate, provided he could bring along his friend, Rini.

The next step was to find a man who knew the highways around Independence, so Lemantia persuaded Deamore to join the party. Deamore asked Bocchio to join them, and the six men set out for Independence.

According to Leona, when the party approached the bank shortly after midnight, Leona and Rini climbed out of the car, leaving the others behind. Rini, however, did not accompany Leona but circled the block in another direction.

"I tried to get near the bank through the rear yard of Mr. Calmes' house," Leona's confession continued. "As I jumped over the fence, one of the pickets broke, and the noise must have awakened Mr. Calmes. He opened the door and shouted, 'Halt!', and fired four shots at me. Surprised and frightened, I fired two shots in the direction that the fire of Mr. Calmes' revolver came from, but unfortunately for him, and me, I killed him. I was alone when Mr. Calmes shot at me, and I alone returned the fire, which killed Mr. Calmes."

When the newspapers made Leona's confession public, Tangipahoa parish authorities, attorneys, and the widow of Calmes pronounced it "a trumped-up affair" in an attempt to save the lives of Leona's five partners. Prosecutors said the evidence did not support the confession, and Mrs. Calmes insisted that she had seen two men that night.

There also was a question concerning the shots Leona supposedly fired. Investigators found bullets that could not have come from Leona's pistol or the one Calmes fired.

Another feature dwelt upon by those who placed little faith in the confession was that it came after all hope to escape execution had vanished. Leona had contracted tuberculosis during his long confinement, which physicians said would prove fatal within a few months.

Governor Parker referred to this in a formal statement on April 23, 1924, in connection with his declaration that no reprieve would ho granted. After stating that the convicted men had the benefit of counsel, the governor added:

"At the eleventh hour one of their number, now afflicted with tuberculosis, seeks to assume responsibility, but in his statement, convicts every man proven to be a member of his party.

"Keeping up with every detail of these cases and having watched the trial, I realize mine is an executive duty, and I am determined to back up to the fullest extent, the decision of the courts. After having considered all the evidence, in my opinion, these men are guilty of deliberate conspiracy and willful murder, and the law shall take its course without interference from the governor. This decision is final."

However, the governor didn't know what he didn't know.

The Bootleggers

With new information from readers and other sources, this chapter evolved from the Bayou Justice column entitled "Bootleg house links Calmes murder to two in New Orleans," initially published in south Louisiana newspapers on Tuesday, September 10, 2019.

ON A SUNDAY NIGHT, May 8, 1921, New Orleans police found Dominick Di Giovanni and Joseph Gaeto shot dead. Their bodies slumped in the front seat of an automobile, and a trail leading back to a foiled bank robbery and the Sunday morning murder of Independence restaurant owner Dallas Calmes.

Newspapers of the day dedicated full pages to the protracted legal fight waged by the six men accused of killing Calmes. Three profligate trials and the dramatic developments that followed overshadowed the New Orleans' homicides. During the Prohibition 20s, shotgun murders happened weekly in the crescent city, but rarely in rural Tangipahoa Parish.

However, to understand the murders of Dominick Di Giovanni and Joseph Gaeto, we must look closer at those ultimately hanged in Amite, the six men accused of murdering Calmes after he prevented them from robbing the bank that Sunday morning.

Initial newspaper reports said bloodhounds tracked the getaway car and cornered all six men in the woods a few yards from the vehicle. The nationally syndicated story said the men all pretended to be campers. That story was false.

Firstly, on the Sunday afternoon following the murder, the sheriff's posse apprehended an additional six people without charging them. They were Nick D'Armore, Pietro "Peter" Leotto, Joseph Riachico, Frank Pisciotto, Natalie Giamalva, and a 10-year-old boy, "Little Joe" Leotto.

Tangipahoa Parish Sheriff Lem H. Bowden told reporters he felt confident that these six were innocent of the murder, but all had interacted with the slayers leading up to the crime. He said his office would hold each of them in protective custody until they could take the witness stand.

Police arrested the majority of the accused nowhere near Independence.

That Sunday afternoon, in Ponchatoula, Town Marshal E. S. Tucker arrested Joseph Bocchio and charged him with murder. Angola trustee M. E. Garrison used bloodhounds from the state prison to capture Joseph Rini and Andrea Lemantia in a swamp between Albany and Holden in Livingston Parish.

Inside the getaway car, Tangipahoa Parish sheriff's deputies found a quantity of nitroglycerine, several dynamite caps, two drills, and a hacksaw, tools they planned to use to rob the Farmers and Merchants National Bank in Independence. They found Natale Deamore hiding in a tree nearby, six miles east of Tickfaw.

New Orleans police grabbed Rosario "Roy" Leona and Joseph Giglio Sunday night as they entered their rooming house at 1601 Tulane Avenue, a block from Deamore's auto repair shop. The men said they had walked the railroad tracks from Independence to New Orleans in just under 15 hours.

That week, a Tangipahoa Parish grand jury indicted Rini, Lemantia, Giglio, Deamore, Bocchio, and Leona for murder, and Judge Robert S. Ellis set a special session to try them. After a 17-day trial, the jury found all six guilty, and Judge Ellis sentenced them to hang. The accused, represented by an expensive attorney from New Orleans, appealed to the Louisiana Supreme Court, who ordered a new trial, citing Judge Ellis for not putting the charges in writing when requested to do so by the defense team.

That defense team included most of the highest-priced lawyers from Orleans, St. Tammany, and Tangipahoa Parishes: B. B. Purser, A. B. Henriques, Louis H. Morgan, J. Sidney Fredericks, George Gullotta, and W. B. Kemp.

The first trial began June 13, 1921, and ended June 29. The second trial started on May 1, 1922, and lasted another seventeen days. Again, a jury returned a capital verdict against the six, and once more, Judge Ellis sentenced them to death.

The defense team appealed again to the Louisiana Supreme Court, but this time, the court upheld the jury's verdict, rendering that decision on December 29, 1922.

On February 24, 1923, the Defense then appealed to the United States Supreme Court. That court, on January 21, 1924, handed down a final mandate, dismissing the appeal citing a lack of jurisdiction.

The Louisiana Supreme Court accepted that mandate on March 19, 1924.

A few days later, Governor John Parker signed the death warrants, and Roy Leona signed a confession, saying he alone fired the two shots that killed Dallas Calmes and absolving his companions of any connection with the murder.

Following Leona's confession, the Defense applied to the Board of Pardons for commutation of sentence to life imprisonment. Attorney General Adolph Coco voted to commute the sentences, while Lieutenant Governor Delos Johnson and Judge Ellis voted against commutation.

Turned down by the pardon board, the Defense appealed to Governor John Parker, who refused to intervene.

Next, the condemned men's well-paid defense team applied for a writ of habeas corpus in the United States district court, which refused the application and barred the attorney from making further appeals.

Now, the critical question: who paid for the defense team? Those accused and condemned to die all claimed to be automobile mechanics and day laborers.

One *Times-Picayune* newspaper photo featured defense attorney B. B. Purser opening a large package of gold coins, sent by "anonymous, but concerned Italian-American individuals and organizations." Sheriff Bowden later charged Purser with attempting to bribe a jury and jailer with some of those same coins.

The murders of the two Italians in New Orleans occurred on or about 11:30 p.m. Sunday, May 8, 1921 — roughly twenty-one hours after the Calmes murder.

Police found the bodies of Dominick Di Giovanni, a 25-years-old stevedore of 1201 North Roman Street and Joseph Gaeto, a 27-year-old garage mechanic of 1361 Tulane Avenue. Both were riddled with buckshot and shotgun slugs, slumped forward in the front seat of an automobile at 843 Tupelo Street, the home of Leonardo Cipolla, a 38-year-old native of Palermo, Italy.

A curious trail from the Independence crime led to the discovery of these bodies. When New Orleans detectives arrested Joseph Giglio at 1601 Tulane Avenue, inside a pocket, he had a letter addressed to him at 903 St. Maurice Avenue, New Orleans.

Assistant District Attorney Thomas Craven met the detectives at that address, a corner grocery with the owner's residence above the store.

Questioned by Craven, the grocer said that "some of the boys" had their correspondence and packages addressed in his care, and that Leonardo Cipolla, or his wife, usually collected the mail for them. He said Cipolla lived at 843 Tupelo Street.

At that address, Craven and the police discovered a Ford touring car and two corpses. Inside the house, police found evidence of a hasty departure, but no Mr. or Mrs. Cipolla.

On the second floor, police discovered ten barrels of wine, a 10-gallon copper whiskey still, sixteen automobile tires, and four auto license plates, all from vehicles stolen within twenty-four hours. Near the still, they found two shotgun cases, one shotgun, and 300 hundred rounds of ammunition. From a desk, they collected a telegram for Andrea Lemantia, a postcard sent from Joseph Rini's Chicago address, and canceled checks written for thousands of dollars, each payable to cash.

Inside a trunk, shipped to Joseph Giglio at that address, police found corks, cognac labels, and other bootlegging supplies. They also found several shotgun shells, loaded with buckshot and slugs matching the type that killed Di Giovanni and Gaeto.

On the floor, they found monogrammed clothing belonging to Joseph Giglio and Roy Leona.

This evidence linked Cipolla to four of the men arrested for the murder of Dallas Calmes: Giglio, Leona, Rini, and Lemantia.

Several days later, police found Cipolla hiding above a grocery store owned by Jake Bucaro at the corner of Clio and Magnolia streets. Police said their evidence showed Bucaro acted as the go-between for Cipolla and

George J. Gullotta, his attorney in New Orleans, and one of those high-priced attorneys working for the six men ultimately hanged in Amite on May 9, 1924.

Next, we complete this puzzle, adding the missing piece, the name of the grocer, who received everyone's mail.

Courtroom Burlesque

With new information from readers and other sources, this chapter evolved from the Bayou Justice column entitled "Women entertain at Dallas Calmes murder trial," initially published in south Louisiana newspapers on Thursday, September 12, 2019.

I FIRST HEARD THE NAME Dallas Calmes in 1979. That year, sent by Editor Nicholas R. Murray of the Daily Sun to write a feature marking a Livingston Parish resident's 90th birthday, I met Elwood Varnado, a former Kentwood farmer who served on the jury in one of two Dallas Calmes murder trials.

The juror told me that three days before the hanging, one condemned man attempted suicide, cutting himself multiple times with a knife, and another nearly died from tuberculosis. The hangman hung both men, he said, seated on strawberry crates inside wooden chairs.

On the day of the hanging in Amite, huge wooden blinds surrounded the gallows, preventing the execution from being a public one and leading local conspiracy theorists to wonder if the men who died that day were the same six the jury found guilty.

Varnado described those days as "a morbid circus" and said the most outrageous events occurred inside the courtroom.

"Local newspapers then were different," he said. "They reported the facts when they thought the public would believe them, but anything the least bit sensational, they left that out, thinking it might hurt their credibility." As an example, he told me of the day two young women disrupted the trial, but at the time, he said, no one complained.

"The papers covered the ladies being there," he said, "But when we told them what happened after the girls left, they wouldn't print a word of it."

On June 14, 1921, *The New Orleans States* related the following:

"Mrs. Anabelle Bocchio, 18, is the wife of Joseph Bocchio, and Miss Katherine Rini, 19, is a cousin of Joseph Rini, two of the six Italians on trial in Amite for the murder of Dallas Calmes at Independence. On this day, these women were the center of interest at the trial. The two young women regularly cheered the somber-looking and serious-faced defendants who were fighting for their lives. They tried unsuccessfully to prove that they did not kill Dallas Calmes when he interfered with their robbery of the Farmers and Merchants Bank near the railroad tracks in Independence."

"Miss Rini, the shapelier of the two women, wore a one-piece translucent gown of pink and white checkered cloth, accented by a broad-rimmed black hat attached to a big bow of white ribbon with a streamer flowing from the side. She is of medium build, and a natural brunette with a beautiful smile and a loud giggle."

"Mrs. Bocchio, the redhead, dressed well; nattily attired with fancy lace tied at her waist over a dark checkered skirt. She carried a serge coat on her arm and a turban hat of white and black feathers on her head, parading around the courtroom in a pair of stylish black pumps. She weighs 125 pounds and is pretty."

"Since the accused — Natale Deamore, the Tulane Avenue garage owner; Andrea Lemantia of Brooklyn; and Roy Leona and Joseph Giglio, bachelors from New Orleans — all had no wives present to console them, Mrs. Bocchio and Miss Rini had to comfort and speak words of encouragement to the whole six."

"Of the two women, Mrs. Bocchio, who traveled from Chicago to be present at her husband's trial, appeared the most expressive. Even the stoic Judge Robert Ellis commented upon her carefree manner."

"She kissed her husband every time he entered or left the courtroom while Miss Rini bestowed her glances, occasional touches, and whispered words of encouragement to all of the accused men."

"The smiles of the young women, seated just behind the six defendants, brightened the courtroom. Almost continuously, jurors saw a wrinkle of laughter about Mrs. Bocchio's mouth while now and then Miss Rini joined her, giggling at some bantering remark."

According to Varnado, the attending crowd left "standing room only," with Miss Rini and Mrs. Bocchio, the only women in attendance. "Every man in the room felt well entertained," he said, "Hot and sweaty, sitting in a depressing trial, but all smiling ear to ear. Those two brightened everything up, and that Rini girl's giggle, the high-pitch gave you chills."

When the jurors met after the trial that day, Varnado said, the jury room had changed. Deputies stood in the hall outside the door all day, but someone had slipped passed them, perhaps while they focused their attention elsewhere.

On the dark wood wall inside the jury room, in fresh white paint, someone had scrawled the words "Not Guilty!" and below the words, the intruder had drawn the rough shape of a gun.

As Varnado predicted, I found no mention of the incident in the jury room in the newspapers. Still, I did find interviews where Judge Robert Ellis complained that he and his family had received several "black hand" extortion letters throughout both trials threatening the life of his wife and his daughter.

The State Times reprinted in full a letter postmarked "New Orleans" and addressed to "Mr. Judge Robert Ellis, Amite Prison."

The letter read:

"Mr. Judge Ellis, I write to ask you for clemency for the six Italians to save their lives. You, Governor Parker, Lieutenant Governor Johnson, and Mrs. Calmes have until Friday to change your mind if you all care for your life. If not, you all shall die next."

"Don't take this as a joke. It is a shame to hang six for one, so think it over. If you all don't do the right thing, we are going to make four pairs of shoes out of your skin."

"Get together with the people of Amite to ask for clemency for those six condemned men. Tell them if they don't save those men from hanging, we will explode the whole town of Amite, and it will be a great mystery how we do it."

A handprint adorned the back of the letter in black ink smeared so deeply that it soaked through the front.

The Baton Rouge Advocate tried to locate Mrs. Bocchio and Miss Rini to ask if they knew anything about the extortion letters. Still, the newspaper — and the police — were unable to identify them.

Three weeks after "Mrs. Bocchio" made her debut in court, the Associated Press questioned her identity, reporting that Joseph Bocchio, alias Joey Luciano of Chicago, actually never married.

A columnist in *The Hammond Vindicator* newspaper suggested gangsters had hired the young women through Thelma Hines, a Ponchatoula madam.

However, according to *The New Orleans Item*, the two entertaining women walked into the courtroom in Amite, escorted by one of the witnesses subpoenaed from New Orleans. This escort was the St. Maurice Street grocer and fruit importer whom New Orleans police said received and forwarded telegraphs and mail to and from four of the men on trial.

Next, we learn more about that grocer, a man named Tony Carollo, whom the *Times-Picayune* described as running "a clearinghouse for rum-runners and racketeers" and causing a "gang war rivalry" in New Orleans.

With this final piece of the puzzle in place, we will recount what happened in 1921, showing who most likely planned the bank robbery, and who killed Dallas Calmes.

Tony Carollo

With new information from readers and other sources, this chapter evolved from the Bayou Justice column entitled "Mob responsible for Dallas Calmes' death," initially published in south Louisiana newspapers on Thursday, September 17, 2019.

THOMAS V. CRAVEN, ASSISTANT District Attorney of Orleans Parish, believed he would solve the Dallas Calmes case before the Tangipahoa Parish Sheriff's Office. Four of the men deputies arrested there worked for Leonardo Cipolla, a leader in one of the New Orleans' hoodlum gangs, representing a new, younger breed of mafioso, specializing in stolen cars and illegal alcohol instead of the tired old extortion rackets.

Another young group, this one led by Vito Di Giorgio, preferred bank robberies to extortion. Suspects in bank jobs throughout South Louisiana and Mississippi, the gang followed the same method of operation at each location. Find a closed bank with no late-night guards, preferably in a small, rural town, just before crops come to market and farmers lineup for payday. Set fire to a local official's home as a diversion, and then hit the bank, using nitroglycerin to blow the vault and escape without anyone getting hurt.

Di Giorgio lost two men following a Mississippi heist, both arrested for being drunk and disorderly and then shipped back to Chicago on outstanding warrants. Craven suspected Di Giorgio needed new muscle and offered Cipolla a piece of the action in Independence in exchange for the loan of two men.

After finding the bodies of Joseph Gaeto and Dominick Di Giovanni outside Cipolla's home, Craven theorized Cipolla made that bank deal without consulting his boss, a produce merchant named Tony Carollo.

When the Independence job went south, Craven believed, Carollo retaliated, sending men to shoot up Cipolla's car, expecting to hit Cipolla, but killing Gaeto and Di Giovanni instead.

After the shooting, Cipolla vacated his home and hid from the police and Carollo. Detectives began searching the homes of suspected mob associates and found Cipolla four nights later, hiding in a storeroom above Guesepe Bucaro's grocery at 1200 Magnolia Street.

Police charged Bucaro with harboring a fugitive and storing large quantities of high explosives in his home. The officers took Bucaro to a cell but brought Cipolla directly to Craven for interrogation.

"State your name and what brought you to New Orleans," Craven began.

"Leonardo Cipolla, 38, married, no children. Born in Palermo, Italy. I came to America when I was 21, lived in Brooklyn until I came to New Orleans almost four years ago."

"Were you with Di Giovanni and Gaeto the night they were murdered in front of your house?" asked Craven.

"Yes."

"What were you doing?"

"They took my wife and me for a ride around the city," Cipolla said.

"Did you stop in front of Deamore's garage at 1561 Tulane Avenue?"

"No," Cipolla answered.

"Bring those detectives in here," Craven shouted, and two officers stepped in and identified Cipolla as the man they saw in a car with Di Giovanni in front of Deamore's Auto Garage the night Gaeto and Di Giovanni died.

Mechanic Natale Deamore was one of the six men arrested in Tangipahoa Parish.

"No. You've made a mistake," Cipolla insisted.

"That clinches it," said the tallest detective. "He's the same man; he speaks the same broken English. No mistake."

"I don't want to talk any longer without my lawyer," Cipolla said, but Craven continued.

"What were you doing in front of Deamore's place Sunday night — the night after they tried to rob the Independence bank and killed Dallas Calmes?"

"I wasn't there, Mister," Cipolla said, "You've got that wrong."

Next, Craven asked about the double murder in front of Cipolla's house, and Cipolla said he and his wife were there, talking to the victims when it happened.

"How could you be in a car full of buckshot holes and not be injured?"

Twisting a white handkerchief in his hands, Cipolla shook his head and said, "No, I wasn't in the car. Before the shots fired, I jumped down in the grass."

"Where was your wife?"

"She was standing there behind me."

"What did you do?"

"I crawled through the high grass, jumped the back fence through the garden, and climbed that Burgundy Street fence and ran."

"Really?" asked Craven. "What became of your wife?"

Cipolla frowned and shrugged his shoulders. "How should I know?"

"Why did four of those men arrested in Independence get mail at your house?" Craven asked.

"I don't know. They just do. That is all I know. The mail comes there, and I give it to them when they stop by."

"You just let them get their mail at your house, and you don't know anything about it?"

"How can I help it if people send mail to me addressed to someone else?" Cipolla asked.

"They didn't send it to you. They sent it to Tony Carollo's fruit stand, and you called for it and kept it for them. Remember that telegram to Lemantia that we found at your house. How do you explain that?"

"I don't know," Cipolla said.

Next, Craven asked about the stacks of stolen tires and the barrels of wine and whiskey found in the house. Cipolla shrugged again.

"And what did you have all that wine for — about 10 barrels today, but how many did you sell?"

"No, I didn't sell any. That's all for my personal use." Cipolla said.

"What did you have all those cognac labels and bottle caps and cognac flavor for?"

"That ain't mine," answered Cipolla. "Belongs to Giglio."

"It was in your house in a trunk full of bootlegging supplies."

Cipolla shrugged again.

"Well, what were you doing with that ten-gallon whiskey still in your house?"

"Still?"

"Yes, a still. You heard me." Craven pounded the table between them.

"What still?" Cipolla asked again.

"Oh, hell," replied Craven, "You know what still, the ten-gallon copper whiskey still we found hidden in the china closet in your front room."

"Oh, that still?" Cipolla said, smiling now. "Sometimes, I make a little whiskey for myself in case of sickness. That's no crime. Everyone does that — right? You pick up every man what makes wine and whiskey, and you'll have everybody in jail."

"Why did Joe Giglio and Roy Leona leave all their clothes in your house?" Craven asked.

Another shrug from Cipolla. "I don't know. They just leave them there."

Craven questioned Leonardo Cipolla until 3:00 a.m., Thursday morning with Cipolla alternating between grinning and shrugging. Before sunrise, Cipolla revealed he had a .32 caliber revolver in his boot, and he offered to sell Craven four tires and a case of sardines.

"You say you are innocent of any connection to these murders?" Craven asked, pointing to photos of Gaeto and Di Giovanni.

"Right. I am innocent." Cipolla said.

"Why were you hiding, then?"

"I wasn't hiding. I was going to surrender when my lawyer told me to," Cipolla said.

"No, it looks as if you were afraid," said Craven, "locked up in that hole with a gun, food, and water. If you're innocent, why not call the police? Why call a lawyer and try to make a deal through him?"

Again, Cipolla shrugged. "I don't know."

Craven ordered the guards to escort Cipolla back to his cell.

On May 16, 1921, a grand jury indicted Leonardo Cipolla for bootlegging, the murders of three men, and involvement in the Independence bank robbery. After the court released him on a $5,000 bond, he vanished.

Vito Di Giorgio fled New Orleans immediately after the murder of Dallas Calmes. Police said he lived on the run in Los Angeles, New York, and Buffalo before hitmen caught up with him in Chicago.

From the Associated Press, May 14, 1922:

"Vito Di Giorgio, a wealthy New Orleans grocer, and James Cascio of Buffalo were shot and killed by mysterious assailants in a barbershop in the Italian quarter of the city today. Police are mystified as to the motive for the shooting, but are inclined to believe it was the result of a Black Hand feud."

"The two men were killed without warning when two armed men stepped inside the barbershop and fired half a dozen shots. The assassins then fled."

The six would-be bank robbers died on gallows in Amite on May 9, 1924.

Antonio "Tony" Carollo — described by *The Times-Picayune* as a "well-known fruit merchant" — actually died three years before the failed bank robbery.

The "Tony Carollo" in this story was most likely his nephew, son-in-law, and heir, Silvestro Anthony Carollo, later known as "Silver Dollar Sam" Carollo, the predecessor of Tomato Salesman Carlos Marcello.

Lynn Nunez

With new information from readers and other sources, this chapter evolved from the Bayou Justice column entitled "Someone's secrets died with Lynn Nunez," initially published in south Louisiana newspapers on Tuesday, September 24, 2019.

SUNDAY MORNING, MARCH 15, 1998, a pedestrian in New Orleans found a corpse slumped over the steering wheel of a car in Mid-City. By mid-afternoon, Chief Coroner's Investigator John Gagliano identified the deceased as 51-year-old Lynn Vessier Revere Nunez of Covington.

Her family and friends called Lynn Nunez "compassionate," partially because she housed and helped friends and relatives when they had nowhere else to turn. However, they said, she also had a reputation for defending her convictions, for standing up for what was right, and for speaking her mind.

Occupationally, Lynn was a respected court reporter for the 22nd Judicial Court. She worked in St. Tammany Parish, the same parish where murdered attorney Donna Bahm worked briefly before her death and the same parish where murdered attorney Margaret Ann Coon made her career and her home.

The night Lynn died, Saturday, March 14, 1998, investigators believe she parked her car, a beige 1996 Nissan Altima, just down the street from her son's home. There, near a curb in the 200th block of South Hennessey Street, before Lynn had time to kill the engine, someone shot her in the head.

Lt. Marlon Defillo said Lynn was on her way to visit her son, Pete Revere, his wife, and their newborn son when the homicide occurred. He said that witnesses told the police that Lynn had left a wedding reception at the Musee Conti, a wax museum on Conti Street in the French Quarter, less than an hour before her murder.

Pete told the police his wife got a phone call from his mom that night. He said that Lynn told her daughter-in-law that she was leaving a wedding at the Hotel Monteleone — on Royal Street, five minutes from the Musee Conti — and would make the 10-minute drive to the Revere home after the reception. When she never arrived, Pete said he and his wife assumed she had gotten tired and decided to drive back to Covington instead.

The next morning Pete heard police sirens nearby, but he didn't learn what happened until an aunt phoned him with the news. By the time the call came, the crime scene next door had been cleaned up, and his mother's car removed.

"It must have happened 30 feet from our house, and I didn't hear anything," he told *The Times-Picayune*, surrounded by family in his mother's home that Sunday evening. "I know what a gunshot sounds like, and I didn't hear a thing. It has me, perturbed."

A former detective in the New Orleans Police Department told me last year that Lynn's assailant locked the doors of Lynn's Altima after the hit.

In 2016, Detective Winston Harbin, with the New Orleans Police Department's Cold Case Division, spoke with WDSU-TV's Randi Rousseau. "According to a witness, the victim's car was in that same spot at 11:15 p.m.," he said, "but it was about 9:30 p.m. or so when the same witness indicated that he heard some gunshots."

Harbin said it was not until the next morning that a passerby discovered Lynn's body in the car. Because nothing appeared to be missing, he said that investigators did not consider robbery as the motive.

"All it does is illuminate the fact that she was the target and that the motive was to harm her," Harbin said.

The detective I spoke to last year said investigators could not prove anyone had removed anything from the vehicle, but suspected that someone had rifled through her trunk and glove compartment shortly before or after the murder.

Pete Revere said he has no idea why someone would want to kill his mother.

"This is just ridiculous," he told reporters that weekend. "It's uncalled for. Now, my mom can't watch her grandson grow up. I'm glad she had those days with him, but she could have had many more. Some bastard took that away."

Although she lived in Covington, Pete Revere said his mother knew his neighborhood and had visited their home several times.

He said he and his wife moved to Hennessey Street in September of 1997. He said that neither had heard of nor witnessed any violence in the community and that a New Orleans police officer lived on the corner where Lynn had parked the car.

The Monday following the murder, flags flew at half-staff over the St. Tammany Parish Courthouse in Covington, where Lynn worked nearly 30 years.

"There are two types of people in this world, givers and takers," said Judge Brady Fitzsimmons. "And she was a giver. She was tough on the outside, but warm, gentle, and compassionate on the inside. She demanded excellence from the judges she worked for and demanded excellence from the people who worked around her."

Before seeking a judgeship, Fitzsimmons served as an Assistant District Attorney, alongside Margaret Coon, who later lived in his neighborhood.

Lynn Nunez also worked with Margaret Coon.

Lynn served the 22nd District Court nearly three decades, first as a deputy clerk of court and then as a court reporter. In her last 18 years, she served as a court reporter for the court of now-retired Judge Fitzsimmons, as well as the courts of Judges Thomas Tanner and Patricia Hedges.

"Her murder makes no sense. I can't think of anything that has shocked me more," Judge Hedges told journalists in 1998. "Everyone loved Lynn. She was an efficient, excellent court reporter with a wonderful sense of humor."

"Of all the people this could happen to." Judge Hedges said Lynn, the mother of two grown sons, was the "backbone of her family," who helped raise nieces and nephews.

Many at the courthouse recalled talking to Lynn the Friday before she died. She said she looked forward to the weekend visit with her only grandchild, Thomas Parker Revere.

"She was showing me pictures of her grandbaby, and she was so excited," said deputy clerk of court Theresa Duck, who had known Lynn for 34 years. "What happened was awful," Theresa said, almost crying. "I still can't believe it."

"It was horrible and senseless," former state Judge A. Clayton James said. "It was like she was just in the wrong place at the wrong time."

One fellow court reporter said she felt shaken by Lynn's death, but declined to discuss her colleague with reporters. "I'm just sickened by this," she said. "But I want to keep [what I say] personal."

Detective Joseph Catalanotto, who led the murder investigation, told reporters in April of 1998 that police removed nothing from the car, and, he believed, that no one else had either. He said investigators had no motive; no clues as to who might have killed Lynn Nunez, and today, more than 20 years later, New Orleans police confirm that nothing has changed.

Lynn's family held her funeral on Wednesday following her death. The E. J. Fielding Funeral Home hosted the service at 2260 West 21st Avenue in Covington.

They buried Lynn in Pinecrest Memorial Gardens next to the funeral home, and with her, many believe, they buried someone's secrets.

Peter Revere

With new information from readers and other sources, this chapter evolved from the Bayou Justice column entitled "Police suspect son in Lynn Nunez murder," initially published in south Louisiana newspapers on Thursday, September 26, 2019.

ON A SUNDAY MORNING in 1998, Gary Nunez took a call from an officer with the Covington Police Department. The caller told Gary his mom's car had been involved in an automobile accident in New Orleans. Gary asked if his mom was in the car, and the officer responded, "No."

Multiple thoughts filled Gary's mind. His mom had left for a wedding in New Orleans the night before. Having worked around the St. Tammany Parish courthouse for nearly 30 years, she knew not to leave the scene of an accident. Even if at fault, Lynn Nunez knew too many influential people not to stay and face the music. Gary decided something must have happened to his mother.

At that moment, the caller asked, "Is there another family member in the house with you?"

"I knew what that meant," Gary told me Monday night, as we sat in what was once his mother's dining room. "I gave the phone to my dad and watched the look on his face, and then I just kind of lost it."

As a 20-year veteran of the St. Tammany Parish Sheriff's Office, Gary said he could never imagine delivering news in that manner. "Not so much as a knock on the door," Gary said. "Just a phone call."

"Afterwards, they told me Mom never had a chance to get out of the car, never saw it was coming," Gary said. "She didn't have a chance to turn the car off."

Later that same Sunday morning, Pete Revere received a similar call from Covington PD at his home in New Orleans. The officer told him the lie about the accident and asked if he knew his mother's location or the reason for her trip to the city.

Pete told the officer he expected his mother the night before; following a wedding reception, she planned to spend the night with him, his wife, and their newborn son, but she never arrived. Pete assumed his mother had changed her mind and drove home instead.

The officer hung up the phone without telling Pete that someone had shot his mother in the head with a small-caliber weapon the night before, or that the shot came as she parked her car less than 30 feet from Pete's driveway.

Sometime later, Pete's aunt called Pete's wife with the news. By then, the Orleans Parish Sheriff's Office had cleaned up the crime scene, removed Lynn's body, and had her beige 1996 Nissan Altima towed to impound.

"The next time I heard from the police," Pete told me Monday night, "Orleans Parish read me my rights and asked me to take a polygraph test."

"All these years," Pete said. "They haven't found who killed Momma because they haven't stopped looking at me." When Lynn Nunez died, Pete worked at a strip club in the French Quarter and wondered if police profiling had led investigators to decide his guilt without judge or jury.

"We seldom hear from investigators," Gary said. "About five to seven have contacted me at different times over the years, usually when they pass the case to someone else, but it always ends the same. They come back saying my brother did it. I tell them I don't think so, that her death had something to do with her job, something she knew. They always seem to listen and leave headed for the courthouse. Shortly after, they stop returning my calls."

A few years back, Gary and Pete decided the only way to get the police to look for their mom's real killer was for Pete to clear his name. "I offered to take the polygraph, whatever they wanted," Pete said, "But they wouldn't give me the time of day. They'd made up their mind and took the easy way out instead of doing their jobs."

"I think Lynn knew something that someone didn't want to get out," Lynn's sister, Gale Bennett, told a television station in 2016. "We still pray this will be solved," she said. "Sometimes, I go down the road, crying, praying God will send someone to help us."

Gale's daughter, Kelly Bennett Feltes, lived with Lynn Nunez before her murder. "I had lived with Aunt Lynn almost three years when it happened," Kelly told me this week. "We were very close."

"I think about her looking down on us sometimes," she said. "I know she's proud of the boys. I hope I've made her proud, too. She used to tell Mom that I was the daughter she never had."

"Aunt Lynn was so charismatic and loyal to a fault, but a force to be reckoned with once you upset her. She'd make it her business to let you know it."

However, Kelly said something at work had her aunt unusually stressed in the weeks leading up to her death. "She kept things to herself until she had to go to the emergency room with health issues related to work," Kelly said. "She had been upset about something. I don't know what, but she said something once about always looking over her shoulder. Anyway, the hospital said she had a TIA, a mini-stroke caused by stress."

A mini-stroke or transient ischemic attack (TIA) occurs when part of the brain experiences a temporary lack of blood flow. This event causes stroke-like symptoms that usually resolve within 24 hours.

"I asked her why she was so stressed," Kelly said, "But all she'd say was 'I can't tell you, Baby Girl. I don't want anything to happen to you.' "

Gary Nunez recalled his mom worrying about a grand jury investigation in the months leading up to her death. "I'm not lying to the grand jury for them," Lynn told her son. "And I'm certainly not going down for them."

"Momma knew a lot of stuff about a lot of people around here," Pete added. "That's why she's not here."

This week, I also spoke with Margaret Coon's first cousin, Henson Coon, III, and his wife, Tamie Mosley Coon, residents of West Monroe.

"With most of the older ones gone," Henson said, "We're all that's left to see justice for Margaret Ann, and we are determined to do what we can. My uncle fought too hard just to let it go."

"Margaret Ann and Lynn Nunez were very close," Tamie told me. "They worked together and had lunch together often. They probably had dirt on the same people, and we think that's what got them killed."

Henson Coon talked about his uncle, how much time and money "Web Junior" had spent attempting to track down his daughter's killer before his death in 2004. "He felt certain it was a mob hit, but he didn't know who hired it done," Henson remembered.

St. Tammany Parish Sheriff's Deputy, Sergeant. Gary Nunez echoed Henson's words. "Mom's [homicide] was a professional hit. I am certain of that."

Next, Bayou Justice looks more closely at the 22nd Judicial District judges and attorneys who Lynn Nunez and Margaret Ann Coon worked with, starting with the grand jury investigation underway when someone murdered Lynn Nunez.

Judge Brady Fitzsimmons

With new information from readers and other sources, this chapter evolved from the Bayou Justice column entitled "DA wanted Lynn Nunez to talk," initially published in south Louisiana newspapers on Tuesday, September 30, 2019.

IN THE SPRING OF 1998, 51-year-old Lynn Nunez, a veteran court reporter for the 22nd Judicial District, told relatives she expected the district attorney to subpoena her to appear before a grand jury. There, she planned to surprise authority and tell the truth no matter who suggested she do otherwise.

Unfortunately, before Lynn's subpoena arrived, someone took her life.

This week, Bayou Justice recounts the history of that grand jury investigation and the indictments that followed, as we consider how the case might have ended differently had Lynn Nunez lived to testify.

Four years earlier, Walter Reed, District Attorney for both St. Tammany and Washington Parishes, sent letters to all justices of the peace and constables in those parishes. He asked each of them to vote for Brady Fitzsimmons in his bid for a 10-year term in the state's First Circuit Appeals Court in Baton Rouge. The letter went on to ask all 22 JOPs to support Fitzsimmons and to promote his credentials among their constituents.

In addition to being unethical, the letter was also illegal, according to Shirley Gottschalck, then President of the Louisiana Justices of the Peace and Constables Association.

"It was more than against the law," she said. "This was a DA. He should know the law. It was embarrassing."

On October 1, 1994, Judge Fitzsimmons won that District C seat on the Appeals court and vacated his position with the 22nd Judicial Court, where he had worked closely with Court Reporter Lynn Nunez.

When a family member asked her why she worked so hard supporting the judge's Appeals court campaign, Lynn responded, "I couldn't think of another way to get the bastard out of here."

In 1995, two of Reed's sitting assistant district attorneys ran for Fitzsimmons' vacant seat, along with a former assistant district attorney, a Madisonville defense attorney, and a Slidell law clerk named Patricia Hedges.

Sheriff Pat Canulette and DA Walter Reed endorsed former Assistant District Attorney David Knight. However, Patricia Hedges told voters, "I am not a politician, and I am not part of their good ole boy network here. Cutting no deals, I am asking for your vote purely on my experience working as a clerk for Judge Clayton James and on my strong desire to make the judicial system here independent from the controlling influence of the sheriff and the DA."

In campaign ads, Hedges' supporters wrote, "There are three separate and distinct branches of our government: legislative, executive, and judicial. We violate the spirit of our constitution when any single branch controls or infringes upon another. District Attorneys and sheriffs should not control judges. We must stop this in the 22nd Judicial District."

Patricia Hedges entered a runoff with David Knight, and the other lawyers formerly in the race endorsed the Walter Reed favorite. However, Patricia Hedges still won the race, and Lynn Nunez loved working with her.

All went well until October 20, 1997.

On that day, Walter Reed retaliated, calling a press conference to tell reporters that he had asked the state to appoint a special prosecutor from northeastern Louisiana to investigate allegations of wrongdoing involving Judge Hedges.

Reed said his office had recused itself from the investigation and turned the matter over to the attorney general's office, which named District Attorney James D. "Buddy" Caldwell of Madison Parish to head the investigation.

Reed then introduced Caldwell, who announced, "The findings of my investigation will be presented to a grand jury early next year."

Judge Hedges told reporters the following day that no one had told her anything about the investigation. Still, investigators with the DA's office had questioned her staff, co-workers, and colleagues close to her.

The judge told a *Times-Picayune* reporter, "This investigation is nothing more than a political vendetta by Walter Reed, who's been out to get me ever since I defeated David Knight when the DA backed him in the 1995 election."

Judge Hedges said she did nothing improper, unethical, or illegal, and that she had never taken money or been influenced by any other means regarding decisions she made on the bench.

"The reason I ran for this job is to be a good, independent judge," she said. "And if the powers-that-be here find that disturbing, then so be it. If they want a fight, I know how to fight."

The judge also explained to journalists how differences between her and Reed continued after she defeated the district attorney's candidate for her judgeship. Shortly after she took office, she said, Judge Hedges found prosecutor Chip Bankston in contempt of court for not concluding a misdemeanor case.

The next day, the judge said, Reed stormed into her office. "He physically threatened and verbally abused me," she said. "He pitched a fit."

Judge Hedges said she let the incident go and did not file a complaint nor talk to the press when reporters questioned her about the incident.

Walter Reed told *The St. Tammany Farmer* that he vaguely remembered an incident in which he and Hedges had "a misunderstanding and disagreement."

"But that incident is over," he said, "And we do have a working relationship. I try to maintain working relationships with all the judges."

Reed insisted that the special investigation was not politically motivated.

"I'm trying to stay out of this," he said. "So, I just can't say anything more about it."

Six months after Reed's press conference, Lynn Nunez told family members that someone wanted her to lie to a grand jury, but she had no plans to do so.

One month later, an unidentified assailant shot Lynn in the head with a small-caliber weapon, and six months after Lynn's murder, *The Baton Rouge Advocate* reported:

"Judge Patricia Hedges of the 22nd Judicial District Court was named in a seven-count indictment Thursday that included allegations of public bribery, extortion, conspiracy to commit extortion, and malfeasance in office."

"Hedges' lawyer, Lewis Unglesby of Baton Rouge, said the indictment was the result of 'some kind of goofy vendetta by a group of bizarre prosecutors who don't understand the legal system and are running rampant in St. Tammany and Washington Parish.' "

"When this grand jury investigation began, Hedges said she had done nothing unethical or illegal, and that the probe was the result of a political vendetta against her by District Attorney Walter Reed.

Reed subsequently withdrew and referred the case to the state Attorney General's Office, which assigned the investigation to Madison Parish District Attorney James D. Caldwell, who said this week that Hedges had been under scrutiny by a special grand jury for the past year."

When Lynn's family members told me of Lynn's fears related to "some grand jury investigation," they had no evidence that a grand jury investigation had been underway at the time she died.

Today, at least, we can confirm that Lynn Nunez's fears were justified.

Walter Reed

With new information from readers and other sources, this chapter evolved from the Bayou Justice column entitled "Judge exonerated; Walter Reed jailed," initially published in south Louisiana newspapers on Thursday, October 3, 2019.

JUST MONTHS AFTER DISTRICT Attorney Walter Reed launched what became a grand jury investigation of Judge Patricia Hedges, Lynn Nunez, the judge's primary court reporter, told relatives someone was pressuring her to lie to a grand jury — and then someone killed her.

For a year and a half, Patricia Hedges went to work amid allegations of being a crooked judge and that she had accepted money in exchange for her rulings. She ignored accusations that she treated criminal defendants differently, based on her friendships with specific attorneys, and that she had attempted to ruin the reputation of a political opponent.

That all changed less than a year after Lynn Nunez died.

On February 26, 1999, without warning and with little explanation, ad-hoc District Attorney James D. "Buddy" Caldwell of Madison Parish dropped all of the charges against Patricia Hedges.

That morning, he stood on the front lawn of the St. Tammany Parish Courthouse "Justice Center" explaining to reporters — and a handful of people wearing "I Love Judge Hedges" buttons — why he had decided to drop the charges.

He said he had been duty-bound to take up the case and to seek an indictment against the judge after reviewing evidence from Walter Reed's office that suggested her guilt. Information recently provided by the defense, he said, convinced him that reasonable doubt would prevent a conviction.

"Everything's been explained now," Caldwell said. "It was all a mistake. It's as simple as that."

Caldwell then insisted that the indictments were not the fruit of a vendetta by longtime pal District Attorney Walter Reed and said Reed did the right thing seeking the grand jury investigation.

When the grand jury brought the seven-count indictment against the judge in October of 1998, her attorney, Lewis Unglesby, said his client felt like the bewildered protagonist of "Alice in Wonderland."

"It did feel like I had fallen down the rabbit hole," Hedges told reporters from an office at the Washington Parish Courthouse. She said allegations that she was a corrupt judge who played favorites angered her.

From the beginning, many in St. Tammany were skeptical that the charges against the judge were legitimate, and so she remained popular. In fact, following her indictment, a deputy at the parish jail booking desk greeted her with a hug when she arrived for fingerprinting.

"It bothered me," she said. "I think anybody who's accused of a crime would feel the same way. I was completely incensed that anybody would think that I would take a bribe."

Investigators had accused Hedges of not only two counts of public bribery but also extortion, conspiracy to commit extortion, malfeasance of office, attempted malfeasance of office, and the destruction of public records.

Walter Reed, who kept a low profile after Buddy Caldwell took over the case, was conspicuously away from the courthouse that day. The DA was in Franklinton, a guest speaker at the inauguration of state Senator Jerry Thomas.

Judge Hedges was not at Caldwell's press conference either, but her husband attended, taking pictures to send to their children.

"I was attending a conference in New Orleans and called the office to check-in," the judge said later. "My secretary told me the charges were dropped. I felt stunned. I didn't know what to say."

Although the court had barred her from hearing criminal cases following the indictment, she never stepped down as district judge. The state Supreme Court granted her request to swap her criminal docket for Judge William Burns' civil docket, and she continued working.

Following her vindication, Judge Hedges said she held no grudges against Walter Reed. She said when she resumed her spot on the criminal bench, she planned to listen to each case dispassionately and apply the law regardless of the attorney representing the state or the defense.

"All people are equal before the law," she said.

In 2000, the court ordered the state of Louisiana to reimburse Hedges nearly $200,000 in attorney's fees, the same amount in salary the 22nd Judicial District paid Walter Reed his last year in office. To date, Reed remains the highest-paid official in St. Tammany Parish history, and Hedges is on record as the first woman judge to hold court in the 22nd Judicial District.

In 2016, a jury found Walter Reed guilty of 18 federal counts in a corruption trial, where, according to the Associated Press, prosecutors portrayed him as "a greedy, grasping conniver who repeatedly sought to use his public office for private gain."

In the end, a trial that lasted only two weeks destroyed a public service record of 30 years.

The jury found Reed guilty of mail fraud, wire fraud, money laundering, making false statements on his federal income tax returns, and conspiracy to commit wire fraud and to launder money.

Federal sentencing guidelines called for a sentence of 12 years, but the judge sentencing Reed, US District Judge Eldon Fallon, was not bound by those guidelines, and he had a reputation for being hard on white-collar criminals.

According to former Federal prosecutor Matt Chester, Judge Fallon typically took a dim view of white-collar defendants with advanced degrees, high public positions, or other advantages. He told *The Baton Rouge Advocate* that Fallon sentenced former New Orleans City Hall tech vendor Mark St. Pierre to 17 years in prison for a minor role in a kickback scheme.

In court, Chester said, the judge harped on the various privileges St. Pierre had enjoyed because of his position in the public trust.

However, surprising everyone, Judge Fallon treated Walter Reed somewhat differently. Still, at that time, the public knew nothing of Fallon receiving the following letter from a retired friend in Sarasota, Florida:

"Dear Judge Fallon:"

"I pen this letter regarding Walter Reed. I have told Walter that I believe he committed numerous ethics violations. However, I do not believe that he committed any crime(s)."

"While it has been many years since we have seen each other, I have, and will always, hold you in great esteem. I believe you to be both a scholar of the Law and a good-hearted person. Thus, when you sentence Walter, as a person who worked for him for several years, I implore you to call upon those two outstanding traits I know that you have, knowledge and empathy. I humbly request that you consider this comment that a distinguished black gentleman told me when I first ran for judge: I don't want Justice for my people; I want mercy."

"I am grateful to you for reading this note and for the tremendous impact you have had on my life."

"God bless you, Judge Brady Fitzsimmons, retired, Louisiana Court of Appeals."

Judge Fallon sentenced Reed to only four years in the minimum-security federal correctional institution Forbes Magazine described this way:

"Perched amid the rolling Blue Ridge Mountains of West Virginia, Morgantown is one of the most picturesque camps in the system. Inmates say it is not unusual for them to awake in the morning to the sight of deer grazing on the compound."

Lynn Nunez died on a Saturday night, March 14, 1998.

According to relatives interviewed by police detectives, investigators believe Lynn parked her car, a beige 1996 Nissan Altima, near a curb in the 200th block of South Hennessey Street.

Then, as she put the car in park, someone fired a shot through the glass of her drivers-side door. Lynn ducked, forcing her upper body down in the direction of the passenger-side floorboard. As she did, a second shot rang out, piercing her neck and severing her carotid artery.

Police found Lynn's car running. Both the glove box and the vehicle's trunk appeared to have been opened, but Lynn's purse and valuables remained untouched.

Another family member, one who worked at the courthouse with Lynn, warned me about Walter Reed.

"Someone may have hired the hit, but it wasn't Walter," she said. "He loved our family. Whenever someone in the family got into trouble, Walter was the one she called, and he always did what he could. Somebody else killed her or hired it done."

Evidence is difficult to come by in this case, but rumors abound.

Some tell stories of Lynn's handyman neighbor, a stalker so obsessed with Lynn that she filed a protection order against him. Others suggest I look into the theories of Rusty Burns and his subsequent "suicide."

Three different acquaintances of hers claimed Lynn had a personal relationship with a married man, and according to one of them, the man's wife learned of the affair less than two months before Lynn's murder.

I'll have to revisit this case when I have something more concrete.

Frankie Richard

With new information from readers and other sources, this chapter evolved from the Bayou Justice column entitled "Did book talk nearly get Frankie Richard killed?" initially published in south Louisiana newspapers on Tuesday, October 8, 2019.

ON A MONDAY AFTERNOON, July 29, 2019, after weeks of discussion through social media, I met Frankie Richard at the Denham Springs rental property, off Eden Church Road, where he lived for over a year.

"I got out of Jennings after my mother died," he told me. "I lived in Morse, but the press found me there after a while. I moved in with family here and told everybody I was in Baton Rouge. Life got peaceful when people couldn't find me no more."

Frankie described his health as bad, saying he did not know how much longer he had to live and wanted the truth reported while he still had his faculties. Frankie told me he wanted to document his knowledge of the eight infamous unsolved murders in Jefferson Davis Parish and the events that led up to them, including all he knew about the parish's dirty cops, prostitution, and the Jennings drug trade.

Before our meeting ended, I agreed to help Frankie record what he knew; ultimately organizing and editing his recollections into manuscript form.

Two weeks later, Frankie sent me a text saying he had moved back to Morse. He ensured me that he planned to continue working on his book, but that he had to take care of some business first.

In Morse, he bragged to friends and family about the publishing project and his goals, and then he overdosed on Heroin.

One relative told me, "He started running his head. That's why they gave him the bad dope. He thinks they won't take him out because of what he knows. He's just been lucky so far."

According to an affidavit dated September 11, 2019, Morse Police responded to a 911 call that evening, a woman saying Frankie had gone into convulsions. Arriving at the home, officers allegedly found a meth pipe and torch, along with other drugs, including crack cocaine, oxycodone, methamphetamine, and Xanax.

The woman at the house, according to the police report, told investigators that Frankie Richard had been paying her in Roxicodone pills to have sex with other men.

Law enforcement authorities in the Jennings Police Department and the Jefferson Davis Parish Sheriff's Office long-ago labeled Frankie, a person of interest in the unexplained deaths of eight women. Residents discovered the bodies in drainage canals and along rural backroads between May 2005 and August 2009.

These women, Loretta Lynn Chaisson Lewis, 28; Ernestine Marie Daniels Patterson, 30, Kristen Gary Lopez, 21; Whitnei Dubois, 26; Laconia "Muggy" Brown, 23; Crystal Shay Benoit Zeno, 24; Brittney Gary, 17; and Necole Guillory, 26, according to the sheriff's office, all knew each other and walked the streets near Frankie Richard's neighborhood.

When doctors released Frankie from the hospital in September, police took him to the Acadia Parish jail, where he remains today pending an $86,000 bond — coincidentally, that's one thousand dollars more than the current Crime Stoppers reward offered for information on the eight homicides.

Another coincidence: Frankie's arrest came on the same day that Showtime aired part one of "Murder in the Bayou," a five-part documentary series on the Jennings Eight murders. The series was based in part on author Ethan Brown's book, "Murder in the Bayou: Who Killed the Women Known as the Jeff Davis 8?"

According to Ethan Brown, Frankie Richard had relationships with six of the eight victims and was the last person to see at least two of them alive. However, contrary to police assertions, Brown does not believe these killings were the work of a serial killer.

A multi-agency police task force filed charges against Frankie and his niece, Hannah Conner, in May of 2007, when a witness accused the two of killing Kristen Lopez. The witness later recanted, saying police investigators coached her to lie.

Police released Frankie and Hannah quietly late one night, and the witness later moved to California.

"I have told them everything that I know, and that is not a lot when it comes to what happened to them girls," Frankie told reporters after his release. "But God knows I didn't do that."

In his book, Ethan Brown says some of the women spoke to the police about the murders and ended up dead themselves. He cites three anonymous sources who said politician Charles Boustany, a U.S. Representative from 2005 to 2017, hired some of the murdered women, who he believes were prostitutes and drug addicts.

"Murder on the Bayou" describes a motel where some of the victims applied their trade, and according to the book, Martin Guillory, a field representative for Boustany, ran the motel.

Brown depicts Frankie Richard as a pimp working out of the motel's bar. In the Showtime documentary, Brown refers to the bar as an ATM for withdrawing drugs and sex with Frankie Richard, the bank manager.

Both Brown and Showtime investigators also interviewed members of the police task force.

"Frankie Richard was somebody who was known to associate with known prostitutes in the area. He was known to be involved in the drug world in the Jennings area and also had a violent past," Commander Ramby Cormier of the Jefferson Davis Parish Sheriff's Office said in the Showtime documentary.

Frankie admitted on camera that he knew all eight women, but he insisted that he did not kill them.

"I did not have anything to do with any of them girls' deaths," he said. "These girls lost their lives because they saw something, heard something, knew something that they were not supposed to know."

Jennings

With new information from readers and other sources, this chapter evolved from the Bayou Justice column entitled "9 deaths in Jennings, what we know so far," initially published in south Louisiana newspapers on Tuesday, October 10, 2019.

IN LATE JULY 2019, Frankie Richard, suspected by some to be a serial killer, met with me in Denham Springs and asked me to edit his memoirs documenting his relationship with the victims of eight mysterious deaths in Jefferson Davis Parish.

According to police, a little over a month later, he overdosed on a bad — perhaps "tainted" — batch of Heroin.

Today, Frankie Richard lives behind bars, and concerned relatives worry he may not leave the Acadia Parish Jail alive.

Tomorrow night, Showtime concludes a 5-part documentary series recapping the presumed murders of the eight victims found near Jennings in Jefferson Davis Parish.

Today, Bayou Justice recaps what we know so far.

The documentary series — "Murder in the Bayou" — tells the stories of eight women who lived near the small town of Jennings, Louisiana. Each died between May 2005 and August 2009, and someone dumped their bodies into bayous and drainage canals alongside the rural backroads of Jefferson Davis Parish.

However, the documentary pointed out, in 1998, near the same rural town, police found another woman, Sheila Comeaux, savagely beaten and left for dead — hospitalized for a year before eventually succumbing to her injuries.

Sheila's daughter, Lakesha Myers, told Showtime cameras that even though the brutal attack occurred seven years before the first known victims, she believes someone in Jennings can connect her mother's death to the others.

From 2005 to 2009, residents found the bodies of eight women in or around Jennings. All of the women moved in the same social circles and lived what Jefferson Davis Parish Sheriff Ricky Edwards deemed a "high-risk lifestyle" that included drugs and prostitution.

Lakesha Myers believes her mother led a similar lifestyle and worked as a police informant — as did the other victims.

Sheila Comeaux died on March 19, 1999.

Loretta Lynn Chaisson-Lewis died six years later, shortly after telling family members that the Jennings police arranged for her to spy on a drug deal for them. She was 28-years old.

A fisherman found her nude body floating in a canal five miles outside of Jennings in the east fork of the Grand Marais off Louisiana Highway 1026. Although examiners reported finding significant amounts of cocaine and alcohol in her system, Loretta's cause of death remains unknown.

On June 18, 2005, the body of 30-year-old Ernestine Marie Daniels Patterson turned up in a canal near Louisiana Highway 102, just five miles south of Loretta's location. Like Loretta, examiners found drugs in her system. However, someone had also cut her throat, and the wounds on her wrists suggested she fought violently before death. Police do classify Ernestine's case as a homicide.

Police believe 21-year-old Kristen Gary Lopez died on March 18, 2007. Like Loretta, they found her nude body in water, wearing a single sock on her left foot. Decomposition, police say, prevented an official cause-of-death determination.

A driver spotted 26-year-old Whitnei Dubois's naked body hurriedly discarded near the side of a public road south of Welsh on May 12, 2007. Again, examiners found drugs in her system but listed the cause-of-death as undetermined.

On May 29, 2008, another driver found Laconia Shontel "Muggy" Brown, 23, near a roadside with her partially nude body doused in bleach. Like Ernestine, someone had slit her throat. She had seven slashes on her neck and another three cuts behind her right ear.

On September 11, 2008, hunters reported a foul smell in a wooded area, where authorities following up found 24-year-old Crystal Shay Benoit Zeno's skeletal remains. Due to the state of the body's decomposition, examiners did not identify the skeleton as Crystal's until November 7. The examiner listed her cause-of-death as undetermined.

A video camera recorded 17-year-old Brittney Gary at a dollar store on November 2, 2008. Two weeks later, police found her body near a highway in Jennings.

In both cases, Crystal's and Brittney's, a police officer claimed to have identified the victim by a tattoo, although the medical examiner said both corpses had decomposed too much to determine the cause-of-death.

In 2007, while Frankie Richard was in jail on an unrelated rape charge, police reportedly questioned him regarding the murder of Ernestine Patterson and later the death of Kristen Lopez. In the Lopez case, they filed second-degree murder charges.

Later, Police dropped both the rape and second-degree murder charges when the witnesses against him recanted.

Since that day, Frankie has vehemently denied involvement and insisted that he had no evidence against the perpetrators.

Sheriff Edwards, now out of office, said in a recorded interview that Frankie knew the victims and met with two of them just days before they went missing. However, the former sheriff said, Frankie was in a rehab center in Shreveport when one of the women died and in jail when one of the others came up missing.

In December 2008, 14 local, state, and national law-enforcement agencies formed a multi-jurisdictional task force to investigate the Jennings deaths. Police hoped establishing this team would ease the fears of residents and assure the victims' families that investigators had not forgotten their loved ones.

Unfortunately, the task force had the opposite effect.

The team was barely a month old when the Louisiana State Police reportedly investigated two of its members. Ultimately, a state ethics board fined veteran Jefferson Davis Parish detective Warren Gary $10,000 after he purchased a truck allegedly involved in one of the deaths. Also, Jennings PD fired another task force agent, Detective Paula Guillory, after she reportedly misplaced $3,000 confiscated in a raid.

Interviewed on the Showtime documentary, Lorritta Elizabeth LaCoste later named Chief Investigator and Parish Jail Warden Terrie Guillory in a wrongful death suit. Officers shot and killed her boyfriend, a police informant named Steven Thomas Gunter, in his Lake Arthur home in June of 2007.

On August 19, 2009, seven hours after family members in Jefferson Davis Parish reported her missing, highway workers discovered the body of 26-year-old Necole Jean Guillory at the bottom of a hill near Egan Ballpark in Acadia Parish. She was the only victim found outside of Jefferson Davis Parish and the only victim killed after the creation of the task force. Examiners have released no official ruling on Necole's cause-of-death.

Concluding Friday night, the Showtime documentary series, "Murder in the Bayou: Who Killed the Women Known as the Jeff Davis 8?" follows Ethan Brown's book of the same name while adding new information uncovered by Ethan Brown since the book's publication.

As of this writing, Frankie Richard remains alive and incarcerated in Acadia Parish with family members concerned that he could be the next to die.

Next, I share my interview with Toby Leger, the man who leased the now-infamous Boudreaux Inn, a small motel and bar where Frankie Richard and "the Jennings Eight" allegedly conducted business.

The Boudreaux Inn

With new information from readers and other sources, this chapter evolved from the Bayou Justice column entitled "Owner recalls Boudreaux's drugs, sex, and video poker," initially published in south Louisiana newspapers on Tuesday, October 15, 2019.

JUST WEEKS BEFORE THE 2016 election, book publisher Scribner, a Simon & Schuster imprint, released a book accusing Dr. Charles Boustany, the Republican frontrunner in a Louisiana congressional race, of sleeping with prostitutes.

Coincidentally, years earlier, David Vitter, another respected Louisiana Republican, had vacated that same bible belt congressional seat to run for governor. He lost when a pricey Washington, D.C. call girl named Wendy Ellis publicly accused him of sleeping with her, getting her pregnant, and forcing her to have an abortion.

Unlike the high-priced sex worker in Vitter's case, Boustany's accusers had no identification. They were simply three "unnamed sources" in a book released less than two months before the election.

Of course, with little time to refute the claims, Boustany lost the election, and his opponent, John Neely Kennedy, insisted that he knew nothing about the book or the accusations against Boustany.

Kennedy won the election, and Boustany, who had served four terms in the United States House of Representatives, left politics in disgrace.

"Politics as usual in Louisiana. All part of the game." That is how former Police Juror Toby Leger of Church Point described these events when I spoke to him last month. "The October Surprise has been sinking political campaigns as long as I can remember, but this is different because the lie muddies the water, preventing families from getting justice for eight murdered girls."

Between 2005 and 2009, Jennings, Louisiana residents found the bodies of eight women, all involved with drugs or prostitution, according to police, dumped in swamps and canals, most in a state of decomposition that made the cause of death difficult or impossible to determine.

According to Author Ethan Brown in his book "Murder in the Bayou: Who Killed the Women Known as the Jeff Davis 8?" Boustany slept with two of the victims at 15189 Highway 26, the location of a little motel called the Boudreaux Inn.

From November 1999 to January 2009, Toby Leger was Chief Executive Officer of Tri-Tech, LLC, the partnership company that leased the motel.

"It makes no sense to me," Toby said. "This author had a solid reputation as an investigative reporter. My name appears in his book, so tell me why, after all these years, have I never gotten a phone call from the guy. You are the first journalist to ask to speak to me."

Instead, Ethan's book focused on Toby's partner, longtime Boustany aide, Martin "Big G" Guillory, who worked part-time for the congressman.

"I feel bad sometimes," said Toby. "Leasing a place was my idea, just a side job to make some extra money. I talked Big G into finding us a location, and then he introduced me to Justin Boudreaux, who he knew from his route. After that book came out, Big G offered to resign, but Boustany's people fired him, just for show, when Boustany sued the book publisher. Big G lost his job all over nothing, just gossip."

The "coda" chapter in Ethan's book appears at the end and reads disjointed from the buildup in the rest of the book. Toby believes someone pulled strings to get Ethan's book published after lying to the author about Boustany's sexual escapades.

"Big G and I worked for an amusement company, servicing video poker machines," Toby said. "We each had a route and could see all the money being made by the customers on our route. We didn't make all that much servicing the machines, so I got the idea to rent a building somewhere and lease our own machines. That was the whole business idea right there."

In Ethan's book, he wrote there was no evidence that Martin Guillory or Charles Boustany were involved in the murders, saying three anonymous individuals told him that the congressman had slept with two of the victims at Toby's motel.

The Boudreaux Inn, according to Toby, had 14 small rooms, a small café, and a bar. The small bar, he said, had 12 barstools, three tables, and nine chairs.

"Dr. Boustany was a heart surgeon turned politician," Toby said. "The man lived in Washington, D.C. When that happened with Vitter, the networks interviewed several Washington prostitutes on TV. They looked like Playboy models. You tell me. If Boustany wanted to pay for a good time, why would he come all the way to Jennings?"

In 2005, Louisiana voters elected Dr. Boustany to represent the state in Congress. He served the Seventh Congressional District, which included Jefferson Davis Parish, until 2013, when redistricting merged that territory into a redrawn Third Congressional District.

Boustany served on the House Ways and Means Committee and championed tax-cuts and boosting energy production in Louisiana. No one accused the congressional representative of any impropriety before the release of Ethan Brown's book.

The author said in a recent television documentary that he learned of a possible connection between Boustany and the eight murder victims from Frankie Richard, whom police describe as "a person of interest" in the murders. Richard told Ethan on the phone, "Boustany, you need to investigate him." Then he asked if Ethan was recording the conversation and hung up.

"Someone said Boustany stopped at the café once on the campaign trail, answering questions, and shaking hands," Toby said. "I don't know; I didn't see him, and politics was something Big G and I both enjoyed. I think he would have told me if Boustany had been there."

"I went to the Boudreaux Inn usually once a week for payroll," Toby said. "Frankie Richard was always there. He lived in the motel for some time, but he hung out in the bar even after he moved out."

"Big G saw him more often than I did, but not that much," he said. "We had managers running the place. We kept a day manager and a night manager. Big G just stopped by a few times a week to service the poker machines, since they were on his route."

"From what I could tell, Frankie was just a lowlife hustler, always bragging about drugs and women," Toby said. "The only time I talked to him was when he borrowed money, which was often, but I've got to say this. He always paid me back when he said he would."

I asked Toby Leger if he knew any of the eight murdered girls.

"Loretta, the first victim," he said, "I called the cops and had her removed at our grand opening. After that, she kept coming around, always arguing with somebody. That kind of thing happened all the time, and not just with her."

"Customers drank and did drugs. They even had a dice game going in one of the rooms, but this wasn't some organized crime operation where the owners got a cut. We rented single rooms for $29 and double rooms for $34. Our profits came from that and those few poker machines."

According to Dun & Bradstreet Corporation, a company that provides financial data, analytics, and insights for businesses, the Boudreaux Inn motel, café, and bar averaged $270,000 in sales annually. It maintained a staff of less than one dozen people.

"In that guy's book, he talks about the police reports, listing fistfights and catfights, jealous husbands finding their wives at the motel in a threesome. I want to challenge him to pull police reports on any other rural motel and bar. See if he can find one that doesn't have those same headaches."

"In interviews, Frankie Richard said he ran women out of the Budget Inn and Holiday Inn. I don't know why they try to make the Boudreaux Inn seem any different."

The Boudreaux Inn closed in 2009 after the owner died, a new truck stop siphoned business, and the owner's family sought to discontinue Toby's lease.

"There is one thing that puzzles me, though," Toby said. "One of the victims, Ernestine Patterson, worked for us, cleaning rooms. She was a real sweetheart, always happy, wouldn't hurt a fly."

"The book describes all the victims as prostitutes and druggies, but Ernestine was so strait-laced, always talking about church or her kids, taking care never to show any skin. I think she was Seventh Day Adventist or something. She wore more clothes than Pentecostals, for sure."

"I always wondered how she made the list. Did she really make such a drastic lifestyle change, or was her killing something else altogether?"

Regarding the murders of the Jennings or Jeff Davis Eight and the question of whodunit, Toby said, "In South Louisiana, when sex and drugs and police graft lead to murder, the trail usually goes back to the crime syndicates and cartels. Anybody serious about this case needs to look at this I-10 drug traffic and follow the money."

Next, Bayou Justice introduces readers to two suspects in the Jennings Eight murders not mentioned in Ethan Brown's book or any of the various documentaries and news stories on the crimes.

The Other Suspects

With new information from readers and other sources, this chapter evolved from the Bayou Justice column entitled "Jeff Davis 8 suspects nearly forgotten by investigators," initially published in south Louisiana newspapers on Thursday, October 17, 2019.

BETWEEN 2005 AND 2009, someone murdered eight women in Jennings, Louisiana, cutting at least two of their throats and dumping their bodies on roadways and in canals in Jefferson Davis Parish.

Frankie Richard — a suspected drug dealer and admitted drug addict — is the most well-known of the Jeff Davis Eight suspects. Police assert that a witness saw him with victim Kristen Lopez shortly before her death. Some Jennings residents have accused him of being a police informant, and two female jail inmates claimed the Sheriff's Office disposed of the evidence, including a 2006 Chevy Silverado pickup truck, at Frankie Richard's behest.

Often, our news media forgets there are other suspects in this case, "persons of interest" who seldom make the news, including two that writers and producers have never mentioned in the various books and documentaries on the case.

In 2010, Louisiana's 17 Judicial District Court sentenced one of them to 30 years in prison after police accused the man of wielding a knife in two sexual assaults. The accused pleaded guilty to aggravated burglary connected to one of the attacks instead of facing trial.

In 1991, that same man — Brian K. Lasage — lived in Jennings, where a Jefferson Davis Parish court that year convicted him of forcible-rape and sentenced him to 15 years in prison, providing a release date of 2006.

However, an article in the Basile Weekly had him back on the streets of Jennings by November of 2003, and an employee at Allen Correctional Center in Kinder, Louisiana, remembers him still incarcerated there for at least part of 2005.

In 2005, Jennings Police interrogated another "person of interest" after raiding a room at the Holiday Inn in connection with the death of the first victim, Loretta Lewis.

From this man, Brandon Joseph Hebert, Police collected a saliva sample, a Walmart receipt, and two pieces of tissue paper, a black shirt, a pair of blue jean shorts, and a white shirt with cut-off sleeves. From the motel room, they collected an LA ID card, a video poker receipt, two note pads, at least a half dozen rolls of 35-millimeter film, a green cigarette lighter, two beer bottle caps, and a Fujifilm Hi8 videotape.

Two years earlier, investigators charged Brandon Joseph Hebert, then 23-years-old, with possession of child pornography. Today, "Joey" Hebert remains a registered sex offender and resides in Sunset, Louisiana.

In the death of Ernestine Patterson, Police initially charged Byron Chad Jones and Lawrence Nixon — a cousin of the fifth victim, Laconia Brown — with second-degree murder. Unfortunately, the sheriff's office did not test the alleged crime scene until 15 months after Patterson died and found it "failed to demonstrate the presence of blood."

In Jennings, an FBI profiler told reporters in 2007 that the murders there were not likely the work of a serial killer as serial killers typically chose women who did not know or live near each other.

Prostitutes Mary Ann Nichols, Annie Chapman, Elizabeth Stride, Catherine Eddowes, and Mary Jane Kelly would likely disagree. They all lived in the same neighborhood and knew each other well. They drank and did drugs together and occasionally slept under the same roof.

The most infamous serial killer murdered these five women in history, a monster in the newspapers called "Jack, the Ripper."

Authorities never charged Brian K. Lasage with serial murder, only serial rape while wielding a lethal weapon.

In 2010, Lasage, then 40-years-old, lived in Mamou and, if convicted, would have faced a mandatory life sentence for the aggravated rape of a 24-year-old woman assaulted the first week in January of that year. The victim lived on East 37th Place in Cut Off, Louisiana.

Lasage also faced charges of aggravated burglary and sexual battery in connection with an attack on another 24-year-old woman four days later.

As part of the plea bargain, the Lafourche District Attorney's Office agreed not to prosecute him on three charges — aggravated rape, sexual battery and failure to register as a sex offender.

The two women who alleged that Lasage sexually assaulted them agreed to the plea deal provided Lasage would not be eligible for parole.

"To avoid an emotional and lengthy trial, we took a plea agreement which omitted a few of the charges but guaranteed him 30 years behind bars," one of the victims told reporters after the plea hearing concluded.

State law defines aggravated burglary, as it pertains to Lasage's case, as the "unauthorized entering of any inhabited dwelling," where the attacker is armed with a lethal weapon. Lasage approached both women with a knife and received the maximum penalty for that charge.

Though he did not plead guilty to either of the sexual-assault charges, Lasage did admit under oath that he attacked the women with the knife. However, Assistant District Attorney Joe Soignet told District Judge Jerome Barbera that, if Lasage did not agree to the plea bargain, the state would present evidence at trial. He said they would prove the defendant confessed to investigators that he committed both sexual assaults as charged.

"I told [the victims] when I presented the terms he pleaded to, that if they were not 100 percent behind it, I'm not going through with it, and I'm going to trial," Soignet said, and he described both women as "brave."

One of the alleged victims read to the court a victim-impact statement, saying her life forever changed due to Lesage's actions. She and her husband, she said, moved from their home due to the trauma associated with the sexual assault Lasage allegedly committed.

"My sense of security is gone," she said. "For the rest of my life, I will always look over my shoulder."

Lafourche Parish authorities charged Lasage with the sexual assaults in March of 2010 after receiving results from the State Police Crime Lab that proved a footprint lifted from one of the alleged victim's homes matched a shoe Lasage wore during his arrest.

Lafourche Parish Sheriff Craig Webre said Lasage called his victims by their first name, brandished a knife, and concealed his face with an article of clothing during the attacks.

"I am convinced that the streets of Lafourche Parish are much safer because Mr. Lasage is now behind bars," the sheriff said. "And they have been safe since his apprehension."

Following the second alleged assault, deputies released a description of a 2007 Chevy Silverado pickup truck they believed was connected to the case. Webre said a deputy stopped a car matching that description a day later north of Bollinger's Shipyard and identified the driver as Brian K. Lasage.

"The deputy said he appeared to be nervous," Sheriff Webre said. "And in addition to that, when he produced his driver's license, there was a sex offender notification on it. So, cueing in on those factors, the deputy escorted Mr. Lasage here to the Criminal Operations Center as a potential suspect."

Today, Brian K. Lasage resides in Angola at the Louisiana State Penitentiary. Still, in 2010, he was incarcerated at the Elayn Hunt Correctional Center in St. Gabriel, where he allegedly told a fellow inmate, "I'm looking forward to Angola. It will give me time to write a book on my girls in Jennings."

Tuesday, Bayou Justice revisits Louisiana's most infamous nautical disaster, a collision that took 78 lives, including 18 from Tangipahoa Parish.

In 1986, one survivor of the crash asked me this question: was the Luling-Destrehan Ferry disaster of 1976 indeed an accident?

The Luling Ferry

With new information from readers and other sources, this chapter evolved from the Bayou Justice column entitled "Some believed 1976 Luling Ferry crash no accident," initially published in south Louisiana newspapers on Tuesday, October 22, 2019.

ACCORDING TO ONE SURVIVOR of the event, one of the most chilling sights in life is to be on a ferry in the middle of the Mississippi River and suddenly see that a ship is going to run you down.

The Luling-Destrehan Ferry disaster was a nautical disaster that occurred in the Mississippi River in St. Charles Parish, Louisiana, United States, on the morning of October 20, 1976. Traveling upriver, the Norwegian tanker SS Frosta stuck the George Prince ferry.

The collision occurred at milepost 120.8 above Head of Passes, less than three-quarters of a mile from the construction site of the Luling Bridge, which replaced the ferry seven years later. The boat was crossing from Destrehan, Louisiana, on the East Bank to Luling, Louisiana, on the West Bank. Ninety-six passengers and crew were aboard the ferry when the tanker hit, and at least seventy-eight people perished.

Survivor George Lingo, of Hammond, 32-years-old at the time of the Luling-Destrehan Ferry Accident, talked about that moment until his death in 2009.

George boarded the ferry George Prince on that fatal Wednesday morning, just one of the still-sleepy people making their way to work in plants across the river, but George was among the 18 who made it ashore alive.

He told me in 1982 that something he saw before the ferry moved into the path of the oil tanker still puzzled him.

"Someone walked by the cabin window in a yellow raincoat and hood," he remembered. "This got my attention because I didn't expect rain, but then as I watched the person go by, I realized it was a woman. You could see bare legs under the coat, and I swear she had on high heels. Nothing could be more out of place on the ferry."

"I watched her go into the pilothouse and laughed to myself, imaging a party going on inside," he said. "The next thing I knew, we were moving."

6:30 a.m. Sunrise would come at 7:05. The wind blew hard and cold with temperatures in the lower 50s.

Unlike most passengers who drove vehicles onto the ferry and stayed in them, windows closed against the wind, radios playing, George left his car and ducked into the warm passenger cabin, filled with "walk-on" passengers.

Five minutes into the 10-minute ferry ride from Destrehan, on the east bank to Luling on the West, the ferry moved into midstream, and George noticed people running across the deck. He left the cabin to find out why.

"I was the first one out the door," George told me. "By then, the ship was right on us. I mean, it was just right there, looking huge. I just froze, almost in shock. The next thing I remember, I was overboard."

A 664-foot Norwegian Tanker, the SS Frosta, whistles blaring in alarm, rammed the 120-by-55 George Prince Ferry, and flipped it over like a toy boat.

Some of the 35 vehicles thrown off the ferry deck by the impact floated in a swirl a few seconds, sinking gradually. In a horrible scene, the cars continued to whirl and bob in the current as the terrified occupants fought to open the doors against the water pressure.

The Coast Guard convened a board of inquiry from headquarters in New Orleans, working to determine the cause of the crash. How could such a thing happen to two well-lit vessels equipped with radio communication, radar, and watchful men at the helm?

Most of the survivors who testified at the hearing in 1976 remembered less than George did in 1982, as each described only a moment of confusion, followed by terror and an abrupt plunge into a cold river.

The Mississippi is about three-quarters of a mile wide at the location of the ferry crossing. Most of those who survived did so by clinging to the overturned ferry. Her sister ferry, the Ollie K. Wilds, rescued them minutes later, just before sunrise.

As the light appeared, rescuers saw the sharp bow of the SS Frosta had smashed a V-shaped gash in one pontoon of the catamaran-style ferry. Though most of the George Prince sunk below water, the upside-down boat remained afloat with one corner, guard rails, and life vest still attached, protruding from the river.

Before the search for survivors concluded, the river current moved the hulk a mile downstream, near the riverbank, where the ferry ran aground against the muddy bottom. The SS Frosta anchored about a mile upstream from the point of collision, before eventually continuing to Baton Rouge after the Coast Guard interviewed the pilot.

Hours later, officials estimated how many had been on the free ferry.

An estimated 78 people drowned that morning, including the ferry's captain and crew. Although the free ferry had no official record of how many boarded that morning, investigators collected 96 floating hard-hats, along with lunch boxes and similar debris, and the George Prince's vehicle deck had been loaded to capacity, 35 cars.

"As time passes," George Lingo told me in 1982, "You think all kinds of crazy things. Thinking about the girl in the yellow raincoat, I got to wondering if someone might intentionally want to cause the wreck, maybe to drown someone on board or something. Then I remembered one of the Union guys on board, working in one of the plants, he was supposed to be mob-connected."

In 1992, after filing a Freedom of Information Act request with the United States Federal Bureau of Investigation, I received a copy of the FBI file on the ferry disaster. I discovered that George Lingo was not the only person interested in the party going on inside the pilothouse of the George Prince.

The United States Coast Guard solicited the FBI's help in 1976 to determine whether the accident involved foul play. Officially, the Luling-Destrehan Ferry Crash remains the deadliest ferry disaster in United States history.

Girl in the Yellow Raincoat

With new information from readers and other sources, this chapter evolved from the Bayou Justice column entitled "Search for mystery woman continues," initially published in south Louisiana newspapers on Thursday, October 24, 2019.

THE LULING-DESTREHAN Ferry disaster was a nautical disaster that occurred in the Mississippi River in St. Charles Parish just before dawn on the morning of October 20, 1976. On a fogless morning, traveling upriver, a Norwegian oil tanker, the SS Frosta struck and flipped the George Prince ferry, killing 78 of the estimated 96 passengers onboard.

Hammond Survivor George Lingo told me in 1982 that he saw someone he believed to be a young woman in high heels and a yellow raincoat entering the pilothouse just before the ferry began to move into the path of the ship.

Vincent Pardo of Tickfaw had just climbed aboard, he told me in 1989.

Pardo, a carpentry supervisor, worked for Monsanto at the chemical plant. Among a group of workers that carpooled from Tangipahoa Parish to St. Charles Parish, Pardo said his group left cars on both sides of the river and rode the ferry as pedestrians. He almost missed the boat that morning, waiting for a co-worker to finish a cigarette.

"We came running. A dockhand had to pull the gate back down to let us on," Pardo said. Pardo stood on an outside deck watching the ship approach, blowing a whistle several times.

"I saw the ship, and I knew an accident was about to happen," he said.

Pardo said the ship toppled the ferry as he attempted to climb up to the pilothouse to alert the crew.

He said he and others yelled, and many sitting in cars blew horns, but they got no response from the ferry captain. Like George Lingo, Pardo soon found himself in the water, clinging to the capsized ferry.

An investigation would later show the pilot was intoxicated and someone had closed the windows of the pilothouse. The pilot likely never heard the warnings.

"Sometimes, I still think about that girl in the raincoat," George Lingo said. "They said the captain might have passed out. I wondered if the girl could have driven us in front of the ship."

Vincent Pardo said he vaguely remembered someone oddly out-of-place in a yellow raincoat, but he never got close enough to see if the person had been male or female or whether the person entered the pilothouse.

In May 1978, the Coast Guard released a Marine Casualty-Report saying the SS Frosta radioed two warnings to the George Prince and repeatedly blasted its whistle as a warning. Although the report said the crews of both vessels could have done something to avoid the crash or lessen the impact, most of the attention focused on Captain Egidio P. Auletta, the pilot of the George Prince.

From the Coast Guard investigation report:

"The George Prince, under the control of Egidio Auletta, departed and turned almost immediately to cross the river, because the current was slow and the volume of automobile traffic made it attractive to cross as quickly as possible."

"The departure into stream traffic created a situation where the risk of collision could exist, but Auletta did not signal his intent to cross the river by radio or horn. Had he announced his departure with the proper signal, and signaled his intent to cross in front of the SS Frosta, he would have made an impolite but acceptable crossing of the river."

"Due to complacency, fatigue, or the effects of alcohol, Auletta failed to detect the approaching ship until the final seconds before the collision, when she disappeared from the view of the SS Frosta's pilot, by which time the collision was inevitable. The investigators concluded that he had time to maneuver to lessen the collision by making it a glancing blow. Still, the forward momentum and downstream current made the collision beyond human remedy."

"The primary cause of the tragedy was the navigation of George Prince into the channel without due regard to, or awareness of, river traffic and the risk of collision. The investigators stated that they could not imagine a more vivid example to prove that keeping a proper lookout is the first rule of seamanship."

The report also recorded six violations against Auletta: (1) failure to sound a horn upon departing a dock, (2) failure to keep a proper lookout, (3) failure to slacken speed, or, if necessary, stop and reverse when approaching another vessel to avoid risk of collision, (4) failure to signal intentions when crossing, (5) failure to navigate with caution until danger of collision is over, and (6) use of a vessel in a negligent manner to endanger life, limb, and property.

The real mystery is why Auletta never heard or did not heed the SS Frosta's warnings. Near the end of his shift, perhaps the captain was tired and fell asleep? That would seem more likely if there were not a full crew of 18 on board the ferry, including inside the pilothouse, where investigators found a near empty bottle of Seagram's VO.

In 1992, after filing a Freedom of Information Act request, I received the FBI files on the ferry accident. The Coast Guard solicited the bureau's help to determine if the liquid remaining in the Seagram's bottle contained anything more than alcohol. The Coast Guard needed to rule-out foul play and did so. The FBI found no drugs or poisons, just Canadian whiskey, and the coroner's report showed Auletta's blood-alcohol level at .09 percent just short of the legal limit.

The Coast Guard report concluded that "Due to complacency, fatigue and-or the effects of alcohol consumption, Auletta failed to detect the approaching SS Frosta until seconds before the collision."

That leaves only one mystery remaining. Who was George Lingo's mysterious girl in the yellow raincoat?

"I don't talk about that anymore," George told me in 1989. "Vince Pardo told me there were no women on the ferry, and that makes sense. Just plant workers crossing the river to work."

However, there were three women on board the George Prince that morning.

The Coast Guard found Anita Stadler's body among the dead. She came from St. Rose, as did most of the ferry's crew. Although no one knows for sure, it is plausible that she was visiting a friend inside the pilothouse. I caught up with a cousin of Stradler's in 1996. He said he did not know why she boarded the ferry that day, but he never knew her to wear heels and had no idea why she might wear a raincoat on a cloudless day.

Another woman on board, Mary Lightsey of Destrehan, worked as a bookkeeper for a scaffolding company, a contractor in one of the plants. Rescuers found her body still in her car at the bottom of the Mississippi River.

The third woman on board is perhaps the most mysterious.

All of the passengers on board the George Prince Ferry that morning resided in Tangipahoa, Livingston, Ascension, Jefferson, or St. Charles Parish, all except one, 18-year-old Anastasia Wanko of New Orleans. Wanko did not work in the plants, and no one has stated publicly why she boarded the ferry that night.

Of the 96 passengers boarding the ferry that morning, 18 survived. The Coast Guard lists Anastasia Wanko among the dead in their official report, and it is visible on the marble monument erected near Luling in 2009. However, after 43 years, the body of Anastasia Wanko has never been found.

Skulls, Ghosts, and Devils

With new information from readers and other sources, this chapter evolved from the Bayou Justice column entitled "Halloween conjures Skulls, Ghosts, and Devil Worship," initially published in south Louisiana newspapers on Tuesday, October 29, 2019.

LAST AUGUST, I MENTIONED Tangipahoa Parish Sheriff Eddie Layrisson's dispute with television news anchor Bill Elder in New Orleans. This mention prompted several readers to write, asking that I recount the full devil dog history and tell all I know about the great Satanists scare of 1988. I haven't been ignoring those requests, just saving the story for Halloween.

For me, the backstory begins in the 1970s. A junior high student in Livingston Parish, I found my first summer job in Hammond at a newspaper called *The Daily Sun*. Editor Nicholas R. Murray had an idea for a new column he wanted wrote from a young person's perspective. For three years, I wrote a column for him entitled "Adventures in the Unknown," essentially playing Scooby-Doo, invalidating folklore and urban legends in South Louisiana.

I wrote about the infamous Albany Light, the Pink Lady of Wardline Road, and a railroad siren in Manchac, the Tickfaw River Goddess, and the Honey Island Swamp Monster. I visited allegedly haunted boneyards in Springfield, Independence, Baptist, Arcola, and Loranger. Not once did I find a real ghost or swamp monster, nor did I provoke anyone to say, "And I'd have gotten away with it too if it weren't for that meddling kid."

However, those adventures introduced me to the Bankston Cemetery between Hammond and Robert. Back then, locals called it "the Skull Creek cemetery," telling the tale of a post-Civil War lynching alongside the creek next to the cemetery. As the legend went, if you parked in front of the graveyard at midnight and flashed your headlights three times, the oldest grave in the group would glow once the lights went out.

Amazingly, of all of the tales, I investigated, this one I could reproduce. Following the headlight ritual, one grave did glow for 15 minutes or so and then faded. Phosphorus, I suspected. The greenish glow resembled the glow-in-the-dark T-shirts kids popularized in the 70s.

Whatever the cause, it was a repeatable experience, and my teenage friends and I routinely brought dates out to see the scare, just as previous generations watched submarine races on Lake Pontchartrain.

A few years later, during my senior year at Holden High School, I worked part-time for *The Hammond Vindicator*, where I told Sports Writer Jimmy Henderson about the glowing grave. He insisted that I take him there, and he said, if I did, he would introduce me to his girlfriend's sister — a college girl! — And we would make the trip on a double date.

The following weekend, there we were, Jimmy Henderson, the Katt sisters — two beautiful redheaded Southeastern students from Natalbany — and me, riding through a black forest at midnight, searching for Skull Creek and its glowing grave.

Unfortunately, I hadn't been there in years, and on a moonless night, every tree looked the same. Making a long story short, we passed the graveyard and found ourselves lost on some backwoods dirt road.

Eventually, we rounded a curve and saw a bonfire not far off the road. Brave for the college girls, I assured them the fire belonged to fox hunters and volunteered to walk into the woods and get directions back to the highway. For the record, that was a stupid idea. As I write about it today, the hair still crawls on the back of my neck.

However, into the woods, I went, while Jimmy stayed in the car, he said, to protect the ladies, but somehow, the closer I got to the light of the bonfire, the better I felt. Soon, some hunters would have a great laugh at my expense, but at least we would find our way out of the darkness.

That's what I thought before the people in black robes saw me and gave chase. Today, I probably weigh double what I did then, but in 1982, I could run.

I think I only hit one tree on my way out.

I dove into the car, and Jimmy punched the gas, anxious to get out of there, still protecting the ladies, of course. Five minutes later, we passed Bankston Cemetery.

It felt like we rounded the curve in front of it doing 80. Glenda, one of the girls from Natalbany, said, "Hey, I saw the glowing grave." But Jimmy didn't slow down until he bounced into the parking lot of the Hammond Police Department.

We sat in the parking lot 20 minutes, never going in.

The next day, Jimmy decided I'd made the robed mob up to scare them, and the more I told the story over the years, the less I believed it myself. Eventually, I decided that I had imagined the whole thing.

That all changed in the summer of 1988.

By then, I was working afternoon drive at 14 Country.

"This is H. L., your A-OK DJ at WFPR."

Yes, it sounded just as corny back then.

However, I got to spend the first half of my eight-hour day with my first love, the News. News Director Pirosko managed newscasts in the mornings, but I took over from noon until my afternoon drive shift began.

One morning, I'm in the newsroom recording a sound bite from Chuck Reed — then Chief Information Officer with the Tangipahoa Parish Sheriff's Office — when Music Director Richard Dees tapped on the glass.

The Newsroom, the Production Studio, the adjoining conference room, and the Control Room, all had partial glass walls. Richard stood in the conference room, three walls down. I didn't hear him tapping; I saw him. By the time I finished with Chuck, Richard was waving his arms beckoning me down there.

I called him on the phone instead. He answered, saying, "You really want to get down here."

Mary Pirosko's twice-weekly call-in talk show, Hammond America, was in full swing, and Richard had been listening in the conference room. When I walked in, Mary had two teenagers on the line, talking about finding men in red and black hooded robes with torches bowing before a fiery pentagram inside the Bankston Cemetery.

Next to Richard, WHMD's Catfish Phil Colwart sat, reading the *Daily Star*, and grinning. "H. L., maybe you're not as crazy as we thought," he said.

That's when Mary took another call.

"Good morning, Hammond America, you're on the air."

"Mary," the voice on the line said, "This is Betty Allen Hebert in Ponchatoula. I think those kids are telling the truth," she said. "My mom and I have had nine cattle killed overnight at our ranch on Sisters Road. We think its devil worshippers. They stabbed our animals with sticks, drained their blood, and cut their hearts out. The sheriff's office won't take us seriously, but we're really scared over here."

On Halloween day, I will recount my visit to the Rose Allen ranch.

Cattle Mutilation

With new information from readers and other sources, this chapter evolved from the Bayou Justice column entitled "Halloween cattle mutilation in Ponchatoula," initially published in south Louisiana newspapers on Thursday, October 31, 2019.

SOMETHING MUTILATED the last of the Allen Ranch livestock on Halloween 1988, seven months after I met the ranch owners, and approximately two months after the television talk shows and tabloid newspapers stopped calling them.

In April of that year, I drove down Sisters Road to the Allen cattle ranch in Ponchatoula for the first time. Betty Allen Hebert and her mother, Rose Allen, met me in front of the house. After exchanging greetings, Rose Allen thanked me for coming out as she climbed aboard a 3-wheeled all-terrain vehicle and sat next to her shotgun.

Betty Allen Hebert unstrapped a holster and handgun from her hip, and said, "You're with me," before dropping both into the back of a pickup truck.

En route to the back pasture, Betty told me how the two widows ran the cattle ranch and a small vegetable farm together and with little outside help. She said the property had been mainly self-sustaining until the morning they found the first of mutilated cow. When I arrived, they had lost seven cattle over a 4-week period. They lost two more before the year ended.

When we reached the back pasture, Rose had climbed off her ATV and stood, looking down at the freshest carcass. The heifer had died two nights earlier. Her eyes and ears were gone, and she had a gaping hole in her chest, the size of a basketball.

"What makes you certain someone did this?" I asked.

"That first morning," Betty said, "We lost a calf and thought maybe a coyote or something got it. We've seen vultures take the eyes and ears before."

"But take a look at this hole," Rose said, pointing, "That's wasn't coyote or buzzard."

Stooping down, I looked at the edges of the cavity, expecting teeth or claw marks of some kind, but to my surprise, the outer edge of the circular cut appeared burned, cauterized.

"We've got a neighbor working for us," Betty said. "He claimed a laser did that. He's watched too many X-Files, believes aliens killed our cattle." She shook her head and grinned broadly.

"Betty don't tell him that," Rose said. "That guy's not all there. He claims we've had black helicopters circling the pasture at night, too." She looked at me. "We don't think the government or little green men killed these cows. People did this, crazy people, but people, plain and simple."

Rose picked up a straight limb from the pasture and marked the width of the hole in the cow's chest. After breaking the stick to that length, she flipped it 90-degrees, demonstrating the same circumference at any angle.

"Pretty smart coyote, huh?" Rose asked, looking up at me.

As we walked or road from carcass to carcass, she brought along the stick and repeatedly confirmed that all seven cattle bore precisely the same size hole in the same location.

"We've both called the sheriff's office at different times," Betty told me. "I guess they think we're crazy. They won't send anybody out, and we're outside of the Ponchatoula Police Department's jurisdiction."

"We did get a game warden out," Rose said. "He took samples, said he'd get LSU to run some tests, but we never heard back from him."

"That was about three weeks ago," Betty added.

"So," I finally got the nerve to ask, "How did you conclude that devil worshippers did this? Did you see a movie or documentary or something?"

"No. None of that," Betty said. "That game warden told us about kids in a cult, worshipping Satan and killing animals, and then we found where kids painted graffiti in an old shack at the back of the property."

"Kids painted those signs," Rose said, "But they didn't kill these cattle and cut that kind of hole. My doctor couldn't cut a circle that precise."

The following week, the front page of *The Ponchatoula Times* newspaper featured the first of my four-part series describing Satanism in general and examining reports of suspected cult rituals in South Louisiana. In addition to the events at the Allen ranch, the series described rituals near Hammond High School, including the incidents at Skulls Creek, including the mutilated animal carcass found nailed to a tree and circled with candles in Bankston Cemetery.

A Livingston Parish sheriff's deputy brought me a handbook of satanic symbols, explaining that Chief Deputy Wayne Sanders distributed the material after attending a Louisiana State Police training on the subject. In turn, Sanders reprimanded the deputy, who I had known since we were children. My friend did not speak to me for over a decade after the reprimand, but the handbook he provided proved that the symbols found in the shack on the Allen property did not originate with Satanists.

After the first part of the series ran, the phones started ringing, readers stepping forward — on-the-record and off — reporting ritual sightings, animal mutilations, and satanic graffiti found across three parishes. The anonymous calls were the worse. They came with threats against my life and the lives of my family and others at the newspaper.

Imagine my relief the day WWL-TV's Bill Elder called, volunteering to take the heat off and to investigate these stories with the full power of the CBS television network behind him. Eventually, that put him in front of an Amite grand jury, explaining what he knew about human sacrifice on the north shore of Lake Pontchartrain.

Sheriff Eddie Layrisson finally sent deputies to the Allen ranch, but by then, the livestock remains had decomposed to only hide and bones. The sheriff held a press conference attacking Elder, where he produced photos of a cow killed by a dog in Natalbany and insisted the Allen's cattle had been killed by "a pack of wild hounds," prompting the spread of "devil dog" jokes parish-wide.

Lab results from LSU eventually came back inconclusive. The examiner would not rule out or confirm the sheriff's wild dog or coyote attack. Still, he did suggest a more sinister possibility, believing the circular holes were consistent with shotgun exit wounds. The sheriff's office followed up with a report suggesting the cattle may have been killed by neighbors, angry with the Allen's concerning a dispute over a bridge on ranch property.

After the last cow died that Halloween, the Allen cattle faded from the headlines. However, the Bankston Cemetery at Skulls Creek did not. Three months after the previous cattle mutilation, mourners found the lifeless body of a 30-year-old Ponchatoula woman in the graveyard, shot four times in the chest and abdomen.

The Cemetery Slayer

With *new information from readers and other sources, this chapter evolved from the Bayou Justice column entitled "Vandals, cemetery slayer escape justice," initially published in south Louisiana newspapers on Tuesday, November 5, 2019.*

A MAN VISITING A CEMETERY in the dead of winter found the body of a 30-year-old Ponchatoula woman in the woods behind Hammond High School. The body was six feet from the gravesite where — eight months earlier — Tangipahoa Parish sheriff's deputies reported finding an animal carcass, black candles, and painted Satanic symbols.

Investigators that January afternoon identified the victim as Bonnie Sue Pannier and said someone had shot her four times with a small-caliber weapon, twice in the chest and once in the abdomen and neck. They said Bonnie had been dead less than 24 hours when a mourner at the Bankston Cemetery found her body — fully dressed in casual clothing — around 3 o'clock that Monday afternoon, January 23, 1989.

"We've got some good suspects," Detective Mike Sticker of the Tangipahoa Parish sheriff's office told reporters within days of the murder.

"For the record, there is no truth to the rumors that this woman's death had anything to do with Satanism or human sacrifice, and there was no robbery involved. We think she was killed in anger, on the spur of the moment."

Six months earlier, attempting to assuage what he termed a near panic, Sticker's boss, Tangipahoa Parish Sheriff Ed Layrisson, held a press conference to refute rumors of satanic rituals taking place at the Bankston Cemetery.

"There has been almost hysteria in the parish," the sheriff said. "Some people will believe almost every rumor, and I think as sheriff, I am obligated to inform the public of the facts."

He said incidents involving dead cattle near Ponchatoula and vandalism at Bankston Cemetery precipitated several unfounded rumors.

In April of 1988, Rose Allen, who lived near Ponchatoula, reported someone had killed seven cattle on her property overnight and that she and her daughter, Betty Allen Hebert, had discovered the dead with 9-inch circular incisions in the chest cavities of each carcass.

That same month in McComb, Mississippi, Pike County Sheriff Robert Lawson requested that the local high school cancel or postpone their prom after discovering a mutilated goat and satanic graffiti at the school amid rumors of a human sacrifice on the Black Sabbath, the night of the prom.

"We've spent a lot of time investigating this and dismiss any devil-worshiping," Tangipahoa Parish Sheriff Ed Layrisson said.

"Without a doubt, wild dogs caused the death of every cow on the Allen ranch," the sheriff said, "And that in Mississippi and at the graveyard near the airport, [that was all] just kids getting into a little mischief."

At Bankston Cemetery, the sheriff said, investigators believed Hammond High School dropouts had become intoxicated "drinking cheap wine" and defaced some graves. According to Layrisson, they also may have built a bonfire, butchered a wild animal, and painted "devil worship symbols" on the surrounding trees.

"All of this publicity by the media has created a monster," the sheriff said. "My job as sheriff is to separate real juvenile crime from pranks and rumors."

One month after the Bonnie Pannier homicide, the sheriff of St. Bernard Parish reported events in another graveyard mirroring those at the Bankston Cemetery. However, St. Bernard Parish Sheriff Jack Stephens openly provided details of his office's investigation.

Stephens told *The Times-Picayune* about a decapitated and gutted animal found in the town of Violet beneath trees painted with "symbols associated with devil worship." He said a Violet woman found the animal Tuesday in Monkey Hill Park near the Twenty Arpent Canal. The dog's intestines, the sheriff said, had been ripped out, its head cut off, with one of the dog's legs inserted where the skull belonged.

The woman told police that her husband and some youths watched a group of people, dressed in dark clothing and carrying candles, walk into a wooded area between the Stacey and Oakridge subdivisions, several blocks from where the woman found the dog, the sheriff said.

Nearby, according to *The Times-Picayune*, Sheriff Stephen's deputies found trees painted with pentagrams — five-sided signs often associated with devil-worshiping — and inverted crosses, the Sheriff's Office said.

Sheriff Jack Stephens said his office received no other reports about animal sacrifices in the parish and was not aware of how closely his description of events matched those reported by Hammond residents the summer prior.

Two days after the dog butchering at Monkey Hill, vandals broke open a child's coffin in a cemetery in St. Tammany Parish after painting a pentagram on the cinder block tomb encasing the casket. The St. Tammany Parish sheriff's office contacted the Louisiana State Police, who sent "Satan hunter" Tom Wedge to assist in the investigation.

According to *The Baton Rouge Advocate*, the state police contracted Wedge, an international consultant on the occult, to investigate 17 cemetery desecrations and animal mutilations across the state, including three events in Tangipahoa Parish.

When *Advocate* reporter Zack Nauth asked Tom Wedge whether the three Tangipahoa Parish events included the death of Bonnie Pannier, the consultant declined to answer.

Bonnie Pannier was born Bonnie Sue Henderson in Alexandria, but she lived most of her life in Joyce, Louisiana. She was the daughter of Bill and Irene Henderson of Joyce.

Reverend Durhl Ray Davis — who died in April of this year — officiated services for Bonnie in the chapel of the Southern Funeral Home in Jonesboro, on a Thursday morning, four days after her murder, which police believe occurred Sunday night, January 22.

Bonnie's family buried her in Joyce at the New Jerusalem Cemetery.

The obituary in the Alexandria Town Talk listed Bonnie's survivors, including her husband, Rickey Pannier of Hammond; her parents, Bill and Irene Henderson of Joyce; five brothers, James P. Henderson of Lake City,

Florida; Billy Henderson and Tommy Henderson, both of Joyce, Kenneth Henderson of Downsville, and David Young of Oklahoma; and one sister, Delores Gay of Santa Fe, Texas.

Dr. Vincent Cefalu, the Tangipahoa Parish coroner, spoke with reporters the morning of Bonnie's funeral. He said that in addition to shooting her, Bonnie's assailant had also struck her on the head with a blunt instrument.

Dr. Cefalu admitted that his office failed to determine whether Bonnie's assailant shot her at the scene or somewhere else before dumping her body at the entrance of the cemetery.

However, Deputy Chuck Reed — identified then by the Associated Press as "executive assistant to Tangipahoa Parish Sheriff Ed Layrisson" — told reporters the following day that the sheriff's office had discovered evidence suggesting that someone had moved the body.

Reed told reporters that Bonnie attended four or five churches, played keyboard in a local band, which performed at a local nightclub. He said she had a "normal social relationship" and "had a lot of friends."

Reed said investigators were studying several theories in connection with Bonnie's death. He said that detectives interviewed over a dozen people within 48 hours of the body's discovery but had not collected evidence warranting an arrest and had no suspects at that time.

One week later, Monday, January 30, 1989, Chuck Reed told *The Baton Rouge Advocate* that investigators had a suspect under interrogation that afternoon in the Bonnie Pannier homicide but could release no further details at that time.

The following Thursday, February 2, 1989, Reed addressed reporters again, this time announcing that sheriff's investigators expected to arrest someone within ten days.

Thirty years later, Bonnie's family is still awaiting that arrest — still awaiting justice — while Bonnie Pannier's killer continues to walk free.

The Devil Cult

With new information from readers and other sources, this chapter evolved from the Bayou Justice column entitled "Pedophile members of Satanic cult imprisoned," initially published in south Louisiana newspapers on Tuesday, November 7, 2019.

AT 1:15 P. M. ON MAY 16, 2005, a church pastor strolled into Detective Stan Carpenter's office in Livingston, Louisiana, and provided a confession that shocked everyone working in the Livingston Parish Sheriff's Office that day.

Fifteen years had passed since Tangipahoa Parish Sheriff Ed Layrisson told a press conference that no satanic cults operated near in hometown of Ponchatoula. Former Hosanna Church Pastor Louis Lamonica, Jr. voluntarily walked into the sheriff's office and described in detail how members of his congregation molested several children over years of "dedications to Satan" inside the Ponchatoula church.

Major Carpenter, 62, told reporters from Newsweek magazine, "Lamonica walked into my office and sat down, just as calm as you and me talking now."

"I was Detective Supervisor at the time. When he came in, he thought that after telling us what they did, he was going to go on about his business."

"Listening to him, here where we're all Christian, so it kind of floored me. You're talking about a man who professes to be a preacher, a pastor, and a church leader, admitting to abusing children and worshiping Satan."

"I was an old guy about to retire in a couple of years. I thought I had seen it all. Then something like this happens. It stays with you."

Law enforcement found evidence to support Lamonica's claims in the closed church, including badly rubbed-out pentagrams on the floor and eight boxes of black hooded robes allegedly used both in the abuse and in "morality plays" performed to prepare the young victims for "the evils of our world."

In the days following Lamonica's confession, police charged others, including Lamonica's wife and a Tangipahoa Parish deputy sheriff, who Lamonica said participated in devil worship rituals involving the drinking of warm animal blood while parishioners poured that blood over the bodies of naked children.

One month earlier, a local woman in Ohio accused Lamonica of targeting her child for unlawful acts before she and the child fled the state, concerned for their safety. The woman told police in Ohio that Lamonica led a cult in south Louisiana participating in child abuse rituals, animal sacrifices, and orgies.

In his confession, the 45-year-old Lamonica named his fellow perpetrators, and he listed their child victims. He explained to Detective Bonita Sager how the ceremonies began and continued for nearly a decade. He also told of having sexual relations with several other children inside the Hosanna Church.

Lamonica described how, from 1999 until 2003, he led church elders, whom the prosecution later labeled a pedophile ring, in rituals with several dozen juveniles that involved sex, including oral, anal, and vaginal intercourse with children ranging from infants to teens.

Several of the participants, he said, including him and his wife, offered their own children as victims. The group sexually assaulted a dog, according to Lamonica, and they sacrificed several cats to Satan. These elders, he said, also forced the children to simulate sex acts with one another and with the animals.

Police arrested Louis Lamonica following the confession, booking him with one count of aggravated rape and one count of crimes against nature.

Two days later, police booked four more.

Louis Lamonica's wife, Robbin D. Lamonica, 45, then a resident of Holden, charging her with one count of aggravated rape.

Nicole Bernard, 36 — the woman who phoned the police from Columbus, Ohio — was booked on one count of aggravated rape of a juvenile under age 13.

Paul Fontenot, 21, of Baton Rouge, was booked with one count of aggravated rape of a juvenile under age 13.

Lois Ann Mowbray, 54, of Ponchatoula, was booked with obstruction of justice, failure to report a felony and accessory after the fact to aggravated rape.

The following day, police arrested another three suspects.

Police booked Former Tangipahoa Sheriff's Deputy Christopher Blair Labat, 24, of Hammond, on charges of aggravated rape and malfeasance in office; and Allen Pierson, 46, of Hammond, with one count of aggravated rape, along with Austin Bernard III, 36, of Hammond.

Ultimately, Patricia Pierson, who pleaded guilty to obstruction of justice, and sheriff's deputy Christopher Labat had all charges dismissed.

Lamonica told Sager he voluntarily turned himself into police because "the guilt of all of this" weighed on his heart and because his wife, he said, was still involved in cult activity. "I know she is," the pastor said, "She is still molesting the children."

At his trial in 2006, jurors heard audiotapes of Lamonica's two confessions, describing how the Hosanna Church switched from Christianity to Satanism in 2000. Without the knowledge of the general congregation, they heard him say, eight church elders sacrificed animals and drank blood in ceremonies that included sex with children.

Lamonica described the pentagram police later found in the middle of the floor at the church, along with a book of "Spells and Temptations." He also described "the youth room" with all windows covered in black. There, they dedicated a baby to Satan, he explained, putting the infant in a black dress in the middle of the pentagram, while playing mystical music, and lighting black candles.

He described how they drained the blood of the cat, each drinking the warm liquid, as the animal died. When the cat stopped breathing, they removed the infant's dress and sprinkled the blood over the baby's body, all while chanting continuously.

When they were not performing rituals on babies, he said, they would pick up girls, the males would line up and have sex with them, and the females would perform oral sex.

"It was orgies. You put one [child] in the middle and took your turn. Everybody got a turn. Nobody missed out, including the women."

The pastor also described the feces and urine scattered on the floor, and how, in some rituals, he would become possessed by Satan, allowing demons to change him into a wild beast.

On the recording, Lamonica said he became pastor of the church in 1993 when his pastor father died. He said that the church closed in 2005, but the rituals continued in the homes of former church elders long after the church closed.

In the trial's opening statements, Lamonica's attorney claimed others in the church manipulated and coerced his client into recording two false confessions. Still, in his second audiotape, Lamonica's voice insisted, "Nobody brainwashed nobody."

Prosecutors also provided jurors with a written confession from Lamonica and contracted a handwriting expert to validate the defendant's 260 pages of explicit sexual text.

Ultimately, prosecutors proved the ritualistic abuse and sacrifice in court but kept the ceremonial aspects to a minimum. Asked why, Tangipahoa Parish Assistant District Attorney Don Wall, explained, "I kept this devil-worshipping stuff to a small portion of the trial. Worshipping the devil is not illegal; Child molestation is, so that's what I focused on."

In 2007, Tangipahoa Parish Sheriff's Office spokesman Chuck Reed told reporters that the sheriff's office did not doubt that some of the abusers believed they were taking part in Satanic rituals. Still, more likely, he said, they were just pedophiles masking their crimes in the "trappings and symbols" of Satanism.

In 2008, Lamonica went on trial for the child molestation charges and received four concurrent life sentences. Evidence of child pornography and child rape helped convict several other members of the group, and all are serving long sentences today.

At one time, Hosanna Church boasted a congregation of 1,000. In the early days of the investigation, police told reporters they had identified more than 25 victims and expected to make at least 40 additional arrests.

Those arrests never came, and police today are closed-lipped regarding how many were involved in the pedophile ring and devil-worship rituals, both before or after the existence of and the horrors at Hosanna Church.

The Bad Cop

With new information from readers and other sources, this chapter evolved from the Bayou Justice column entitled "FBI agent: Louisiana bad cop problem easily corrected," initially published in south Louisiana newspapers on Tuesday, November 11, 2019.

HIRED TO FIGHT POLICE corruption in the New Orleans Police Department, a seasoned government agent moved to New Orleans after retiring as Special Agent in Charge of the Federal Bureau of Investigation's Chicago office.

The mayor of the crescent city hired the former FBI chief after hearing the top agent speak at an Illinois mayor's conference, where he told attendees that corrupt cops existed for one reason only and that citizens could quickly resolve the problem.

Last month, Louisiana State Police arrested Livingston Parish Sheriff's Deputy Dennis Perkins, 44, of Denham Springs. The State Attorney General's office charged him with 60 counts of production of pornography involving a juvenile. They also charged him with two counts of first-degree rape, three counts of possession of child pornography, two counts of video voyeurism, two counts of obscenity, and obstruction of justice. He threw his cell phone from a bridge into a river in North Louisiana.

The investigation began with a tip from the National Center for Missing and Exploited Children, where a whistleblower reported seeing the couple's videos on Porn-Hub, a website claiming to have streamed 75 gigabytes of data per second last year to 87.8 billion viewers, more per month than Netflix, Amazon, and Twitter combined.

Contests on Porn-Hub offer large sums of money to viewers who upload the most outrageous pornography videos.

Last Thursday, police moved Perkins to a state prison amid rumors that trustees had served him contaminated food. That afternoon, state investigators reported the fired officer's schoolteacher wife had allegedly offered tiny square cupcakes, known as petit fours, tainted with Perkins' seminal fluid to more than 50 middle school students.

Unfortunately, Louisiana police officers are not alone making money with this outrageous side-hustle. Last Wednesday, the Maryland State Police charged Officer Anthony Mileo of the Maryland National Capital Park Police Department with 17 counts of child pornography. In California, the Cypress Cove Police Department arrested one of its own for allegedly attempting to rape a woman in a bar while capturing the assault on video.

Likewise, pornography is not the only vice attracting law enforcement professionals.

Yesterday, according to the Escambia County Sheriff's Office, Mannford, Oklahoma Police Officer Michael Patrick Nealey and Mannford Police Chief Lucky Miller, 44, were in Florida attending a conference when Officer Nealey shot and killed Chief Miller.

In October, the interim chief of the Fort Worth Police Department apologized to the family of Atatiana Jefferson after a police officer shot and killed her in her own home. Aaron Dean, the officer who shot Atatiana, resigned from the department and has been charged with murder. Interim Chief Ed Kraus asked the Fort Worth community not to allow the incident to reflect poorly on his department.

According to the McClatchy News Agency, more than 80 law enforcement officers working today in California are convicted criminals, with rap sheets that include everything from animal cruelty to manslaughter. The review found 630 officers convicted of crimes in the last decade, an average of more than one per week.

Law enforcement agencies continue to employee criminals because not enough people will pin on a badge and risk their lives for the small salaries afforded police officers.

Last Tuesday, former Lake Charles police officer Robert Hammac pleaded guilty to a charge stemming from a May 2017 incident of police brutality. In Chicago that same day, police arrested an officer who beat up a co-worker while dressed as a circus clown.

The day before, Monday, November 4, deputies arrested former Tangipahoa Parish sheriff candidate Arden Wells on one count of unauthorized entry for allegedly sneaking through a gap in fencing to retrieve political signs earlier confiscated by the sheriff's office.

In July, the Louisiana State Police arrested former St. Tammany Parish Sheriff Jack Strain on charges of aggravated rape, sexual battery, incest, and indecent behavior with a juvenile.

In December 2016, the FBI raided the offices of the Tangipahoa Parish Sheriff Daniel Edwards and the Hammond Police Department. They arrested longtime DEA agent and former Tangipahoa Parish Sheriff's deputy Chad Scott, who the courts subsequently convicted on seven counts that included perjury, obstruction of justice and falsification of government records.

With Scott, the FBI also arrested former Tangipahoa Parish Sheriff's Office Deputy Karl Newman, who pleaded guilty to corruption charges in 2017. Newman was the second member of the task force arrested. Agents also charged former Tangipahoa Deputy Johnny Domingue and former City of Hammond police officer Rodney Gemar.

Chad Scott was far from the only DEA agent to go rogue. Investigators have busted many on the payroll of Mexican drug cartels. In 2016, a Federal judge convicted agents Glen Glover of New Jersey and David Polos of New York of hiding a strip club they owned and operated on government time.

In a feature article entitled "Good Cops Gone Bad," Newsweek magazine reported that the bulk of law enforcement officers that break the law do so in exchange for drug money. Speaking under the guise of anonymity, police officers interviewed in New York, Brooklyn, Los Angeles, and New Orleans reported they could make four times their salaries by merely looking the other way at pertinent times.

That brings us back to that retired FBI chief who moved to New Orleans to cleanse the New Orleans Police Department of graft and corruption.

In that Chicago speech, he said, "There are factors that impair good law enforcement. They include inadequate salaries, lack of proper equipment, insufficient personnel, long hours, and poor training facilities."

"All of these are obstacles to good law enforcement," he said, "And when citizens tolerate such unhealthy conditions, they reap a tragic harvest."

It is easy to imagine that he was referring to Dennis Perkins or Chad Scott, but this FBI agent said that in 1954.

Today, his remarks loosely translate to, "You get what you pay for."

If we want trained officers, we have to teach them. If we need skilled, efficient, and trust-worthy officers, we have to pay them what they are worth.

Law enforcement officers in the United States, on average, have lower salaries than our lawn care workers, and Louisiana employs some of the lowest paid officers in the country.

Instead of funding building contractors, buying helicopters, and deploying fully loaded sports utility vehicles as patrol cars, our sheriff's departments should consider investing in their police officers.

Unfortunately, though, that is not how things work in Louisiana.

After Mayor de Lesseps Morrison hired that FBI agent, the city ranked the officer in the number three position at the New Orleans Police Department. The television stations and newspapers cheered his work, calling him a hero, as did citizens writing letters to the editors at those publications.

However, his fellow police officers despised him and his work, calling him a spy for breaking their "code of silence" and crossing their "thin blue line."

In 1955, the former FBI chief submitted evidence to a grand jury indicting 90 police officers for accepting weekly payoffs from mob-controlled gambling interests.

However, before those cases went before judges, a bartender at one of those gambling establishments filed charges against the former FBI agent, saying he came to the bar intoxicated and threatened to pistol-whip the bartender.

The agent resigned and ran for the city council, denouncing the mayor and his cronies for pretending to address corruption in the police department. Still, his candidacy failed when he refused to accept payoffs from organized crime.

That FBI agent died in 1964 accused of everything from living drunk and disorderly to planning the assassination of John F. Kennedy.

That FBI agent's name was Guy Banister.

Ed Asner portrayed him in the movie JFK.

The Mailbox Skull

*W*ith new information from readers and other sources, this chapter evolved from the Bayou Justice column entitled "Missing mother's skull found near Folsom mailbox," initially published in south Louisiana newspapers on Tuesday, November 19, 2019.

AT 5:30 ON A THURSDAY morning, a 27-year-old mother of one arrived home from her newspaper delivery route. She made and drank coffee with her husband and saw him off for work before sunrise. Soon after, Ruth Anne Blake Manguno vanished, leaving her eight-month-old daughter crying alone in a playpen on the back porch.

Before dawn, May 26, 1983, Anne Manguno, a private contractor working for *The Times-Picayune*, delivered 327 newspapers in the Folsom area before completing the route at her driveway in the Wembley Estates subdivision, south of Folsom off Highway 25. Anne had worked at *The Times-Picayune/The States-Item* since the fall of 1980 when the couple married and moved to Wembley Estates.

Arriving home that Thursday morning, Anne made the coffee and changed Baby Ashleigh's diaper, while her husband, Bart Manguno, dressed for work. According to Bart, the couple then visited over coffee until 5:55 when he left for work at Frischhertz Electric Company on Toulouse Street in New Orleans.

Bart kissed Anne, he said, and left her sitting at their table, wearing a red-plaid flannel robe and reading the newspaper issue the working mother had just delivered.

Five hours later, Donna Manguno, Anne's sister-in-law, arrived at Anne's home with a group of children, whom Anne had invited for a swim in the pool.

She found her niece, Ashleigh, wet and crying and in her playpen on the screened-in back porch. On a table next to the playpen, Donna found a partially filled cup of cold coffee and Anne's open Bible.

After searching the home, Donna — certain Anne would not leave the baby alone for any reason — phoned both the sheriff's office and Bart's employer.

Bart returned home when he got the message.

On the phone with the sheriff's office dispatcher, Donna described Anne as a devoted wife and insisted that the dispatcher send a deputy immediately. Before nightfall, the sheriff's office had 50 deputies on foot, horseback, and three-wheelers combing the wooded areas surrounding Wembley Estates.

The following day, four boats and six divers from the sheriff's office drug two ponds a few hundred yards from Anne's home. According to Detective Dennis Larocca, they hoped to find "evidence that might have been discarded during an abduction" rather than Anne's body. He said one pond was about the size of a city block, and the other was about half that size.

Both searches — in the forest and the ponds — proved fruitless.

Detective Larocca spoke to *The Times-Picayune* after the searches concluded.

"It is all very mysterious," he said, "We haven't ruled anything out just yet, but I believe if she had been nearby, we would have found her."

The detective said he believed that the couple's two dogs, a mixed-breed and full-blooded cocker spaniel, would have followed Anne if she had walked away from the home. She often wandered into the woods, Bart Manguno had told him, but the dogs always followed her. Donna Manguno told police she found both dogs inside the house when she and the children arrived for the swimming party.

Bart told Detective Larocca that Anne had been active for some time in a Bible group and enjoyed studying the Bible after work. He said his wife had suffered from headaches and a stiff neck for a few days and planned to call a doctor for an appointment later in the day.

Donna said Anne seemed stressed over a friend's injury in a recent car accident, but ordinarily, she said, Anne was a happy, cheerful person.

Neither Bart nor Donna could find anything missing from the Manguno home that morning.

"Her car, purse, clothes — everything is in place," Bart said.

Early in the investigation, detectives verified reports that a stalker had harassed Anne when she started working for the newspaper three years earlier. She received threatening telephone calls, forcing her to change her home phone number to an unlisted one.

Ultimately, detectives located the man involved in that incident and cleared him of involvement in her disappearance.

"There is a perplexing absence of clues in this case," St. Tammany Parish Sheriff Pat Canulette told television reporters after Anne's disappearance. "But we are 80 percent sure she was abducted," he said.

According to Special Agent Charles Sale, Sheriff Canulette enlisted the aid of the Federal Bureau of Investigation on a presumption that Anne's abductor had taken her across state lines. An FBI bulletin went out to all field offices, describing Anne as 5 feet 6 inches tall, weighing 138 pounds, with brown hair and eyes.

Three months later, Folsom resident Laurinda Anglin walked to the end of her sister's driveway to check for deliveries to a rural mailbox. Her sister and brother-in-law, Pat and Rachele Cunningham, lived a quarter-mile from Anne Manguno's home in Wembley Estates.

In a roadside ditch, near the mailbox, Laurinda found a human skull.

"I just looked down and saw the skull looking up at me through the mud," she told a newspaper reporter.

Dr. Charles Crumpler, a pathologist at Slidell Memorial Hospital, examined the find and believed that a bullet had entered the right base of the skull and exited above the left eye. Anne's dentist, Dr. Mary Beilman in Covington, compared x-rays of the skull to Anne's dental records and made a final match. The skull belonged to Anne.

Dr. Crumpler believed an animal might have uncovered a shallow grave and that police would find the remainder of Anne's body buried within a few hundred yards of the Cunningham's mailbox. Still, using dogs, sheriff's deputies searched a two-mile radius and found nothing.

Four months after uncovering the skull, the St. Tammany Parish Sheriff's Office had the New Orleans Police Department pick up Charles Gandolfo, 44, for questioning.

An anonymous caller told Police that Gandolfo had buried the body of a woman behind his place of business, the New Orleans Voodoo Museum, and according to the caller, the buried corpse had no head.

Voodoo Man and Other Suspects

With new information from readers and other sources, this chapter evolved from the Bayou Justice column entitled "Bootleg house links Calmes murder to two in New Orleans," initially published in south Louisiana newspapers on Thursday, November 21, 2019.

ON SEPTEMBER 20, 1983, the St. Tammany Parish Sheriff's Office booked the owner of the New Orleans Voodoo Museum with purchasing a corpse and transporting a body without a permit.

Six hours earlier, District Attorney Marion B. Farmer of the 22nd Judicial District solicited a judge to hold 44-year-old Charles Gandolfo, and deputies locked him in the parish jail in Covington, where detectives questioned him as a person-of-interest in the murder of Ruth Anne Manguno.

Gandolfo paid a $100,000 bond and walked out the next day.

Initially, investigators questioned Gandolfo as a suspect in the killing of Ruth Anne Manguno, a 27-year-old newspaper carrier, who vanished from her home in Folsom on a Thursday morning, May 26, 1983. Her disappearance left her eight-month-old baby girl, alone and crying on the back porch, next to a cold cup of coffee and an open Bible.

Three months after Anne's disappearance, pathologists identified her bullet-punctured skull. Neighbors had found it partially buried in the mud a quarter-mile from the Manguno home, prompting authorities to search all rural areas for her other body parts.

This search prompted Charles Gandolfo's brother to phone the sheriff's office and confess to helping his brother bury a woman's remains in a vacant lot on the opposite side of St. Tammany Parish.

Later, the brother drove to the sheriff's office with photos of the corpse.

Following Gandolfo's release, St. Tammany Parish Sheriff Pat Canulette said Gandolfo was no longer a suspect in Anne's death. He said the body Gandolfo buried was in a more advanced state of decomposition than Anne's could have been, and despite initial reports, the buried skeleton's skull remained intact.

Canulette would not elaborate further, but Gandolfo's brother, Jerry, told New Orleans television station WWL that Gandolfo found the corpse in caskets donated to the museum for a Halloween exhibit.

Gerald Gandolfo said his brother panicked and buried the remains, which they believed came from a New Orleans cemetery.

Before the arrest of Charles Gandolfo, police had identified another person-of-interest in the murder of Anne Manguno, her husband, Bart Manguno.

The couple had married three years earlier after meeting at the Royal Sonesta Hotel on Bourbon Street in New Orleans, where they both worked. Anne managed the front desk while Bart worked as a hotel contractor, along with Bart's best friend, Gary, the man who provided Bart an alibi the morning Anne died. After three years, the two still rode to work together daily from St. Tammany to Orleans Parish.

When a Covington dentist confirmed the skull found in the mud belonged to Anne, Major Wilmer "Bill" Fandal of the St. Tammany Parish Sheriff's Office told reporters an animal could have drug the skull to the roadside mailbox.

"But another possibility," he said, "is that someone put it there to be discovered for insurance purposes."

In front of television cameras, Bart Manguno angrily denied that he killed his wife for insurance money or any other reason. He told WWL's Bill Elder that authorities had treated him and his family "with no more compassion than the man next door watching the crime on television."

He said he has an almost $50,000 mortgage cancellation policy on his home, meaning the insurance would pay the balance on the house in the event of his or his wife's death. He also had a personal life insurance policy with a $5,000 rider for Anne.

"That's not enough for me to murder my wife," he said.

Reacting to Manguno, Fandal told reporters he did not infer Manguno's guilt when he made his statement. Realizing the victim's family could not collect insurance without a corpus delicti, Fandal imagined, "the murderer could have been watching television, saw Bart and his child on the news, felt sorry for the baby, and dropped the skull as proof of death."

"I never know what the cops are doing," Bart Manguno said, and he complained that he learned how police found his wife's skull by watching television. "I can't afford to miss a newscast," he said. "If I do, I might miss the arrest of the people responsible for all this."

Before testing the skull, Chief Deputy Wallace Laird said, they had no leads to report. Afterward, he said, investigators had told Manguno and his family everything they could without jeopardizing the integrity of the investigation.

By November of 1983, Anne's case had grown cold, and according to a neighbor, Bart Manguno had a new girlfriend living in their Wembley Estates home, helping care for Ashleigh, Bart and Anne's then 14-month-old girl.

Bart married the girlfriend a year later, the neighbor said.

In 1984, a Texas convict named Henry Lee Lucas told Williamson County Sheriff Jim Boutwell and members of the Texas Rangers that he had killed two women before police arrested him as a felon in possession of a firearm. Investigators thought the confession plausible since Lucas had spent 15 years in prison for murdering his mother in 1960.

To keep him talking, investigators awarded him with a steak dinner, cigars, and a road trip, and surprisingly, Lucas began confessing to dozens of additional murders.

"All of a sudden, he became the person that Sheriff Boutwell was looking for," crime historian Robert Kenner explained in a recent television interview. "He had a theory there was a mass killer in Texas, and Henry filled the bill. He became everything law enforcement needed to close their cold cases."

Rewarded with more meals, drinks, and road trips to alleged crime scenes, all with the privilege of roaming around without handcuffs, Lucas confessed to more murders. He admitted to every homicide the Texas Rangers Task Force asked him about, and he encouraged other police agencies to meet with him.

"That was probably the happiest moment of his life, and police filmed most of it," Kenner said. "Lucas was thrilled by the attention, and when you see him ordering milkshakes, and ordering his hamburger, answering the telephone, or putting pins in his murder map, that footage is amazing."

In June of 1984, the Associated Press reported the following:

"Confessed serial killer Henry Lee Lucas has been linked to the death of a housewife from Folsom, according to St. Tammany Parish Sheriff Pat Canulette."

"Canulette said Lucas made a taped confession to the murder and revealed details of the slaying and the circumstances only one involved in the crime would have known."

In February of 1986, after taxpayers flew Lucas to Louisiana, he failed to show investigators where he buried Anne Manguno and others.

United Press International summarized the events this way:

"A special St. Tammany Parish grand jury has concluded after a four-month investigation that mass murderer Henry Lee Lucas did not rob and kill four parish residents."

"In 1984, Lucas told Texas authorities that he and traveling companion Otis Toole had killed 600 people, including four in St. Tammany Parish."

"The St. Tammany grand jury had been studying evidence and hearing testimony about the possible connection of Lucas with the slayings of Sargent Louis Wagner in 1978, teenager Roxanne Sharp and Slidell motel owner Kenneth Broyles in 1982, and homemaker Ruth Anne Manguno in 1983."

"The grand jurors Friday returned no-true bills in all four cases, meaning there will be no indictments. The jurors found insufficient evidence to connect the drifters with any of the homicides."

"In 1985, Lucas recanted all confessions and claimed the only person he ever killed was his mother, but investigators brought him to Louisiana anyway."

The murder of Ruth Anne Blake Manguno remains unsolved nearly four decades later, but a Manguno relative told me this week that Bart's family still forbids the mentioning of Anne's name.

"The family fears facing the truth," the relative told me. "Bart was a different person back then than he is today. Uncertain what occurred, the family has forgiven what could have happened and moved on."

In 1996, Bart Manguno wrote the editor of *The Times-Picayune* in support of capital punishment. The following quotes are excerpts from that letter:

"Being the husband of a murder victim 13 years ago..."

"Since my wife's death, I, myself, have accepted Jesus Christ into my life and know how a person can change."

"Although by most accounts, many will say I have fared well since my wife's death, no one knows what goes through my mind and heart daily."

"Why a society would continue to care for people who choose to commit these kinds of horrendous crimes against other human beings is beyond my comprehension."

"I've heard it said many times that capital punishment is not a deterrent to crime, but I disagree."

"I would be willing to say that most confessed murderers and rapists are not first-time offenders..."

"If my wife's murder is ever solved, should the person or persons responsible be spared death? ...I think not."

Louisiana's Robin Hood

With new information from readers and other sources, this chapter evolved from the Bayou Justice column entitled "Who killed Bloody Tangipahoa's Robin Hood?" initially published in south Louisiana newspapers on Tuesday, November 26, 2019.

STORIES OF THE SWAMP monster in Honey Island Swamp are imaginary tales, fiction, much like the official account of Eugene Bunch's murder.

We never hear about train robberies anymore, but in the 19th century, the most colorful character among that outlaw breed called southeast Louisiana his home. Eugene Bunch stole from the railroads and occasionally shared with the poor. In the 1890s, *The Daily Picayune* newspaper called him the Robin Hood of Bloody Tangipahoa.

We never hear about Honey Island anymore, either. Still, long before hunters reported seeing a swamp monster in the Pearl River marsh, Honey Island was Louisiana's most nefarious sanctuary, a secluded rendezvous for pirates and desperados hiding from the law.

Before, during, and after the Civil War, criminals felt safe in this pathless maze of sloshing muck and impenetrable thickets. Eugene Bunch, who allegedly robbed trains in six states, retreated to Honey Island between crime sprees, and in 1892, shortly after he robbed a train near Amite City, someone shot him in the back at his campsite on Honey Island.

Before I recount what eyewitness-testimony says happened the morning Eugene Bunch died, we must review the official account:

Born in Mississippi in 1841, Eugene F. Bunch was the youngest of a family of two sons and a daughter. His father moved the family to Tangipahoa Parish while the children were teenagers. The boys received a solid education, and Eugene advanced rapidly in his studies.

When the Civil War began in 1861, 20-year-old Eugene enlisted in the Tangipahoa Parish Company. He proved himself a good and brave soldier until he received word that his family back home had all died of consumption. Soon after, he grew quick-tempered and started to gamble and to drink.

At the close of the war, Eugene married a young debutante in Baton Rouge and moved back to the family home in Tangipahoa Parish. He taught school in Amite City until his drinking problems worsened, causing him to lose his job.

He accepted a teaching position in Covington with the same results.

His reputation lost in south Louisiana, he and his wife, migrated to Gainesville, Texas, where he found a career that welcomed drinking and gambling. As a politician, he made many friends, who helped elect him Court Clerk in Cooke County, and as his popularity grew, he even managed to control his drinking.

Eugene and Flavia Bunch lived in Clover, Texas — an exclusive and affluent community. As Clerk, Eugene had access to all government books and filings. He knew when the prime real estate came on the market. He knew the going rate, and at work, he had access to considerable amounts of cash.

By "borrowing" from the county, building, and selling property in Clover, Eugene soon became a wealthy man. Still, county officials noticed the cash discrepancies before Eugene could repay his loans, forcing him to return to Louisiana.

Flavia Bunch chose to remain in Texas.

Living on Carondelet Street in New Orleans, Eugene adopted a new name, found a new spouse, and began two new occupations.

"Captain J. W. Gerald" worked as a riverboat gambler until his Texas real estate riches ran out, and then he took a secret night job robbing trains.

His first night shift was in August of 1889.

Just as the Southern Express from New Orleans got underway, the engineer turned and saw a masked man standing near him. Before the engineer could speak, two big revolvers touched his chin.

The masked man told the engineer to run the train under an upcoming river bridge and stop. After he did, the robber directed him to step out of the engine room and force his way into the passenger express car.

As the engineer entered, the express messenger lowered the pistol in his hand.

The robber standing in the door told the passengers to put their heads between their knees and ordered the messenger to open the safe.

As the messenger loaded money into two sacks held by the engineer, the robber fired shots outside the train on one side and then the other, keeping the passengers looking down and afraid.

With two sacks full, the robber motioned the messenger to the floor and told the engineer to step back out. In the engine room, the robber had the engineer start the train forward, while the bandit dove from the train and vanished into the bushes and the night.

News reports said the robber got away with about $40,000 that night. In today's dollars, that's just over a million and a half.

New Orleans Superintendent of Police David C. Hennessy — whom the New Orleans mafia murdered a year later — tracked the robber on horseback. The trail led to a train station in Covington, where he found a woman named Cora, claiming to be Eugene Bunch's second wife. She was carrying a trunk full of loot, two six-shooters, and a belt filled with cartridges.

Eugene Bunch, however, had made his escape to Honey Island where, in those days, he was safe and his capture practically impossible. With most of the money recovered, Hennessy returned to New Orleans, where he may or may not have known a New Orleans resident gambler named Captain J. W. Gerald.

Just when the police and the public thought Eugene had left the state for some new territory, a lone bandit hit another Southern Express train near Duck Hill, Mississippi. Still, this time, one of the passengers, braver or foolhardier than the rest, was shot and killed instantly by the masked man.

Four months later, the Illinois Central railroad experienced another robbery on the same rail line, this one near Newsome's Mill, and this time, the masked bandit brought four sacks and robbed the train while it was still moving. As before, he had the engineer and messenger load two sacks with money, but afterward, he had them place the other sacks over their heads.

When they laid on the floor, the masked robber pulled the rope to stop the train.

By the time the men removed their sacks, the bandit had vanished. Some speculate he may have removed his mask and returned to his passenger seat, later leaving the train with his luggage heavier than when he boarded.

Fed up with Eugene, the railroad hired Detective Thomas V. Jackson — the only bounty hunter known to have collected bounties in Honey Island Swamp — and they offered a top-dollar bounty for Eugene Bunch, dead or alive. It took Jackson two years, but he eventually did find Eugene's campsite on Honey Island — a highland oasis at the center of the marshland.

On August 17, 1892, a posse of twelve men left Tylertown, Mississippi, heavily armed and on horseback. They traveled all night, reaching Pearl River at dawn. Jackson told his men that a hunter had tipped him off and that he knew precisely where Eugene and his new partner, Colonel E. S. Hobgood, would be camped.

As the posse proceeded, the thick underbrush forced them to leave their horses and walk single file on foot. Jackson warned them to remain on guard against ambush. Eugene Bunch, he said, was a dead shot who swore no one would take him alive.

One step at a time, each cautious step forward followed another as the posse made its way behind Detective Jackson. After several miles, the posse heard voices; the outlaws feeling secure in their hideaway felt no need to remain silent.

The bounty hunters broke through the underbrush, startling Eugene Bunch and Colonel Hobgood at their campsite. The colonel dropped his revolver and raised his hands, while Eugene backed up firing on the group, but hitting no one.

Eugene Bunch fell to the ground dead, riddled with bullets.

Colonel Hobgood later stood trial in Amite City for train robbery, and then again in Mississippi for murder, getting off on technicalities in both courts. Later, the colonel moved back home to St. Mary Parish, where he, like Thomas V. Jackson and his posse, became a bounty-hunting railroad detective.

Next time, we will review evidence suggesting that the actual events only vaguely resemble this historically accepted account.

Colonel Hobgood

With new information from readers and other sources, this chapter evolved from the Bayou Justice column entitled "Hero train robber murdered by partner-in-crime," initially published in south Louisiana newspapers on Tuesday, November 30, 2019.

DURING HIS FIRST OF three murder trials, Tuesday, September 13, 1892, Colonel Edward Scanlon Hobgood told the court he first met the train robber, Eugene Franklin Bunch, five months before his death.

Hobgood described how he escaped the law in Mississippi and fled to Louisiana, knowing Pinkerton detectives feared the marshland near Honey Island.

In the swamp, he befriended Bunch, who paid him to deliver a horse north of Amite City, at a bend in the tracks between Arcola and Tangipahoa. There, Bunch jumped off a train, carrying sacks of cash, and the two laughed back to Honey Island Swamp.

After the robbery, the two men made camp at the old Sheridan Place, a roofless farmhouse on Honey Island, ravaged years earlier by a hurricane.

According to Hobgood, he woke to the sound of whispers just before noon and walked 15 steps to retrieve his Winchester when a posse climbed out of the brush. Hobgood raised his hands to surrender, but Bunch awoke, firing his pistol, and fell dead seconds later.

Hobgood told one jury, "They killed my poor partner before he had time to think about surrendering."

The posse, he said, put four slugs in Bunch's chest and one in his head.

The coroner's inquest found Bunch died of a revolver shot that entered the base of his skull in the back at his neckline and exited his forehead just above the left eye. The other four shots came from rifles and entered through his back.

Several witnesses at Hobgood's trial testified to hearing a single shot fired near 9:00 AM and a volley of shots when the posse arrived at 11:00 AM.

Henderson Dillon testified that Hobgood walked to his house and borrowed a black pony shortly after 9:00 AM, and Wilbur Tullus, 14, said he saw Hobgood riding a black pony towards Charles Crane's house.

Charles Crane told the court, "Colonel Hobgood came to my house Sunday morning, August 21, around 9:30, and asked me to tell his brother Rob to bring money and clothes, because he was going away. I told him he would have to deliver the message himself."

Preston Thomas testified that he saw Colonel Hobgood riding away from Charles Crane's house that morning in the direction of Rob Hobgood's farm.

Colonel Hobgood and his attorney, F. B. Carter, objected multiple times, but the judge, Robert Reid from Amite City, ignored them.

For weeks, Hobgood had told investigators and newspaper reporters that he had slept until almost 11:00 AM that Sunday, awaking only minutes before the posse raided their camp.

Crane also told the court that Rob Hobgood came to his home later that Sunday morning, asking him to deliver a message to Detective Thomas V. Jackson. He wanted to tell Jackson that Bunch was dead and that Hobgood wished to surrender, but he had something to discuss with Jackson first.

Two members of Jackson's Posse, Frank Morris and Whit Pierce, testified that Jackson left the officers eating breakfast around 10:00 AM. When they caught up with him, he was atop a hill, talking to Rob Hobgood.

Will Bartall, 12-years-old, testified, "I know Colonel Hobgood, and remember the day Bunch is said to have been killed. I saw the colonel pass that morning with William Crane around sun-up. Colonel Hobgood had on a black hat and a pair of low quarter shoes. He told me he was leaving the swamps, going back home."

Under cross-examination, Bartall said, "I am certain that it was on Sunday because I went to church that morning, and I know it was the colonel. I have known him ever since I could recollect. I know him and his brother Robert. I am sure it was the colonel. He was coming from the direction of the old Sheridan place."

In closing, he added, "And no one told me what I had to say at this here trial either."

Charles Elliot, 15, told the court he passed the old Sheridan Place three times that morning. The first time, just after sunrise, everything looked normal. The second time, around nine, he noticed a man lying on his side in the grass with his head propped up on his arm and a saddlebag.

"I couldn't tell whether he was awake or asleep," Elliot said. "His right eye looked half-open. I just eased by, not saying nothing, in case he was sleeping, but then I saw he had a hole in his head, just above that left eye. No blood. Just that big hole."

Charles Elliot found the man in the same position on his third trip through, but that time, he had holes in his back and blood covering his clothes.

Mrs. Mary Elliot also took the stand. She confirmed that Charles Elliot, her son, told her about the man with the hole in his head at least two hours before she heard the posse's shots just before noon.

George Sheridan testified that the railroad detectives hired him to haul Eugene Bunch's body in his wagon. He said the detectives refused his help loading the body, leaving him wondering whether the body was warm or cold. Sheridan expressed surprise that a man so recently killed could smell so rotten.

In the end, Colonel Hobgood had a pre-trial, a miss-trial, and a real trial. By the third round, most of the witnesses had fled the state, and the jury had no choice but to find him not guilty.

From there, he went to Amite City to stand trial for the train robbery and got off on a technicality. In Mississippi, the murder charge also went away, and Hobgood launched a successful career as a railroad detective, much like Thomas V. Jackson, the man who collected an $8,000 bounty on Bunch and paid his posse $40 each.

Now, before we leave this infamous murder, there are a few more oddities worth mentioning.

Firstly, no one who testified at Hobgood's trial knew the dead man as Eugene Bunch. They knew him as Bob Grice. They only had Detective Jackson's word that the name Bob Grice was an alias used by Eugene Bunch.

Secondly, genealogists today have records proving that Rob Hobgood lived near Pearl River, but they cannot find evidence that he had a brother.

Finally, photographs of Colonel Edward Hobgood and Eugene Bunch today are scarce. Still, reading old newspaper descriptions and comparing the remaining photos and sketches of the two men, it is conceivable that they were one person.

Jimmy and Diddie

With new information from readers and other sources, this chapter evolved from the Bayou Justice column entitled "Who killed Diddie Cooper?" initially published in south Louisiana newspapers on Tuesday, December 10, 2019.

THE TIMES-PICAYUNE newspaper described Diddie Cooper, a New Orleans television personality and mother of three, as an attractive young socialite from a prominent Louisiana family. Her seven-year-old daughter, the newspaper said, found her mother dead in their home on November 30, 1952.

Someone had strangled and bludgeoned Diddie to death with a blunt instrument, one never identified or recovered by the police. The victim wore a blue translucent negligee, turned inside out, and drenched in blood.

New Orleans police made arrests, and the state tried a suspect, but today, over a half-century later, no one knows who killed Diddie Cooper.

Family members described Diddie as a caring mother of three children. Her older two, Mackie and Allison, came from her first marriage, but Donald, her 9-month-old, was the son of James Leland "Jimmy" Cooper.

Jimmy Cooper was born in Clara, Mississippi, on January 16, 1910. In his teens, he went to school in Chicago, Illinois, and worked nights as a hospital technician. The Chicago Police Department arrested him for stealing a car in 1932, and he served six months in the Cook County House of Corrections before moving to New Orleans in 1933.

In the French Quarter, he worked as a theater manager until 1938 when he bought the Court of Two Sisters Restaurant on Royal Street.

The United States Army Quartermaster Corps drafted him into the army during World War II, where he earned the rank of captain before his discharge. After the war, he returned home to New Orleans and the Court of Two Sisters.

His wife, Mildred Schmidt Cooper, ran the restaurant while Jimmy was overseas, growing the Court of Two Sisters into one of the most popular hotspots in the French Quarter. However, the enterprising couple drifted apart and eventually divorced on June 21, 1951.

On June 30th, Jimmy married Diddie.

Amelie Jane "Diddie" Woolfolk was born on December 2, 1921, in New Orleans, Louisiana. Her father, Robert M. Woolfolk, was an investment banker, and her mother, Ruth Samson Woolfolk, was an accomplished musician. Her socially prominent parents engaged in philanthropic work in the community, and like any proper young socialite, Diddie made her debut in society after high school.

While she attended H. Sophie Newcomb Memorial College at Tulane University, Diddie's activities graced the society pages of all New Orleans newspapers. She made front-page news on September 5, 1942, marrying Macrino Trelles, heir to the Trelles Cigar fortune.

Heiress or not, Diddie actively pursued a career of her own. Focusing on entertainment, she took a position with WDSU-TV in New Orleans, hosting "A Date with Diddie," a weekly variety show called spotlighting local talent.

Diddie and Macrino divorced in 1947.

Diddie married Jimmy Cooper four years later.

Jimmy adored Diddie's children, and they loved him. He paid for their private schools and summer camps and dance lessons. Before long, Diddie was pregnant again and gave birth to Donald Robert Cooper in 1952.

Newspapers described the Coopers as an ideal couple, but patrons of the Court of Two Sisters knew better. Jimmy drank, and when he drank, he abused Diddie and described their bedroom activities to anyone who would listen.

The couple had separated before the birth but reconciled for the baby's sake. After the birth, according to restaurant staff, Diddie seemed afraid of her husband and would not leave no matter how belligerent Jimmy became.

After a festival in April of 1952 called a Night in Old New Orleans, Jimmy and Diddie gave a party in the Creole Room upstairs at the Court of Two Sisters. For a time, all seemed fine. Diddie sat by the piano and sang.

She and Jimmy both drank, but everyone seemed happy.

As the night wore on, however, Jimmy became increasingly intoxicated and belligerent, ultimately provoking a fistfight with a guest, and going home alone. The next morning, Jimmy called the guests and apologized, joking that Diddie would not return home until everyone forgave him.

On May 6, 1952, the New Orleans Police Department arrested Jimmy after Diddie called them. Once again, found intoxicated and abusive, Jimmy went to jail wearing only his undershorts, and the style shirt later called a "wife-beater."

The next morning, Diddie filed for formal separation. In June of 1952, Jimmy moved out of the apartment at 3211 Louisiana Avenue Parkway and began paying Diddie alimony along with her apartment rent. He also spent a weekly salary for Diddie's grandmother, Coralee Samson, to move into the apartment and work as a maid and part-time nanny to the children.

Jimmy refused to accept divorce as inevitable and smothered Diddie with his presence. In October 1952, after the Tulane-Georgia football game, Diddie gave a cocktail party. Jimmy arrived uninvited. Diddie left the party, later telling friends that Jimmy still entered the apartment at all hours. She said he threatened to evict her and her grandmother if she did not take him back.

Eventually, her party guests joined her at Perez's nightclub, including Jimmy, once again drunk and obscene. He begged her to take him back in front of the guests and asked some of them to intercede on his behalf.

On November 29, 1952, the Saturday after a Thanksgiving with relatives in another state, Diddie attended the Tulane-LSU football game at Tulane Stadium with two other couples.

No one invited Jimmy, but he followed anyway.

It was cold and stormy that night. Jimmy, at first happy and pleasant, bought umbrellas and raincoats for everyone. Diddie refused to sit with him and sat in the row in front of him with the other ladies in their party.

Diddie told him she had plans with her friends after the game and warned him that she would call the police if he followed. Jimmy apologized, insisting that he had not been drinking, and asked if little Mackie could spend the night at his house. Mackie adored Jimmy and had spent nights there before, but never on a Saturday night.

Saturday nights were busy at the restaurant, more so after a Tulane-LSU game. Bourbon Street would be crowded, and the restaurant would be packed. However, Diddie reluctantly agreed. Mackie loved Cooper's company and even called him "Daddy."

After Jimmy left with Mackie, Diddie went home and changed shoes, her other pair soggy from the rain. After, she joined friends at Charlie's Steak House on Dryades Street, and later, they migrated to the Key Club on Louisiana Avenue for dancing.

Diddie's evening ended with coffee at her neighbors around 2:00 a.m.

Crossing the street for home, she realized she had forgotten her hat. Yelling back to the neighbors, she said she would pick it up in the morning. The neighbors stood outside, watching her cross Louisiana Avenue Parkway and climb the stairs to her apartment for the last time.

Upstairs, Diddie wrote a check for her babysitter, Cecile Plantagenet, who caught a cab home at 2:10 a.m. after locking Diddie's front door on her way out.

At approximately 3:15 a.m., Diddie's grandmother, Coralee, heard a scream. Climbing from the bed, she looked out the window facing Toledano Street in the back of the house. Under a street light on the corner of South Roman and Toledano, she watched a man in a gray suit get into a light-colored car and drive away.

Seeing nothing else unusual, she returned to her bed.

Near 9:00 the following Sunday morning, Coralee woke to the baby screaming and the telephone ringing. When she answered the phone, the voice sounded muffled, unrecognizable.

"Can I speak to Diddie?" the caller asked.

"Who is this?" Coralee asked back.

"Jimmy," he said.

Coralee told him Diddie was still asleep and to call later.

At 10:00 am, Coralee asked Allison to wake up her mother, but the little girl refused, saying she had tried earlier and that her mother "looked funny." Coralee walked to the bedroom to see for herself, but Diddie's bed stood empty.

In the children's room, the television star's corpse lay half on and half off one of the two twin beds. Naked from the waist down, Diddie's lingerie and quilted housecoat appeared rolled up over her breasts.

Purple finger marks wrapped her throat, and blood covered her hands and clothing. A bloody foam seeped from her nose. Coralee later told police that Diddie looked as if someone had dressed her with her clothes inside out.

Goodbye, Diddie Cooper

With new information from readers and other sources, this chapter evolved from the Bayou Justice column entitled "New Orleans TV star's murder remains unsolved," initially published in south Louisiana newspapers on Thursday, December 12, 2019.

THE 7-YEAR-OLD DAUGHTER of a New Orleans television star found her mother, Diddie Cooper, naked and strangled on a Sunday morning in 1952.

The child alerted her grandmother, who phoned Diddie's brother, Bobby.

When Bobby arrived, he found the back door ajar and the screen door open.

Police on the scene found a thick layer of undisturbed dust on the railing and steps of the back stairs — no evidence of forced entry, and no evidence of a struggle. Neither Diddie's downstairs neighbors or the newspaper delivery boy reported witnessing anything unusual.

The police questioned Diddie's first husband, Macrino Trelles, the father of her two oldest children. Trelles, who paid his wife $100 a month alimony, had been at home with his mother, Mary Venta Trelles, the wife of the Trelles Cigar manufacturer.

"I loved Diddie," he told the police, "But she didn't love me. She was cold."

After an extensive investigation, police arrested Diddie's estranged husband, the owner of the Court of Two Sisters restaurant, Jimmy Cooper. A grand jury indicted Cooper for first-degree murder on August 5, 1953. Jury selection in the case began on January 12, 1954. District Attorney

Severn T. Darden assigned the case to Assistant District Attorney Edward A. Haggerty, who announced that week that the prosecution would seek the death penalty.

The state postulated that Jimmy Cooper — sometimes known as the "Mayor of the French Quarter" or "Mr. Bow Tie of Bourbon Street" — had grown tired of paying alimony to two ex-wives. They also pointed out that he had snubbed by Diddie after a football game earlier in the day and then spurned sexually by her later that night. Based on this circumstantial evidence, the state postulated that Cooper drank excessively and became enraged before attacking and killing his wife.

Crime scene fibers recovered from Diddie's body and analyzed by the FBI were "consistent with" those found on Jimmy Cooper's T-shirt and boxer shorts. The blood evidence on Diddie's hands and clothes belonged only to the victim.

At trial, Orleans Parish Coroner Dr. Nicholas J. Chetta spoke extensively about Diddie's injuries. Her time of death, as evident by her stomach contents, he placed between 3 and 4:30 a.m. on the morning of November 30, 1952.

Pointing to autopsy photos, he showed the jury the bloodstains on the bottom of Diddie's nightgown, explaining how these proved that part of the gown had once covered her head. He said that was the reason her robe was on inside out, and although the position of the body hinted at sexual assault, Chetta said he found no evidence of that.

On projected slides, the jury saw blood streaming from Diddie's nostrils. She had a black eye and frothy red clumps on her lips. Someone had fractured her skull with a blunt instrument. The photos revealed contusions and abrasions on her jaw and marks "like extended fingers" on her neck. Chetta said he found her hyoid bone broken. Strangulation caused her death. However, he explained, the skull fracture alone would have killed her had she not choked to death.

Diddie's grandmother and live-in nanny, Mrs. Coralee Samson, took the stand to tell of the late-night scream she heard. She also described the unidentified man she saw boarding a vehicle on Toledano Street. Coralee said that man was not Jimmy Cooper. However, she also testified that Cooper had entered the apartment and Diddie's bedroom uninvited one week before the murder.

Investigator Pershing Gervais testified that organized crime-controlled Cooper and said the word on the street said a hitman from Chicago killed Diddie at Cooper's behest. The judge ordered Gervais' remarks stricken from the record and instructed the jury to forget he told them.

Mary Augusta, Diddie's maid, testified that per Diddie, she had to be sure the door to the back of the house was locked when she left every night. She explained that the back steps were hard to navigate unless you were familiar with them. She said she didn't regularly clean the railing unless Diddie had house guests staying there.

The night porter, John Washington Merritt, testified that Cooper had borrowed his car overnight, claiming his Cadillac's brakes needed repair. He said that Cooper returned the car before 6:30 a.m.

When police examined the vehicle, they found a cigar wrapper from an El Trelles cigar, a brand sold exclusively in New Orleans at the Court of Two Sisters. The company owned by Macrino Trelles, Diddie's first husband, manufactured the brand.

The porter also testified about a back entrance to Cooper's apartment. He said it was located on the Bourbon Street side of the Court of Two Sisters, where anyone could enter and exit undetected.

The state introduced Yvonne Holmes, who dated Cooper at the request of the New Orleans Police Department, hoping to get a confession from him. She testified that Cooper did not confess but attempted to strangle her when he found out she was working for the police.

The defense painted a different view of the defendant. Putting him on the stand to testify on his behalf, Cooper systematically refuted each point of circumstantial evidence that the state brought against him. Cooper said he was innocent and had stopped drinking for two weeks preceding the murder in hopes of a reconciliation with Diddie.

"Diddie said if I could straighten up and fly right," he said. "I could come home any time I wanted to. That's what I was working on and the reason her boys stayed at my place that night."

The defense also questioned the credibility of Yvonne Evers Holmes. Under cross-examination, she admitted to being a former barmaid and stripper on Bourbon Street before marrying one of the detectives working the Cooper case.

While the city could not get enough of his sensationalized trial, Cooper, twenty years older than the victim, fell asleep twice during his court proceedings. When the defense rested, Cooper predicted — rightly so — that he would be free by the weekend.

When the jury acquitted Jimmy Cooper, the panel joined courtroom spectators, who stood and applauded when the judge announced their verdict.

Unfortunately, the police had no other suspects.

Two years after his acquittal, Jimmy Cooper's son, Mackie, found his father's corpse on the kitchen floor of his apartment above the Court of Two Sisters. Dr. Chetta said Cooper's death was "due to angioneurotic edema" from "a painful swelling of the windpipe due to an allergic reaction."

In other words, he strangled to death.

Diddie Cooper's family buried her on her 31st birthday. Her gravestone names her as simply Amelie Jane Woolfolk, forgetting her famous nickname and the surnames of her former husbands.

Nearly seven decades later, Diddie Cooper's murder remains unsolved.

The Carwash Witness

With new information from readers and other sources, this chapter evolved from the Bayou Justice column entitled "Reed pre-trial continues, carwash witness testifies," initially published in south Louisiana newspapers on Tuesday, December 5, 2019.

MONDAY AFTERNOON, JUDGE Beth Wolfe denied a motion by the Defense to suppress a witness's identification of Reginald Reed within two weeks of his wife's murder.

During her cross-examination of a state witness, the defense attorney left her seat before the bench and walked to the back of the courtroom. There, she looked up at the witness stand with her arms raised and wearing a surgical mask over her face. With all eyes on her, the attorney walked back to her seat, where she asked the witness if the distance she walked had been more or less than seventy-five feet.

Following these theatrics, Assistant District Attorney Taylor Anthony reminded the court that the witness had written down the license plate of the car while the defendant allegedly drove around that carwash, proving she had near-perfect eyesight.

Television's stereotypical public defender is often depicted as lazy and disinterested, leaving the grand-standing to the higher-priced defense attorneys, the Perry Mason and Johnny Cochran types.

LaToia Williams-Simon is not that stereotypical public defender. She waves her hands when she talks and often raises her voice when speaking to judges. Outside the courtroom, LaToia directs activities at a Kentwood bar called Club 81, sometimes while chatting with friends on social media through her "Courtroom Honey" Instagram profile.

LaToia earned her Arts and Communications degree at Louisiana State University in 2011 and her law degree from the David A. Clarke School of Law in 2014. Perhaps, one day, LaToia hopes to win public office, a goal her mother has sought for over a decade.

Vanessa R. Williams of Amite, who has both a law and political science degree, made it into the primary in the 2013 21st Judicial District Court Division H election. She also ran for the District Attorney seat back in 2008, losing to incumbent Scott Perrilloux, who's staff she later joined.

LaToia Williams-Simon was born on April 28, 1989, less than two years after Selonia Reed's assailant dumped her body near a carwash and convenience store in Hammond, Louisiana.

The carwash eyewitness, Crystal Furca of Hammond, told LaToia she thought the defendant might have been a few feet further than the length of the courtroom. She said she saw the defendant at the carwash where a murderer dumped his wife's body later that same night.

"I was sitting in my truck with my three-year-old son in his car-seat," Furca told the court. "I was writing a check for my gas when I saw this car moving slowly through the parking lot."

She said the occupants did not appear to be going into the store, and the car they drove appeared "Spic and Span" clean. She wrote down the license plate number, she said, in case the store was later robbed.

When she walked across the parking lot to the store carrying the check, she saw the two men sitting in the front seat of the car inside the carwash. She saw their faces clearly.

After she paid for her gas and exited the store, she saw the men again, this time standing outside the vehicle.

She described the driver of the car as "a black man, light-complexion, nice-looking, with an athletic build."

She said he wore a muscle shirt and tennis shoes. The license plate and car belonged to Idella Reed, Reginald Reed's mother. From a photo lineup, Furca identified the driver of the vehicle as Reginald Reed and the passenger as the co-defendant in the Selonia Reed murder trial, Jimmy Ray Barnes.

Furca had not planned to testify until the jury trial next year. Still, last month, LaToia Williams-Simon asked Judge Beth Wolfe to suppress her identification of Reginald Reed from a photo lineup. Earlier, retired

Hammond Police Detective Vincent Giannoble told the court Furca identified Reed and Barnes as the two she saw in the carwash on the night of August 22, 1987. She said they were "behaving suspiciously" in the parking lot where police discovered the body of Reed's wife the following morning.

Before Judge Wolfe last month, Giannobile described how Crystal Annette Dimattia (now Furca) sat in front of the gas pumps at John's Curb Market. She wrote a check to pay for gas and noticed what she believed to be a suspicious vehicle circling the parking lot. The shiny, clean car eventually pulled into the nearby carwash, and two black males climbed out.

On a piece of paper from her checkbook, the witness wrote down the license plate number of the vehicle in case someone robbed the store later that night. She told police that she worked nights at another convenience store and trained to watch for suspicious customers.

The next morning, police found the body of 26-year-old Selonia Reed inside her car near that same carwash. When Furca heard the news that afternoon, Giannoble explained, she called the Hammond Police Department. On the phone with Lieutenant Steve Raacke, she provided the license plate number, and Raacke provided the information to the lead detective on the case, Vincent Giannoble.

Running the plates, Giannoble found the car registered to Reginald Reed's mother. He then prepared a Polaroid photo lineup of the men Giannoble believed had access to the vehicle. The included Reginald Reed, his three brothers, and two family friends.

According to Giannoble, on September 10, 1987, he presented the six color photos to Furca, and she took only seconds to identify Reginald Reed and Jimmy Ray Barnes. Both men are now co-defendants in the Selonia Reed murder case.

LaToia Williams-Simon said she filed a motion to suppress the evidence because the photo lineup was "unduly and unnecessarily suggestive." She needed "to protect her client's constitutional rights," she said.

LaToia described the conduct of the Hammond Police Department as "extremely improper" since the suspicious parties in Giannoble's report had been described only as "two black males." She said Giannoble's photo selection should have been based directly and solely on witness descriptions. She also suggested the detective may have been racist in selecting lineup photos.

The State argued that the opposite was true, explaining that the men pictured being of similar build and complexion made the selection less suggestive and more than fair to the suspects pictured.

The Defense also insisted that the witness testifying for the State should have been Lieutenant Steve Raacke since he recorded the initial description from Furca.

Judge Wolfe elected to make no ruling until December 2, allowing time for the prosecution to arrange Furca's appearance.

After Judge Wolfe denied the request to suppress the photo lineup identification, LaToia Williams-Simon requested that additional evidence be suppressed. She wanted the court to ignore, from investigator's interviews with witnesses, all allegations related to arson, insurance fraud, statutory rape, cocaine use, cocaine distribution, contributing to the delinquency of a minor, and participation in homosexual or bisexual acts.

Both ADA Anthony and Judge Wolfe agreed that introducing such information at trial might prejudice the jury and force a mistrial. For this reason, all involved agreed not to introduce these allegations into evidence.

LaToia Williams-Simon also asked the judge to suppress allegations against the defendant related to spousal abuse. The judge denied that request.

Don't miss out!

Visit the website below and you can sign up to receive emails whenever HL Arledge publishes a new book. There's no charge and no obligation.

https://books2read.com/r/B-A-MGBH-KZZCB

BOOKS 2 READ

Connecting independent readers to independent writers.

Did you love *Bayou Justice: Southeast Louisiana Cold Case Files*? Then you should read *Carnal Knowledge: Mafia Strippers and the Hit on JFK* by HL Arledge!

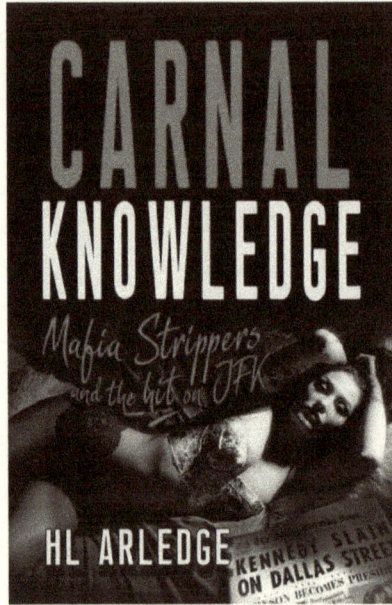

Bourbon Street Burlesque Queen Blaze Starr said, "Barrooms or bedrooms, men can't keep secrets in either place. If you really want to know what's going on, ask a stripper." This book interviews Blaze, Tempest Storm, Candy Barr, and a host of others who made their livings working for the mob—validating their beliefs against public record and the memories of retired law enforcement professionals—in order to reveal what really happened in New Orleans in the Summer of 1963.

Read more at bayoujustice.com.

About the Author

HL Arledge is the author of Bayou Justice, a twice-weekly true crime newspaper column featuring exciting or notable crime-related stories often focusing on cold case files in South Louisiana; stories based on interviews with key players, among them: police investigators, lawyers, victims, and their families. HL Arledge is well established as a journalist, IT Professional, and story teller. Not only is he published in the periodicals and professional journals. HL works in Louisiana state government and lives with his beautiful wife in a farmhouse just north of New Orleans. HL Arledge also writes quirky crime fiction. Literary Agent Elizabeth Pomada said he should describe himself as Elmore Leonard with a southern accent. HL's short stories have been published in Ellery Queen Mystery Magazine, Twilight Zone, and Alfred Hitchcock Mystery Magazine.

Read more at bayoujustice.com.

About the Publisher

Bogart Books is both an independent publisher, specializing in books featuring a crime—real or imaginary—as its central focus. We aim to publish work that makes readers suspicious of everyone.

www.ingramcontent.com/pod-product-compliance
Lightning Source LLC
Chambersburg PA
CBHW021218090426
42740CB00006B/274